Michigan Butterflies and Skippers

A Field Guide and Reference

Mogens C. Nielsen

FIRST EDITION 1999

Library of Congress Cataloging-in-Publication Data

Nielsen, Mogens C., 1926-
Michigan butterflies and skippers : a field guide and reference / Mogens C. Nielsen. — 1st ed.
p. cm.
Includes bibliographical references (p. 237).
ISBN 1-56525-012-5 (pbk. : alk. paper)
1. Butterflies—Michigan. I. Title.
QL551.M5 N53 1999
595.78'09744—dc21

99-6307
CIP

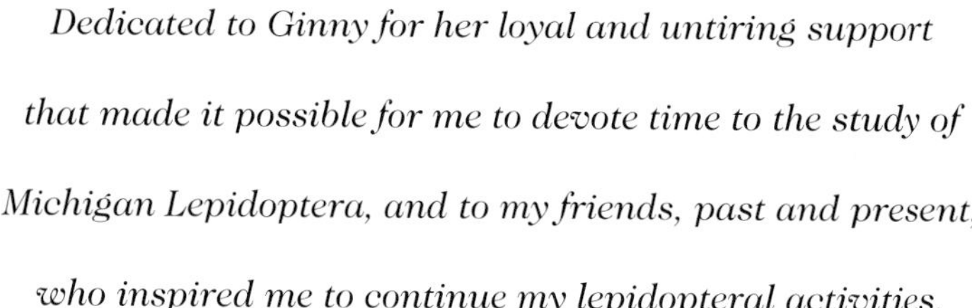

Dedicated to Ginny for her loyal and untiring support that made it possible for me to devote time to the study of Michigan Lepidoptera, and to my friends, past and present, who inspired me to continue my lepidopteral activities.

Mogens C. Nielsen

Issued in furtherance of MSU Extension work in agriculture and home economics, acts of May 8 and June 30, 1914, in cooperation with the U.S. Department of Agriculture. Arlen Leholm, Extension director, Michigan State University Extension, E. Lansing, MI 48824.

Contents

Preface

The collection and study of Michigan Lepidoptera, especially butterflies (including skippers), began some 100 years ago. Wolcott (1892) published the first Michigan list of butterflies and skippers from the Grand Rapids area, recording 79 species. Since that time, others have published various articles and lists, which culminated with Moore's (1960) annotated list of Michigan butterflies and skippers. He recorded 139 species; later Nielsen (1970) added seven more state record species.

Much of what is currently known of the Michigan butterfly fauna, including the life history and distribution within the state, can be credited to the enthusiastic efforts of avocational lepidopterists, private individuals who collect and maintain their own collections. Inasmuch as most of our butterflies are not considered economic pests, very little public funding has been expended in gathering data on Michigan species.

I have been collecting, studying and, more recently, photographing Michigan Lepidoptera for more than 50 years. Since 1947, after returning from military service, I have been very actively studying Michigan species in more than 60 counties, including Isle Royale. Most of my attention has been focused in Cass, Lenawee, Ingham and Otsego counties in the Lower Peninsula and most of the counties in the eastern half of the Upper Peninsula. This guidebook is the result of the cumulative records from numerous published papers, the contributions of many avocational collectors and my records of some 50 years of field activity.

Michigan is fortunate in having many interesting and unique habitats for butterflies, which continue to yield new records, but there are still many areas of the state and unique habitats that have not been collected or surveyed for species new to Michigan. For example, the Olive Hairstreak, *Mitoura grynea* (Hübner), which uses red cedar as its larval host plant, has not been found in Michigan as of this time. Red cedar occurs throughout most of the southern half of the Lower Peninsula; the hairstreak is found in adjacent states and southern Ontario. Many portions of the Upper Peninsula have been poorly collected, especially elevated portions of the western counties; likewise, Isle Royale, which has many features similar to the near shore of Ontario, is still poorly surveyed. The islands of the Great Lakes offer interesting potentials for many special research projects regarding their butterfly fauna.

The aims of this guidebook are to update and synthesize the older works of Moore (1960) and Nielsen (1970), and to provide the background to which additional information may be added in the future. This guidebook provides illustrations of Michigan's recorded butterflies and skippers and comments on their identification, habitat, adult food sources, larval host plants and distribution in the state.

Acknowledgements

This guidebook was originally inspired by the late Wilbur S. McAlpine, who, along with the late George W. Rawson, envisioned an inexpensive guide that would be available to Michigan young people in their quest for information about butterflies and skippers. I was asked to participate in this project in the late 1960s, inasmuch as I had maintained a card-file index of all Michigan butterfly and skipper county records since Sherman Moore's passing in 1954.

Much of the data in this guide came from my field activities, but many additional records have been obtained by examining institutional and private collections. Others have come from the contributions of data and/or examination of specimens from countless avocational lepidopterists. Though the following list of collectors is not inclusive, I do express my deep appreciation to the following, who made significant contributions: George Balogh, Glenn Belyea, James Bess, Thomas Carr, Patrick Conway, Julian Donahue, John Douglass, Erwin Elsner, Richard Fleming, Edward Herig, Jr., Ronald Hodges, Loran Gibson, John Heitzman, Richard Holzman, David Iftner, Harry King, Leroy Koehn, Irwin Leeuw, Elizabeth Littler, Wayne Miller, Steven Mueller, the late John Newman, Daniel Oosting, James Parkinson, David Parshall, John Peacock, Owen Perkins, John Perona, John Shuey, Stephen Stephenson, Bradleigh Utz, Edward Voss, Warren Wagner, Jr., the late Virgil Warczynski, Reginald Webster, Jason Weintraub, the late John Wilkie, Bruce Wilson and William Westrate, Jr.

I am particularly grateful to Charles Oliver and David Wright, who cleared up taxonomic questions and determinations of the Michigan *Phyciodes 'tharos'* and *Celastrina 'ladon'* complexes, respectively.

Special thanks to all those curators and collection managers who allowed me access to their Lepidoptera collections at the Chippewa Nature Center, Midland; Cranbrook Institute of

Science, Bloomfield Hills; Eastern Michigan University, Ypsilanti; Kalamazoo Nature Center, Kalamazoo; Michigan State University, East Lansing; Michigan Technological University, Houghton; Northern Michigan University, Marquette; and the University of Michigan, Ann Arbor.

Most importantly, I give warm thanks to Fred Stehr, who read my manuscript and made many helpful comments; especially his constant encouragement to finally overcome my years of procrastination in holding off this publication until "one more state record" is made! I also thank James Harding and John Wilterding III for their review of the manuscript and helpful comments. Special thanks are extended to Kurt Stepnitz, who so patiently, and with great care, photographed the specimens, and my long-time friend Larry West, a superb naturalist photographer who loaned me many of his prize-winning photographs of Michigan species in natural settings. Without their skills and artistry, this field guide would not have been possible.

I would be remiss if I did not acknowledge with deep appreciation the following well known Lepidoptera specialists who examined questionable specimens over the past years: John M. Burns, the late Harry K. Clench, the late Alexander B. Klots, the late Arthur Lindsey and C. Don MacNeill.

Last but not the least is my deep appreciation to Alicia Burnell, Ken Fettig and Leslie Johnson of the MSU Department of Outreach Communications for their enthusiasm, skill and commitment in producing this guidebook.

Introduction

Butterflies (including skippers) and moths make up the insect order Lepidoptera, whose members have scales covering their wings. Butterflies can usually be distinguished from moths by their day-flying habit; their thin, clubbed antennae, and their manner of holding the wings upright over the body when at rest. Some skippers hold their wings flat against the ground, hold the hindwings at a 45 degree angle or wrap them around a branch. Butterflies go through a complete metamorphosis — i.e., egg, caterpillar, chrysalis, adult. There are one or two generations per season for most species, though some species, such as the alpines and the arctics, may take two years to complete development. Many adult butterflies live from a few days to two weeks; some live longer. Perhaps the two species that live the longest are the Mourning Cloak, a hibernating species that may live up to 8 months, and the Monarch, which migrates to Mexico in the fall and may also live 8 months or longer.

Worldwide, butterfly species number approximately 15,000; some 900 species are found throughout the United States and Canada. Michigan has recorded the 159 species featured in this guidebook, or approximately 17 percent of those that occur in America north of Mexico. Of these species, about 137 (86 percent) can be classified as year-round residents; the others are frequent or accidental southern strays or migrants. It is the purpose of this guidebook to stimulate more interest in the study of our butterflies that will add more knowledge of their life histories and distribution within the state and perhaps record still more species.

Michigan butterflies and skippers have long been of interest to avocational and professional lepidopterists — those interested in studying and collecting moths and butterflies. In recent years, we have seen an increase in nature photographers, butterfly gardeners and lay naturalists, all interested in learning more about Michigan's butterflies and skippers.

Unfortunately, there has never been a guidebook to Michigan butterflies. Several large scientific publications (Howe, 1975; Scott, 1986) and Pyle's *Audubon Society Field Guide to North American Butterflies* (1981) cover America north of Mexico. In recent years, several regional books (Ebner, 1970; Holmes *et al.*, 1991; Iftner *et al.*, 1992; Shull, 1987) have covered the butterflies and skippers of neighboring states and Canada. In addition, Opler and Malikul (1992) published the Peterson field guide *Eastern Butterflies*, a useful guide to the butterflies that occur east of the 100th meridian. This guide, and Opler and Krizek's (1984) *Butterflies East of the Great Plains*, feature color plates and range maps, and include useful information on Michigan species. However, the information is not detailed enough and the distribution maps are too general for a more thorough study of Michigan butterflies.

This guidebook will not repeat many of the basics included in Opler's publications, such as butterfly structures, preparing specimens and making a collection. Anyone interested in making a collection and learning of equipment and techniques in preparing specimens should consult one of these publications.

The primary purposes of this guidebook are to stimulate a greater awareness of and interest in Michigan's butterfly fauna, to assist in the identification of species and to promote their study. It should be pointed out that without collections of properly prepared specimens, complete with accurate data, we would know very little about the butterfly fauna of Michigan. Avocational collecting of insects in a reasonable manner should be encouraged, especially in proximity to metropolitan areas, where habitat is being destroyed by development.

This guidebook provides a brief description of the adult butterfly (male and female), adult food sources, early stages and host plants, distribution and flight period. The dates cited after "Flight period" refer to the earliest and latest dates of capture in Michigan. In those cases where I do not have personal knowledge of any of these features, I have consulted Opler's two publications. Aiding in the identification of each species are color photographs showing the upper and lower surfaces of males and females and a map of Michigan showing the known Michigan distribution. Photographs in natural settings are included for some species. Most of the figured specimens are from my collection and the Lepidoptera collection in Michigan State University's Center for Arthropod Diversity Study. The *Papilio machaon hudsonianus* (No. 3) specimen was borrowed from the Edward Herig, Jr., collection, and the *Erora laetus* (No. 48) specimen, showing the undersurface, was borrowed from the Leroy Koehn collection. James Davidson kindly donated the photograph of the *E. laetus* male on page 14.

The nomenclature and arrangement of species and families, including common names, essentially follows Opler and Malikul (1992), with the exception that I treat Satyridae and Danaidae as separate families.

Physiography and Climate of Michigan

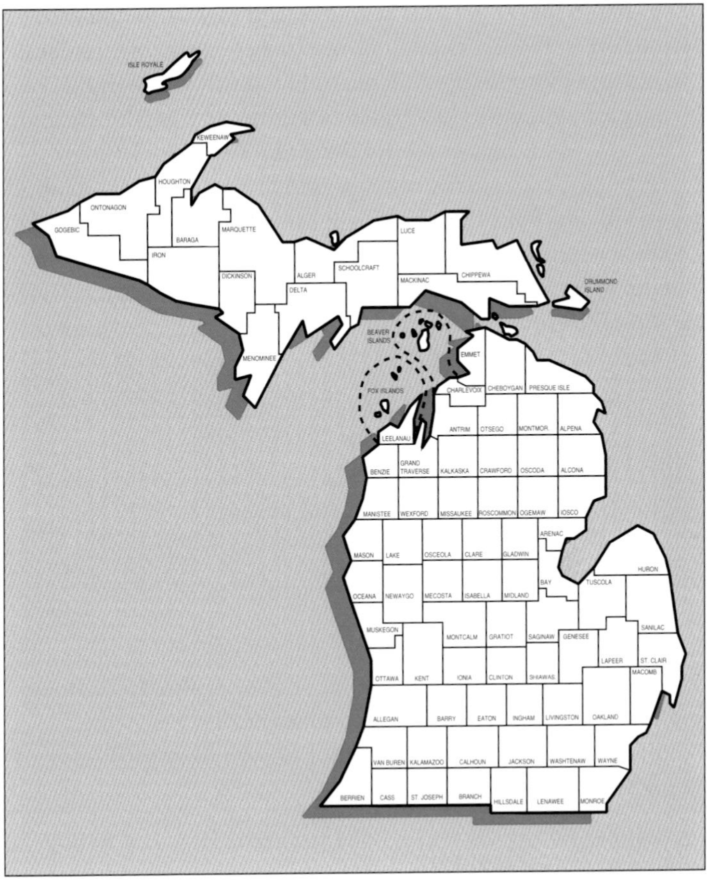

Excluding the area of the Great Lakes, Michigan covers 58,915 square miles (152,590 square kilometers) situated between the 41st and 48th parallels of latitude. The Lower Peninsula extends 277 miles (446 kilometers) from north to south and has an extreme width of approximately 195 miles (314 kilometers), while the Upper Peninsula measures 318 miles (512 kilometers) from east to west and varies from 30 to 164 miles (48 to 264 kilometers) in width. Elevations range from approximately 570 to 1,979 feet

(174 to 603 meters) above sea level, the highest point being Mt. Arvon in Baraga County in the Upper Peninsula. By land, the state is bounded by Indiana, Ohio and Wisconsin; however, by Great Lakes and connecting waters (the Detroit, St. Clair and St. Marys rivers), it borders Illinois, Minnesota, Pennsylvania, New York and the province of Ontario. In all, Michigan has some 3,200 miles (5,149 kilometers) of Great Lakes shoreline, including several small and large islands. The most notable of the islands is Isle Royale in Lake Superior, now a national park.

Geologically, Michigan's two peninsulas vary greatly in origin and in the character of their surface and subsurface formations. The entire state, like much of the north central part of North America, was dramatically affected by past glacial activity. The last glacier disappeared more than 10,000 years ago. All of the Lower Peninsula lies buried beneath a deep layer of glacial drift made up of various mineral materials. Its topography varies from the relatively high, sandy plateau of Otsego County to the rolling moraines and ancient lake beds of the more southern counties. These land features have given rise to various soil types, which result in a great number of distinct plant and animal communities.

The Upper Peninsula can be divided approximately in half, with the eastern half represented by relatively level to gently rolling terrain covered by a more shallow glacial drift, and the western half dominated by numerous igneous rocky hills and other prominent rock formations. Among the latter are the Huron and Porcupine Mountains, with altitudes approaching 2,000 feet (609 meters) above sea level. There are some 11,000 inland lakes, more than 37,000 miles (59,533 kilometers) of streams, and countless bogs, fens and marshes statewide.

The climate of Michigan, generally classified as humid, is further categorized into two types: continental and semimarine (USDA, 1941). The former occurs in the interior counties of both peninsulas and is identified with extremes in temperature. The latter type is found in proximity to the Great Lakes shoreline, where the nearby water serves to moderate temperatures in both winter and summer. Perhaps the most temperate climate in Michigan is found in the extreme southwestern portion of Berrien County, where the average number of frost-free days approaches 180 — 100 days more than in parts of Baraga and Iron counties in the Upper Peninsula! In the Upper Peninsula, the average date for the last killing frost is May 20 along the Great Lakes to June 10 in the interior; in the Lower Peninsula, the dates range from May 1-10 in the southern counties to June 10 in the north-central counties (USDA, 1941). Average temperatures range from 10 to 26 degrees F (-12.2 to -3.3 degrees C) in January to 60 to 72 degrees F (15.6 to 22.2 degrees C) in July. Precipitation averages 30 inches (76.2 cm) a year, with average snowfalls of 115 to 130 inches (292 to 330 cm) in the extreme north to 30 inches (76.2 cm) in the southeastern portion. Prevailing winds are from the southwest in southern Michigan and westerly in the north.

Habitats

The combination of geological and climatic forces has made Michigan one of the most diversified ecological areas east of the Misssissippi River. It would be difficult to find another state that has such a variety of unique habitats, ranging from the cactus prairies of Newaygo County to the sedgy marshes and acid bogs in many counties and the extensive hardwood and pine forests, each with its peculiar flora and fauna. Some of the more prominent ecological areas that offer habitat for many of our more interesting and unusual butterflies are:

Oak-hickory forests of southern counties: Banded and Hickory Hairstreaks.

Beech-maple-birch-hemlock forests in northern counties: West Virginia White and Early Hairstreak.

Jack, red and white pine barrens with blueberry: Hoary and Pine Elfins, Chryxus Arctic and Canadian Tiger Swallowtail.

Sedgy swamps with wide-leaf sedges, buttonbush and mixed swamp hardwoods, found in many southern counties: Appalachian Eyed Brown and Dukes' Skipper.

Sedgy marshes, containing wide-leaf and narrow-leaf sedges, cattails, grasses and other plants found throughout the state: Eyed Brown, Mulberry Wing, Dion and Two-spotted skippers.

Tamarack and poison sumac fens, located primarily in south-western counties: Mitchell's Satyr.

Acid bogs, ranging from small, scattered ones in Oakland to Allegan counties to some covering thousands of acres in the Upper Peninsula: Bog Copper, Bog Fritillary and Jutta Arctic.

Dry tall-grass prairies of Allegan and Newaygo counties, characterized by big and little bluestem grasses, prickly pear cactus and other plants usually found in the Great Plains: Regal Fritillary, Ottoe and Leonard's skippers.

Coastal sand dunes, principally along Lake Michigan, with rock cress, beach grass and interdunal hardwoods and pines: Olympia Marble and migrating Monarchs.

Butterfly Gardening and Conservation Efforts

Butterfly gardening is a relatively recent phenomenon in urban and rural areas. Suddenly, people want to attract butterflies to their yards and neighborhoods by planting a multitude of nectar plants and, perhaps, caterpillar host plants. Part of the reason, I believe, is that many individuals have seen a reduction of native species that heretofore were taken for granted as part of their local environment. They now want to assist in bringing butterflies back into their neighborhoods. Many formal gardens and city zoos are now creating butterfly gardens and presenting information to the public on how and what to plant in their areas.

Local bookstores now carry an assortment of books and other publications on butterfly gardening; many are very instructive on just what to plant in various parts of the country. It is wise to plant flowers that will attract butterflies and skippers throughout the growing season. Spring-blooming lilacs followed by many late spring and summer flowers and ending with butterfly bush, zinnias and marigolds will give gardeners a good start on an attractive butterfly garden. Adult food sources and caterpillar host plants discussed under each butterfly species in this guidebook will give additional ideas on plants to use in creating a butterfly garden.

If the gardener also wishes to attract breeding species, then larval host plants must be planted. One of the most informative books on butterfly gardening is *Butterfly Gardening - Creating Summer Magic In Your Garden* (Xerces Soc., 1990). This book is relatively inexpensive and contains more than 100 exquisite color photographs of butterflies and flowers.

Along with this interest has come a nationwide and worldwide interest in the creation of butterfly greenhouses — i.e., large enclosed structures that maintain a wide variety of nectar plants and live butterflies from local and exotic places. This interest is so strong now that new butterfly houses are being constructed throughout the United States. In fact, Michigan State University was instrumental in creating one of the first butterfly greenhouses in the country several years ago; plans are now underway to build a new and larger facility.

Michigan's Endangered Species Law, Act 451, Public Acts of 1994, currently lists 11 species of butterflies and skippers as "endangered and threatened" in Michigan, along with 14 "species of special concern". While the law draws public attention to these species as a threatened portion of our natural environment, it also authorizes the Michigan Department of Natural Resources (MDNR) to engage in activities to promote their numbers and habitat. However, the policies of the MDNR Wildlife Division greatly restrict the activities of avocational lepidopterists, those who are most likely to assist the MDNR by providing additional knowledge of the life histories and distribution of these listed species. For example, collecting permits will be issued only to individuals affiliated with a public institution, provided a new colony is located and provided that all specimens of endangered and threatened species collected are deposited in a public institutional collection. With these conditions, few if any permits will be issued to avocational lepidopterists. The irony of this situation is that the list is required by law to be reviewed every two years to determine if there has been a change in the status of listed species during the previous period. Without the assistance of avocational lepidopterists, one can wonder where the new data, if any, will come from?

The steady destruction of butterfly habitat by the ever-expanding development of residential subdivisions, shopping centers, bigger and better highways, and expanding fencerow-free agricultural areas will undoubtedly reduce numbers of butterflies and possibly eliminate certain local species. Tougher zoning laws and better enforcement of Michigan's wetland statute and similar land-use laws could help to slow down and curtail much of this destruction in the future. A viable butterfly fauna is one of the barometers of the health of Michigan's natural environment, and facilitating their study should be encouraged.

"See a little blue butterfly fluttering about on the dry brown leaves in a warm place by the swamp side, making a pleasant contrast."

Thoreau

✓ Checklist of Michigan Butterflies and Skippers

	Species Number	Common Name	Scientific Name	Page No.
Family Papilionidae: Swallowtails				
☐	1	Pipe-vine Swallowtail	*Battus philenor* (Linnaeus)	28
☐	2	Black Swallowtail	*Papilio polyxenes asterius* Stoll	30
☐	3	Old World Swallowtail	*Papilio machaon hudsonianus* A.H. Clark	31
☐	4	Giant Swallowtail	*Papilio cresphontes* (Cramer)	32
☐	5	Tiger Swallowtail	*Papilio glaucus* (Linnaeus)	34
☐	6	Canadian Tiger Swallowtail	*Papilio canadensis* (Rothschild & Jordan)	35
☐	7	Spicebush Swallowtail	*Papilio troilus* (Linnaeus)	37
☐	8	Zebra Swallowtail	*Eurytides marcellus* (Cramer)	38
Family Pieridae: Whites, Sulphurs				
☐	9	Checkered White	*Pontia protodice* (Boisduval & LeConte)	40
☐	10	Western White	*Pontia occidentalis* (Reakirt)	42
☐	11	Mustard White	*Pieris napi oleracea* (Harris)	43
☐	12	West Virginia White	*Pieris virginiensis* (W.H. Edwards)	44
☐	13	Cabbage Butterfly	*Pieris rapae* (Linnaeus)	45
☐	14	Large Marble	*Euchloe ausonides* (Lucas)	47
☐	15	Olympia Marble	*Euchloe olympia* (W.H. Edwards)	48
☐	16	Clouded Sulphur	*Colias philodice* Godart	49
☐	17	Orange Sulphur	*Colias eurytheme* Boisduval	51
☐	18	Pink-edged Sulphur	*Colias interior* Scudder	52
☐	19	Dog Face	*Colias cesonia* (Stoll)	53
☐	20	Cloudless Sulphur	*Phoebis sennae eubule* (Linnaeus)	54
☐	21	Orange-barred Sulphur	*Phoebis philea* (Johansson)	55
☐	22	Little Sulphur	*Eurema lisa* (Boisduval & LeConte)	56
☐	23	Sleepy Orange	*Eurema nicippe* (Cramer)	58
☐	24	Mexican Sulphur	*Eurema mexicanum* (Boisduval)	59
☐	25	Dainty Sulphur	*Nathalis iole* Boisduval	60

Family Riodinidae: Metalmarks

Family Nymphalidae: Brushfoots

Species Number	Common Name	Scientific Name	Page No.
Family Hesperiidae: Skippers			
❑ 112	Silver-spotted Skipper	*Epargyreus clarus* (Cramer)	177
❑ 113	Long-tailed Skipper	*Urbanus proteus* (Linnaeus)	179
❑ 114	Hoary Edge	*Achalarus lyciades* (Geyer)	180
❑ 115	Southern Cloudy Wing	*Thorybes bathyllus* (J.E. Smith)	181
❑ 116	Northern Cloudy Wing	*Thorybes pylades* (Scudder)	182
❑ 117	Dreamy Dusky Wing	*Erynnis icelus* (Scudder & Burgess)	183
❑ 118	Sleepy Dusky Wing	*Erynnis brizo* (Boisduval & LeConte)	184
❑ 119	Juvenal's Dusky Wing	*Erynnis juvenalis* (Fabricius)	185
❑ 120	Horace's Dusky Wing	*Erynnis horatius* (Scudder & Burgess)	187
❑ 121	Mottled Dusky Wing	*Erynnis martialis* (Scudder)	188
❑ 122	Columbine Dusky Wing	*Erynnis lucilius* (Scudder & Burgess)	189
❑ 123	Wild Indigo Dusky Wing	*Erynnis baptisiae* (Forbes)	190
❑ 124	Persius Dusky Wing	*Erynnis persius* (Scudder)	191
❑ 125	Grizzled Skipper	*Pyrgus centaureae wyandot* (W.H. Edwards)	192
❑ 126	Checkered Skipper	*Pyrgus communis* (Grote)	194
❑ 127	Common Sooty Wing	*Pholisora catullus* (Fabricius)	195
❑ 128	Arctic Skipper	*Carterocephalus palaemon mandan* (W.H. Edwards)	196
❑ 129	Swarthy Skipperling	*Nastra lherminier* (Latreille)	197
❑ 130	Least Skipper	*Ancyloxypha numitor* (Fabricius)	198
❑ 131	Powesheik Skipperling	*Oarisma powesheik* (Parker)	199
❑ 132	European Skipper	*Thymelicus lineola* (Ochsenheimer)	201
❑ 133	Fiery Skipper	*Hylephila phyleus* (Drury)	202
❑ 134	Laurentian Skipper	*Hesperia comma laurentina* (Lyman)	203
❑ 135	Ottoe Skipper	*Hesperia ottoe* W.H. Edwards	205

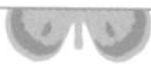

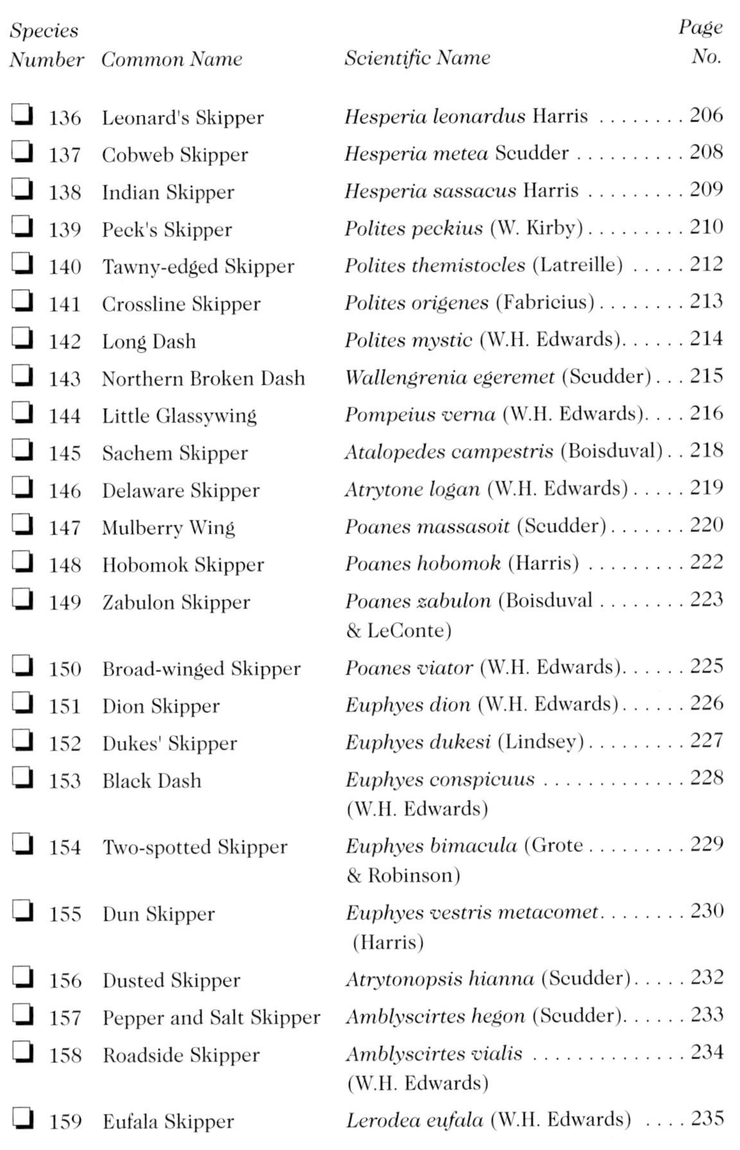

	Species Number	*Common Name*	*Scientific Name*	*Page No.*
❑	136	Leonard's Skipper	*Hesperia leonardus* Harris	206
❑	137	Cobweb Skipper	*Hesperia metea* Scudder	208
❑	138	Indian Skipper	*Hesperia sassacus* Harris	209
❑	139	Peck's Skipper	*Polites peckius* (W. Kirby)	210
❑	140	Tawny-edged Skipper	*Polites themistocles* (Latreille)	212
❑	141	Crossline Skipper	*Polites origenes* (Fabricius)	213
❑	142	Long Dash	*Polites mystic* (W.H. Edwards)	214
❑	143	Northern Broken Dash	*Wallengrenia egeremet* (Scudder)	215
❑	144	Little Glassywing	*Pompeius verna* (W.H. Edwards)	216
❑	145	Sachem Skipper	*Atalopedes campestris* (Boisduval)	218
❑	146	Delaware Skipper	*Atrytone logan* (W.H. Edwards)	219
❑	147	Mulberry Wing	*Poanes massasoit* (Scudder)	220
❑	148	Hobomok Skipper	*Poanes hobomok* (Harris)	222
❑	149	Zabulon Skipper	*Poanes zabulon* (Boisduval & LeConte)	223
❑	150	Broad-winged Skipper	*Poanes viator* (W.H. Edwards)	225
❑	151	Dion Skipper	*Euphyes dion* (W.H. Edwards)	226
❑	152	Dukes' Skipper	*Euphyes dukesi* (Lindsey)	227
❑	153	Black Dash	*Euphyes conspicuus* (W.H. Edwards)	228
❑	154	Two-spotted Skipper	*Euphyes bimacula* (Grote & Robinson)	229
❑	155	Dun Skipper	*Euphyes vestris metacomet* (Harris)	230
❑	156	Dusted Skipper	*Atrytonopsis hianna* (Scudder)	232
❑	157	Pepper and Salt Skipper	*Amblyscirtes hegon* (Scudder)	233
❑	158	Roadside Skipper	*Amblyscirtes vialis* (W.H. Edwards)	234
❑	159	Eufala Skipper	*Lerodea eufala* (W.H. Edwards)	235

Swallowtails: *Family Papilionidae:*

This family contains medium to large tailed butterflies; the Giant Swallowtail is the largest butterfly in Michigan. Most of the species have two broods, with the spring specimens smaller than subsequent broods. Females usually lay single eggs on a wide variety of herbs, shrubs and trees. Young swallowtail caterpillars of most species are black with a small, white saddle patch that makes them resemble bird droppings. All swallowtail caterpillars have an orange, forked, odor-producing, fleshy organ located just behind the head that can be everted when the larva is disturbed or attacked by a predator. They overwinter in the chrysalis, which is suspended by a silk girdle around its middle and attached horizontally or vertically to a twig, tree trunk or other structure.

Pipe-vine Swallowtail

Battus philenor (Linnaeus)

Adults and food sources: The Pipe-vine Swallowtail is an uncommon, large, black butterfly with iridescent greenish blue on the hindwings of the males. Females are essentially black with white marginal spots. Spring specimens are much smaller than summer specimens.

Adults frequently feed on nectar of wild bergamot, thistles, common milkweed, and several other pink and purple flowers. Their wings flutter rapidly while they feed.

Early stages and host plants: Young caterpillars cluster together on the host plant; mature caterpillars are velvety black or dark brown with rows of fleshy red tubercles along the body. They are solitary feeders and may be found crawling on the forest floor searching for the host plant.

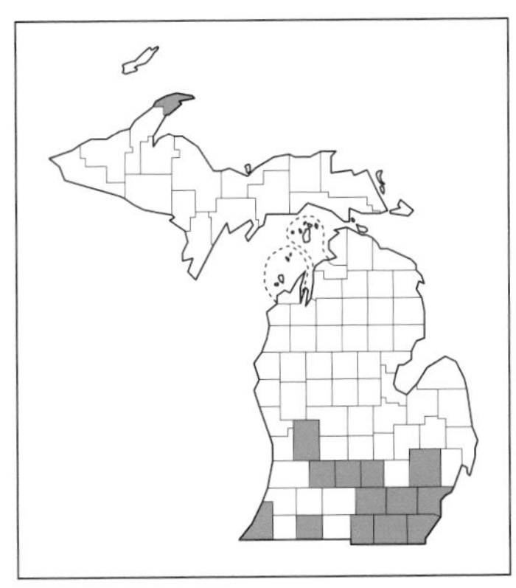

Eggs are laid in small clusters on Virginia snakeroot; another host is Dutchman's pipe, frequently planted as an ornamental vine in southern Michigan counties. They are also reported to use wild ginger.

Habitat: Open fields and railroad embankments near oak-hickory woods. Adults of the spring brood can be seen flying in these woods in late April to early May.

Distribution: Infrequently found in southern counties but very common in Ohio and Indiana. Two stray specimens were collected in Keweenaw County on July 22, 1975, and July 16, 1977.

Flight period: Two broods; April 20 to October.

Remarks: The Pipe-vine Swallowtail is listed as a threatened species by the Michigan Department of Natural Resources Natural Features Inventory, pursuant to Michigan's Endangered Species Law. Its larval host plant, Virginia snakeroot, is also listed as a threatened species. The butterfly, distasteful to birds, is a model for other butterfly mimics such as the Spicebush Swallowtail (No. 7), the dark form of the female Tiger Swallowtail (No. 5), the Black Swallowtail (No. 2) and the Red-spotted Purple (No. 93a).

Male - Upper

Female - Upper

2 Black Swallowtail

Papilio polyxenes asterius Stoll

Adults and food sources: Both sexes are essentially black butterflies with rows of yellow spots on both fore- and hindwings. Males have more distinct rows of yellow spots on the hindwings, while some females have fewer and less distinct spots and more blue on the hindwings than males. Early spring specimens are noticeably smaller than summer specimens.

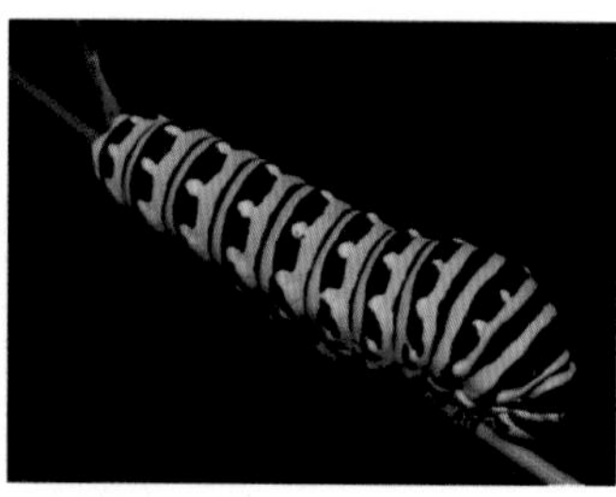

Adults feed on nectars from a wide range of wild and cultivated flowers such as lilac, common milkweed, thistle and zinnia. Males are fond of sipping moisture and nutrients from damp soils.

Early stages and host plants: The mature caterpillar has green and black bands with rows of yellowish orange spots. It is the most often seen swallowtail caterpillar.

Females lay eggs on a variety of plants in the carrot family, usually selecting wild carrot (also known as Queen-Anne's-lace) in southern counties. Larvae can be a minor pest to some gardeners when they feed on parsley, dill and carrots.

Habitat: Old fields, vacant rural and urban lots, farmland and city gardens.

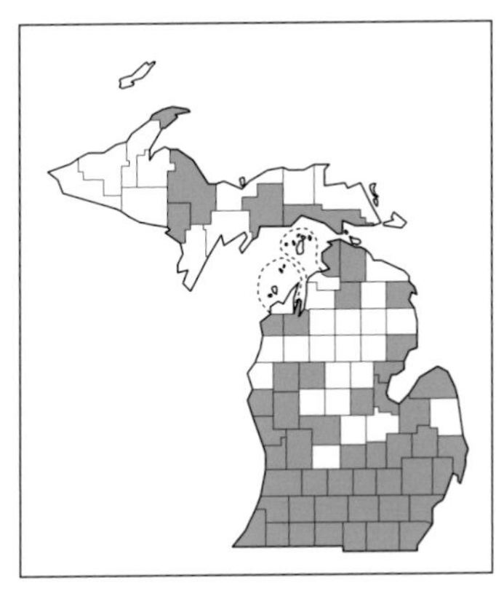

Distribution: Throughout the Lower Peninsula and scattered counties in the Upper Peninsula.

Flight period: Two broods in southern counties; April 10 to September 30.

Remarks: This is one of Michigan's commonest swallowtails. Their chrysalis can frequently be found suspended under windowsills and other ledges around buildings. The nominate subspecies *P. polyxenes polyxenes* Fabricius is neotropical and is not found in eastern states.

Spring male - Upper

Male - Upper

Female - Upper

3 Old World Swallowtail

Papilio machaon hudsonianus A.H. Clark

Male - Upper

Adults and food sources: This is a medium-sized black and yellow swallowtail. I have no field experience with this species in Michigan; one immaculate specimen was collected by a non-resident lepidopterist several years ago in the Upper Peninsula a few miles north of Paradise.

Early stages and host plants: The caterpillar is reported to be similar to the Black Swallowtail larva. It is reported to favor plants in the carrot family.

Habitat: Reported by Opler (1992) and Scott (1986) in barren rocky areas in Canadian and Hudsonian zones. The Michigan specimen was collected in jack pine barrens.

Distribution: A butterfly of subarctic Canada, with only one confirmed Michigan record from Chippewa County in the eastern Upper Peninsula. It may occur infrequently on Isle Royale; it has been taken at Thunder Bay, Ontario, Canada.

Flight period: Reported to extend from late May to July. The Michigan specimen was taken on June 9, 1991.

Remarks: This holarctic, subarctic species may occur infrequently in the northern portions of the Upper Peninsula. It may be mistaken by casual observers for the common Canadian Tiger Swallowtail (No. 6), which would occur at the same time.

4 Giant Swallowtail

Papilio cresphontes

(Cramer)

Adults and food sources: This large, dark brown butterfly has diagonal bands of large yellow spots on the wings. It's the largest butterfly found in Michigan, with some females reaching over 6 inches (15 cm) in wingspread.

Favored nectar sources include teasel and butterfly-bush; it also visits buttonbush, bull thistle and joe-pye-weed.

Early stages and host plants: Mature caterpillars are olive-brown mottled with lighter and darker markings and a large whitish patch in middle and anal areas. They closely resemble a large bird dropping.

Females prefer prickly ash and hop-tree for egg laying in Michigan. Both plants are members of the rue family, which includes various citrus plants. The caterpillar is known as the "orange dog" in the South, where it's sometimes a minor pest on citrus.

Habitat: Forests and woodlots containing the host plants; fields, gardens and roadsides.

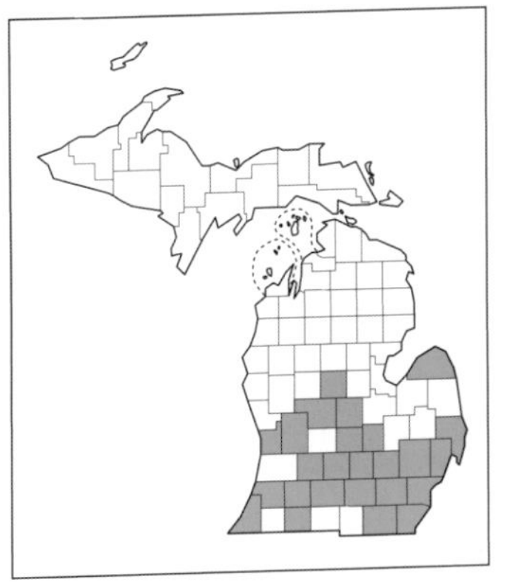

Distribution: Widely found in the southern half of the Lower Peninsula.

Flight period: Usually two broods; April 26 to October 7.

Remarks: Never common in any area. It has extended its range northward to a line running approximately from Bay City to Muskegon during the past 50 years.

Spring male - Upper

Summer male - Upper

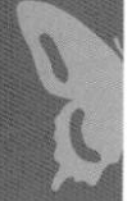

5 Tiger Swallowtail

Papilio glaucus (Linnaeus)

Adults and food sources: This large yellow swallowtail has black stripes; it is one of the state's most familiar butterflies. The undersurface of the forewing has a marginal band of separated yellow spots. Some females are predominantly black, especially in southern counties. These females mimic the unpalatable Pipe-vine Swallowtail.

Adults are fond of a variety of cultivated and wild flowers, including bergamot, buttonbush, red clover, orange hawkweed, honeysuckle, ironweed, lilac, marigold, common milkweed, downy and garden phlox, blazing-star and joe-pye-weed. Males take moisture and nutrients from damp soils, feces and carrion.

Early stages and host plants: The mature caterpillar is dark green with two small false eyespots on the swollen thoracic area. When not feeding, the caterpillar rests on a silken mat within a slightly curled leaf.

The preferred larval host is wild black cherry in Michigan, but ash, chokecherry, lilac, hop-tree and tulip-tree are also chosen.

Habitat: Forest openings, edges, brushy fields, rural roadsides and stream margins; also found in urban parks and gardens.

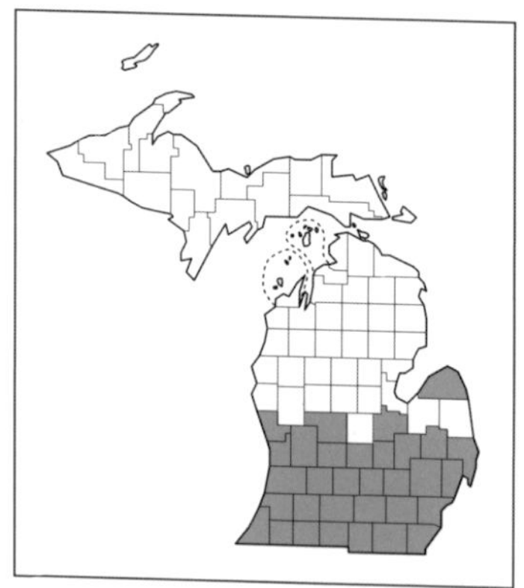

Distribution: Throughout the southern half of the Lower Peninsula.

Flight period: Usually two broods; May 2 to October 6.

Remarks: The Tiger Swallowtail is easily confused with the Canadian Tiger Swallowtail (No. 6) where their populations overlap. The latter swallowtail is slightly smaller and has a continuous yellow marginal band on the undersurface of the forewing and has a narrower black inner edge on the upper surface of the hindwing.

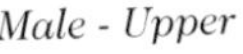

Male - Upper

Male - Under

Female - Upper

Dark female - Upper

Aberrant male - Upper

6 Canadian Tiger Swallowtail

Papilio canadensis

(Rothschild & Jordan)

Adults and food sources: This is a large yellow swallowtail with black stripes that looks very similar to the Tiger Swallowtail. Females are yellow, similar to males. The undersurface of the forewing has a continuous yellow band.

Nectar sources include ornamental cherry, honeysuckle, wild iris, wood lily, lilac, wild-raisin and Labrador tea. Males

frequently congregate in large numbers—40 or more—for moisture and nutrients on damp soils along trails and streams.

Early stages and host plants: The caterpillar is similar to that of the Tiger Swallowtail.

Trembling aspen is the preferred host plant; birch and black cherry are also reported as food plants.

Habitat: Pine barrens, aspen forest openings and edges, roadsides and stream margins.

Distribution: Throughout the Upper Peninsula, including Isle Royale, and the northern half of the Lower Peninsula, overlapping narrowly with the Tiger Swallowtail's range.

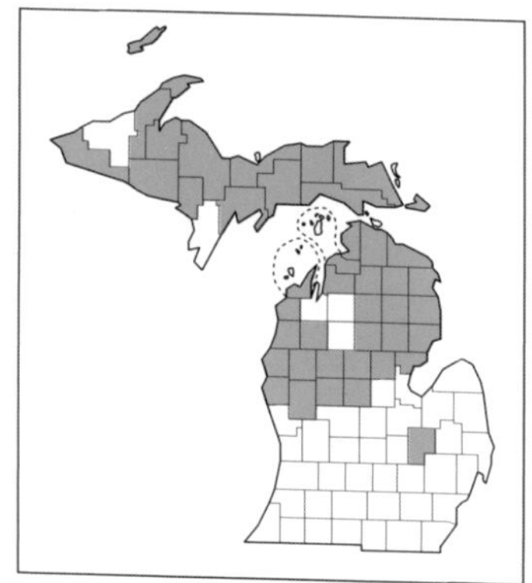

Flight period: One brood; May 12 to August 12.

Remarks: Long considered a subspecies of the Tiger Swallowtail (No. 5), the Canadian Tiger Swallowtail was recognized as a distinct species in 1991 (Hagen *et al.*).

Spicebush Swallowtail

Papilio troilus (Linnaeus)

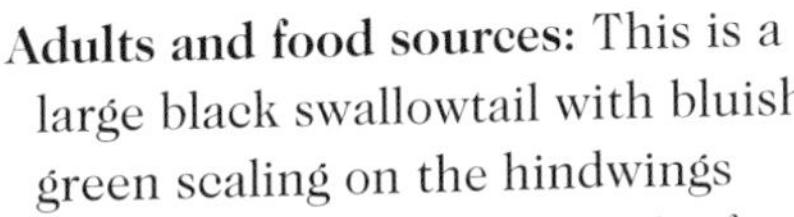

Adults and food sources: This is a large black swallowtail with bluish green scaling on the hindwings that is more iridescent on the female. The undersurface of the hindwing has a marginal row of orange spots. Tails are spoon-shaped. Spring specimens are smaller than those of summer.

Adults nectar on blackberry, blueberry, wild crabapple, dandelion, honeysuckle, lilac, lupine, common and orange milkweed, blazing-star, New Jersey tea, and many other wild and cultivated flowers.

Early stages and host plants: Mature caterpillars are dark green above and whitish below, with two large, black, orange-edged false eyespots on the swollen thoracic area and rows of black-encircled blue spots on the abdomen.

The preferred host plant is sassafras, but spicebush is also used in Michigan. The caterpillar hides during the day on a silken mat within a curled-up leaf.

Habitat: Oak-hickory forest openings, edges, oak-pine barrens, trails and roadsides.

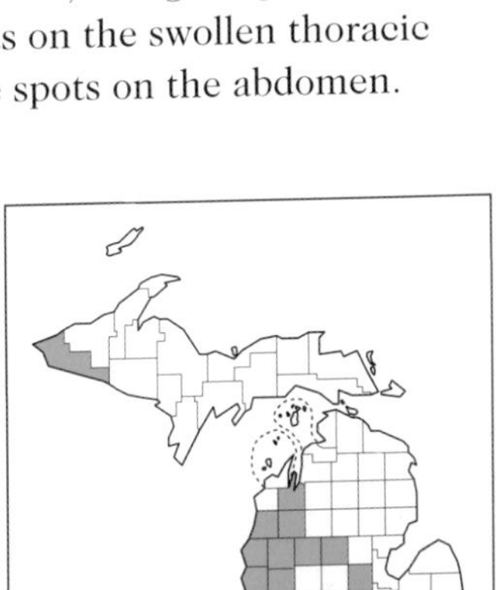

Distribution: Throughout the southern two-thirds of the Lower Peninsula; a single specimen was recorded from Ironwood, Gogebic County, in the Upper Peninsula.

Flight period: Two broods; May 3 to September 23.

Remarks: The butterfly is common in southern counties. It mimics the Pipe-vine Swallowtail (No. 1), which is distasteful to birds.

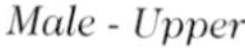

Male - Upper

Female - Upper

8 Zebra Swallowtail

Eurytides marcellus (Cramer)

Adults and food sources: This medium-sized greenish white swallowtail has black stripes and very long tails. Spring specimens are much smaller, with shorter tails and a double red spot on the upper surface of the hindwing.

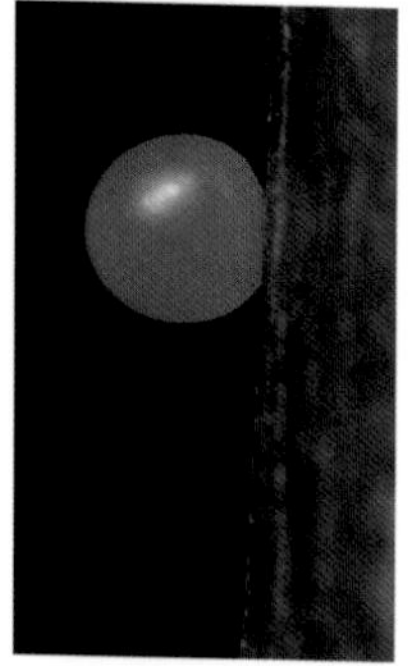

Adults nectar on dogbane, lilac, common milkweed and privet; occasionally males take moisture and nutrients from stream banks and roadside ditches.

Early stages and host plants: The mature caterpillar is pea-green with alternating bands of yellow and black.

The preferred host plant in Michigan is pawpaw; females usually select seedlings and young saplings in openings for egg laying.

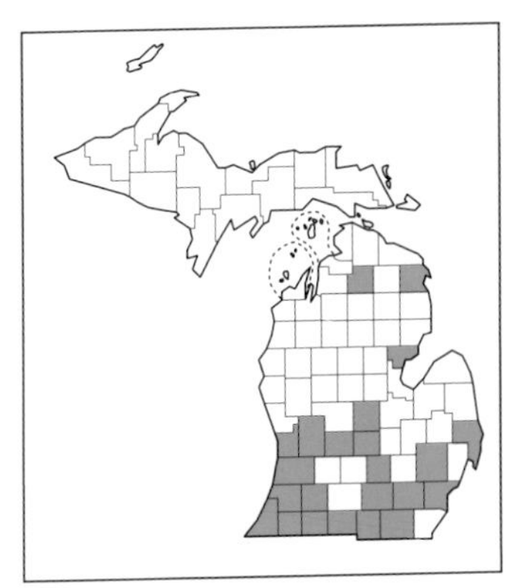

Habitat: Floodplain forest openings, edges, stream margins and, occasionally, rural and urban gardens.

Distribution: Essentially southern counties, extending north to Gratiot County along the Maple River. Strays have been observed in Alpena and Otsego counties.

Flight period: Two broods: April 17 to September 16.

Remarks: An uncommon butterfly. Summer specimens are the fastest fliers among Michigan swallowtails.

Spring male - Upper

Summer male - Upper

Whites, Sulphurs: *Family Pieridae:*

This family contains medium to small yellow to white butterflies, frequently with black borders or markings. The Cabbage Butterfly is a very common example. Females of many Michigan species choose one of the legumes (e.g., alfalfa) or plants in the mustard family (crucifers such as cabbage) for the caterpillar food plant; a few species select other plants, including shrubs. The caterpillars are generally light green and covered with short, fine hairs. The chrysalis is suspended by a silk girdle around its middle and attached to a twig or other structure. They generally overwinter as chrysalids, but some spend the winter as larvae.

9

Checkered White

Pontia protodice (Boisduval & LeConte)

Adults and food sources: The male's forewing has black checkering on the outer half; the upper surface of the hindwing is essentially white. Females have heavier checkering on both wings. Spring specimens are much smaller, with the black markings on the upper forewing much reduced and with greenish scales tracing the veins on the underside of the hindwing.

Adults take nectar from a variety of flowers, including alfalfa, bergamot, bouncing Bet, butterfly-weed, red clover, cockle, goldenrod and thistle. Females frequently seek the flowers of their larval host plant.

Early stages and host plants: Caterpillars are striped alternately with yellow and purple-green and have small black tubercles. For egg laying, females select plants in the mustard family, such as wild pepper-grass and shepherd's-purse.

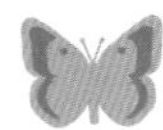

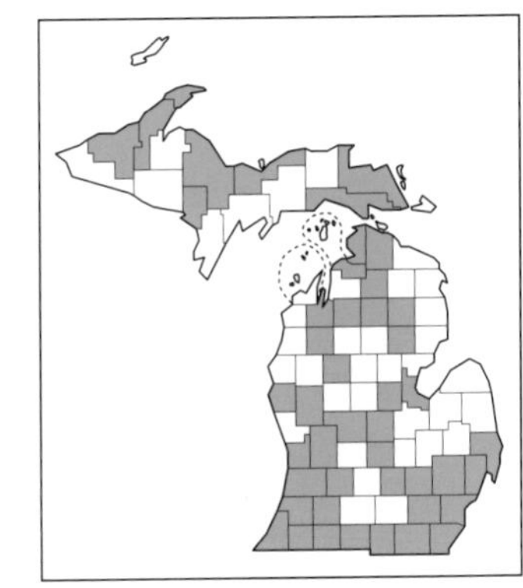

Distribution: Recorded from many counties in the Upper and the Lower Peninsula.

Habitat: Old fields, roadsides, pastures, and other open and disturbed areas.

Flight period: Usually two broods; April 16 to November 30.

Remarks: This butterfly is infrequently observed or not observed for several years in Michigan. It is more common in states south and west of Michigan. Some suggest its scarcity may be due to competition from the very common Cabbage Butterfly.

Male - Upper

Male - Under

Female - Upper

Spring male - Upper

Spring female - Upper

(10) Western White

Pontia occidentalis
(Reakirt)

Adults and food sources: The Western White is similar to the Checkered White (No. 9), but the male has more black markings and gray scaling on the upper surfaces of the wings. Beneath, the hindwings have gray-green veining.

No observations have been made of adults feeding on nectar in Michigan.

Early stages and host plants: These are reported to be similar to those of the Checkered White.

Habitat: Open areas, similar to the habitat of the Checkered White.

Distribution: Only two specimens have been positively reported from widely separated counties: Keweenaw, in the Upper Peninsula, and Montcalm, in the Lower Peninsula.

Flight period: June 29, 1989, and September 17, 1979.

Remarks: It is likely that the Michigan records are strays; it may occur more frequently but is easily confused with the Checkered White.

Male - Upper

Female - Upper

Male - Under

11 Mustard White

Pieris napi oleracea (Harris)

Adults and food sources: There are two seasonal forms. Spring specimens are white above with veins boldly marked with gray-green on the undersides of the hindwings. Summer specimens have wings that are essentially pure white above and below.

Adults feed on nectar of various mustard family plants and blueberries, boneset, ornamental cherry, dogbane, wild plum and thistle.

Early stages and host plants: The caterpillar is green with lateral yellow stripes. Females in Michigan favor mustard family plants, especially water cress, for egg laying.

Habitat: Floodplain forests and other shrubby wetlands and roadsides.

Distribution: Throughout the state.

Flight period: Two broods; April 17 to September 8.

Remarks: Locally common. This butterfly can be confused with the Cabbage White (No. 13) and the West Virginia White (No. 12), but the Cabbage White has one or two black spots on the upper forewing, and the West Virginia White has more rounded tips on the forewing and the lower hindwing veins are not as sharply outlined. The Michigan subspecies occurs essentially in the northern states; the nominate subspecies, *P. napi napi* Linnaeus, is found in Europe.

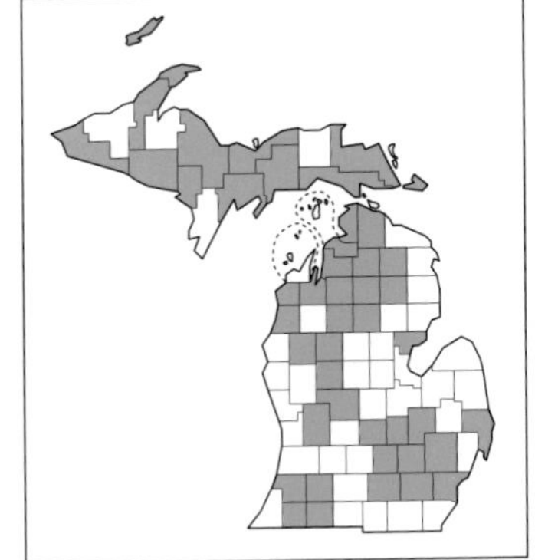

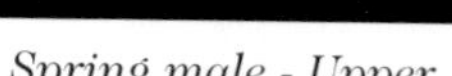

Spring male - Upper

Spring male - Under

Summer male - Upper

12 West Virginia White

Pieris virginiensis
(W.H. Edwards)

Adults and food sources: Adults are generally white and thin-scaled, some with faint dark markings on the upper surface; veins on the underside of the hindwing are faintly lined with brownish scales. It's easily distinguished from the Mustard White (No. 11) by the lack of yellow on the underside at the base of the hindwing.

Adults nectar on toothwort, the common trillium and other spring flowers that bloom in northern hardwood forests.

Early stages and host plants: The caterpillar is yellowish green with a lateral green stripe.

Females prefer to lay eggs on toothworts in Michigan.

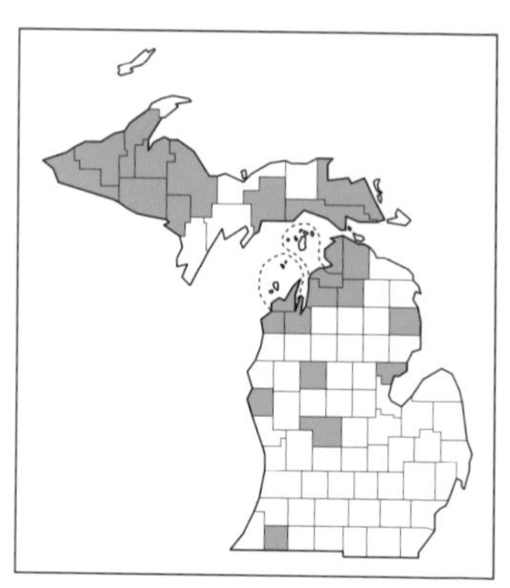

Habitat: Usually restricted to northern hardwood forests and edges. Adults are on the wing prior to full leaf development.

Distribution: Throughout northern counties, extending southerly to Cass and Montcalm counties.

Flight period: Single brood; April 24 to June 19.

Remarks: Locally common. A weak flier, it flies close to the forest floor. It overwinters as a chrysalis.

Male - Upper

Male - Under

13 Cabbage Butterfly

Pieris rapae (Linnaeus)

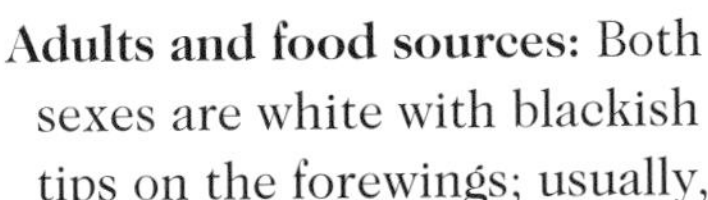

Adults and food sources: Both sexes are white with blackish tips on the forewings; usually, males typically have one black spot and females have two on the forewings. Yellowish scales cover the tips of the forewings and the hindwing on the underside. Spring specimens are frequently all white.

Adults feed on nectar from a wide variety of cultivated and wild flowers, including catnip, goldenrod, knapweed and purple loosestrife; they're also frequently seen at mud puddles sipping moisture and nutrients.

Early stages and host plants: The caterpillar is green with faint yellow lines on the back and sides and covered with short, fine hairs.

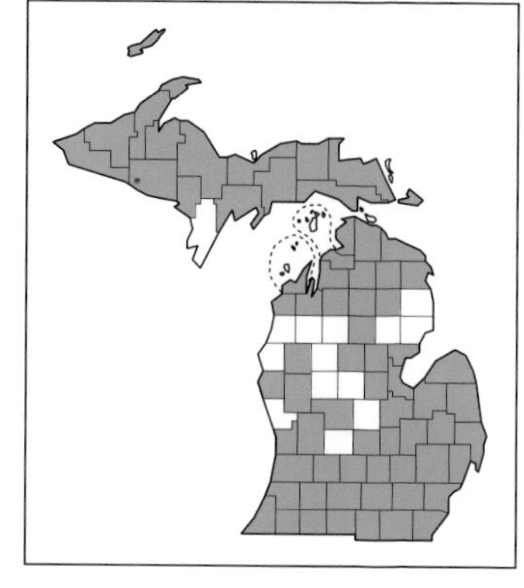

Eggs are laid on a wide variety of wild and cultivated plants in the mustard family. Larvae can be pests of cabbage, broccoli, Brussels sprouts, kale, cauliflower and others.

Habitat: Gardens, old fields, roadsides and disturbed areas.

Distribution: Throughout the state, including Isle Royale.

Flight period: At least three broods; March 25 to December 24.

Remarks: Introduced from Europe, it is now one of the state's most abundant butterflies.

Male - Upper

Male - Upper

Male - Under

Female - Upper

14 Large Marble

Euchloe ausonides (Lucas)

Adults and food sources: The upper sides of the wings are white with a black-patterned apex and a black, crescent-shaped mark along the leading edge of the forewing. The female's hindwing has a yellowish cast. The underside of the hindwing is marbled with greenish gray scales.

No observations of adults feeding in Michigan have been recorded.

Early stages and host plants: The caterpillar is striped with black, yellow and white, similar to the caterpillar of the Olympia Marble (No. 15).

It is found exclusively on Drummond's cress on Isle Royale, where larvae usually eat flowers and developing seedpods.

Habitat: Open areas, rock outcroppings and trails. Frequently on ridge tops.

Distribution: Known only from Isle Royale in Michigan; it should be looked for in the Porcupine Mountains and along elevated portions of the Keweenaw Peninsula.

Flight period: Single brood; June 16-29.

Remarks: First collected on Isle Royale in 1964 near Rock Harbor. Specimens of the Large Marble are generally larger than those of the Olympia Marble. Additional research is needed to determine the status of the Michigan population. It is listed by the Michigan Natural Features Inventory as a special concern species.

Male - Upper

Male - Under

15 Olympia Marble

Euchloe olympia
(W.H. Edwards)

Adults and food sources: The upper sides of the wings are predominantly white. The forewing has a black-patterned apex and a black bar along the leading edge. The hindwing is essentially unmarked, similar to that of the Large Marble (No. 14). The underside of the hindwing is marked with greenish gray marbling that is less extensive than on the Large Marble; it also has a pinkish hue near the base of the hindwing.

Adults nectar on Drummond's cress and rock cress, leatherleaf, lilac, lupine, wild mustard, downy phlox, puccoon and wild strawberry.

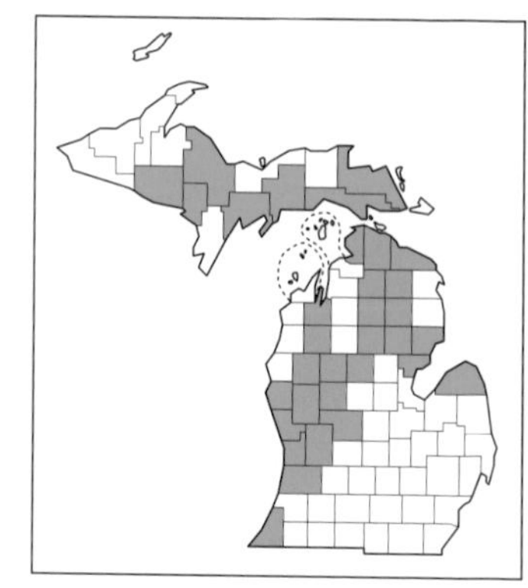

Early stages and host plants: Caterpillars are gray with yellow and white stripes.

Eggs are deposited on rock cresses; larvae eat only flowers and seedpods. Populations along the Great Lakes shores prefer rock cress and inland populations use Drummond's cress.

Habitat: Great Lakes dunes and open oak-pine barrens on sandy soils.

Distribution: Throughout the Upper Peninsula and extending into the Lower Peninsula from the Thumb area to the extreme southwest corner of the state along the Lake Michigan dunes.

Flight period: Single brood; April 23 to July 28.

Remarks: An uncommon butterfly. Coastal specimens are noticeably smaller than those found inland.

Male - Upper

Coastal male - Upper

16

Clouded Sulphur

Colias philodice Godart

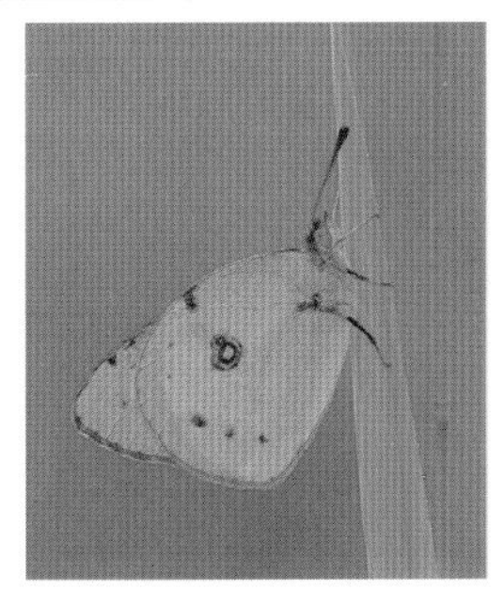

Adults and food sources: Wings of males are yellow with a solid black border; females are yellow with an uneven black border enclosing a few yellow spots, especially on the forewing. Both sexes have a black spot near the leading edge of the forewing and a yellow spot near the center of the hindwing. The hindwing has a silver spot rimmed with pink on the underside. Many females are white marked like the yellow form.

Adults use a wide range of nectar sources, including alfalfa, aster, red clover, cress, dandelion, goldenrod, mint and blazing-star. They can also be found at puddles and wet areas taking moisture and nutrients.

Early stages and host plants: The caterpillar is green with lateral white stripes edged with black. There may be some red spots in the white stripe.

Eggs are usually laid on white clover but may also be deposited on red clover, vetch and other legumes.

Habitat: Open areas, clover and alfalfa fields, roadsides and disturbed areas.

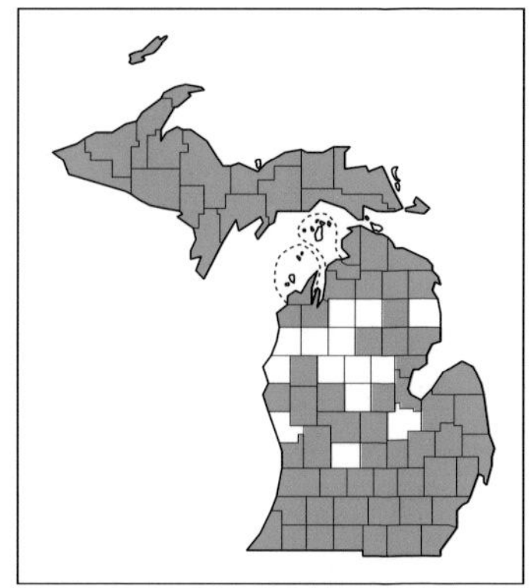

Distribution: Throughout the state.

Flight period: Three broods; April 12 to November 17.

Remarks: Common. Hybrids with the Orange Sulphur (No. 17) are common in late summer.

Male - Upper

Male - Upper

Male - Under

Female - Upper

White female - Upper

Orange Sulphur

Colias eurytheme Boisduval

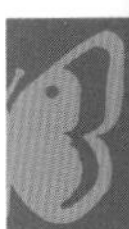

Adults and food sources: Both sexes are marked like the Clouded Sulphur (No. 16) except for having some orange scaling. The summer brood is heavily colored with orange and wings have wide black borders; the discal spot on the hindwing is deep orange. Some females are white, as in the Clouded Sulphur, but with a wider black border on the wings.

Adults utilize a wide range of nectar sources, including alfalfa, aster, butterfly-weed, goldenrod, common milkweed, blazing-star, blue vervain and joe-pye-weed.

Early stages and host plants: The caterpillar is similar to that of the Clouded Sulphur.

Alfalfa is the preferred larval host, though other legumes such as vetch, white sweet clover and white clover are also used.

Habitat: Open areas, alfalfa and red clover fields, rights-of-way and wet areas.

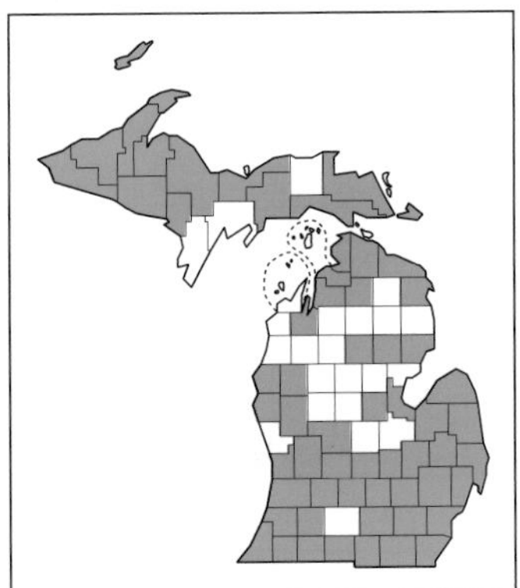

Distribution: Throughout the state.

Flight period: Possibly three broods; May 7 to November 24.

Remarks: Common. Hybrids with the Clouded Sulphur are found in late summer.

Male - Upper

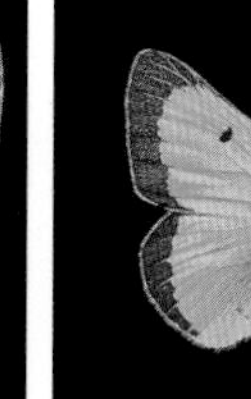

Male - Upper

Male - Under

Female - Upper

White female - Upper

18 Pink-edged Sulphur

Colias interior Scudder

Adults and food sources: Both sexes are yellow with distinct pink fringes. Males are marked similar to the Clouded Sulphur (No. 16). Females have a black apical area and little or no black on the hindwing. The underside of the hindwing has a single pink-rimmed silver spot. Rarely, females are white.

Adults frequently feed on nectar from goldenrod, orange hawkweed, knapweed and common milkweed.

Early stages and host plants: The caterpillar is green with a white and red line on each side.

Females lay eggs on various blueberries.

Habitat: Blueberry bogs and oak-pine barrens. They are also found in recently burned pine barrens with an abundance of blueberry, and along trails and roadsides.

Distribution: The Upper Peninsula and south into the northern counties of the Lower Peninsula, and scattered southeastern counties.

Flight period: Single brood; May 2 to August 21.

Remarks: Locally common. Easily confused with the Clouded Sulphur while in flight.

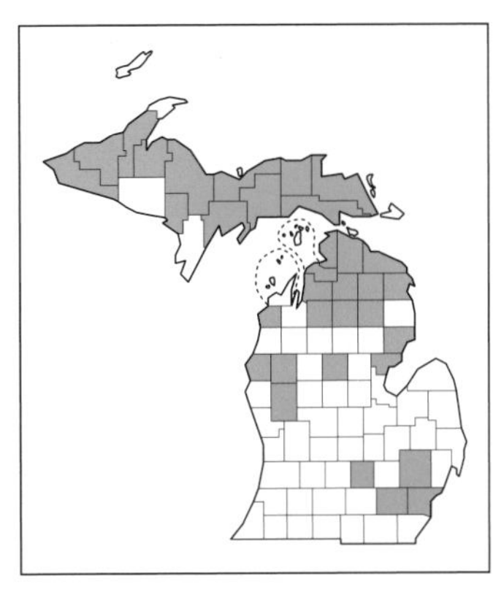

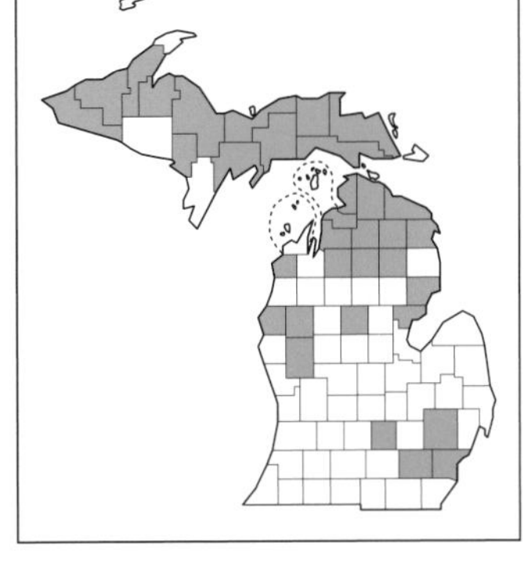

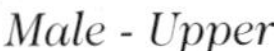

Male - Upper

Female - Upper

Female - Upper

19 Dog Face

Colias cesonia (Stoll)

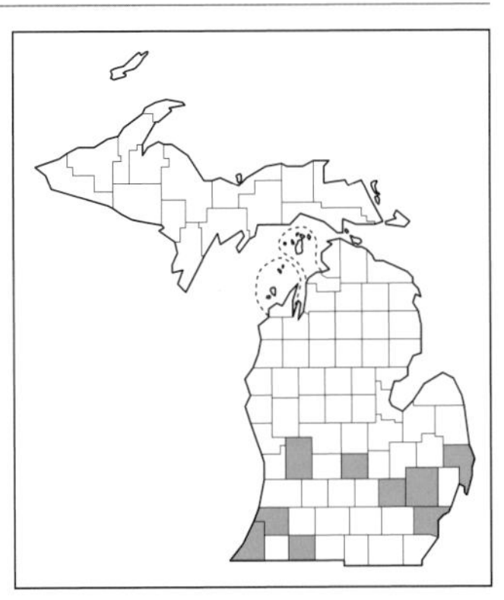

Adults and food sources: The forewing has a pointed apex, and the yellow area almost surrounded with black forms the outline of a dog's head in profile. The female has less black on the forewing. The late summer brood has pink scaling on the underside.

Adults have been reported nectaring on alfalfa and wildflowers.

Early stages and host plants: Caterpillars are reported to be green with blackish tubercles.

No observations of caterpillars feeding have been made in Michigan, but food plants are reported to be several legumes, including lead-plant and clovers.

Habitat: Fields and open woodlands.

Distribution: Occasionally found in southern Michigan; recorded from seven counties.

Flight period: Single brood; May 23 to August 13.

Remarks: A southern species that occasionally enters Michigan and may become a resident in southwestern counties in some years. It may be confused with the Clouded Sulphur (No. 16) in flight.

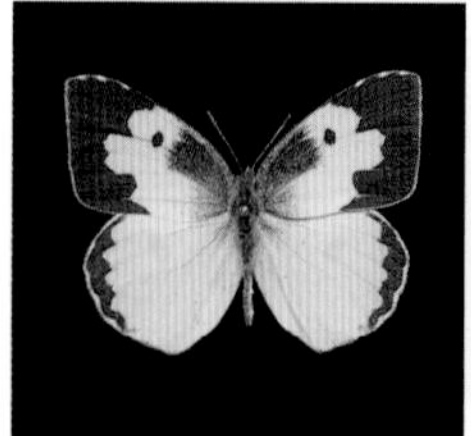

Male - Upper

Female - Upper

Male - Under

20 Cloudless Sulphur

Phoebis sennae eubule (Linnaeus)

Adults and food sources: This is a large yellow sulphur. Males are unmarked on the upper surface; females have a black discal spot on the forewing. Females rarely are white and sometimes have some irregular blackish scaling along the wing edges. The undersides of both sexes have a few scattered darker spots and two pink-edged silver spots on the hindwing.

Adults are reported to use a wide variety of flowers, especially long-tubed flowers such as the cardinal-flower.

Early stages and host plants: The caterpillar may be green or yellow with small black tubercles.

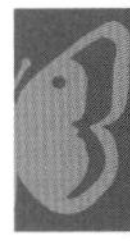

Any wild species of senna is used as the caterpillar food plant.

Habitat: Open areas along roadsides and streams.

Distribution: Scattered locations in Michigan, but most likely to be found in the southern portions of the Lower Peninsula.

Flight period: May 27 to October 13.

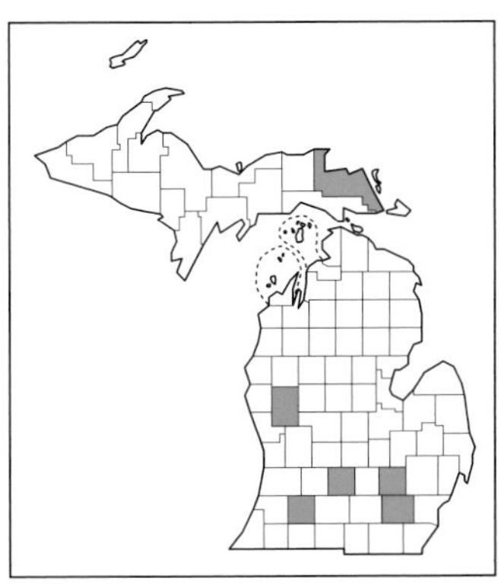

Remarks: The Cloudless Sulphur is considered a rare migrant that occasionally strays into the state. It may be confused with our common Clouded Sulphur (No. 16), except the Cloudless Sulphur is larger and has a very strong and rapid flight.

The subspecies *eubule* is found in eastern United States; the nominate subspecies *P. sennae sennae* (Linnaeus) occurs in tropical America.

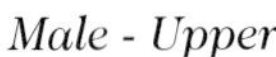

Male - Upper

Male - Under

21

Orange-barred Sulphur

Phoebis philea (Johansson)

Adult and food sources: Slightly larger than the Cloudless Sulphur (No. 20), it has a wide orange bar near the middle of the forewing on males. Both sexes have orange on the outer portion of the hindwing. The female has a black discal spot and some blackish scaling on the outer edge of the forewing.

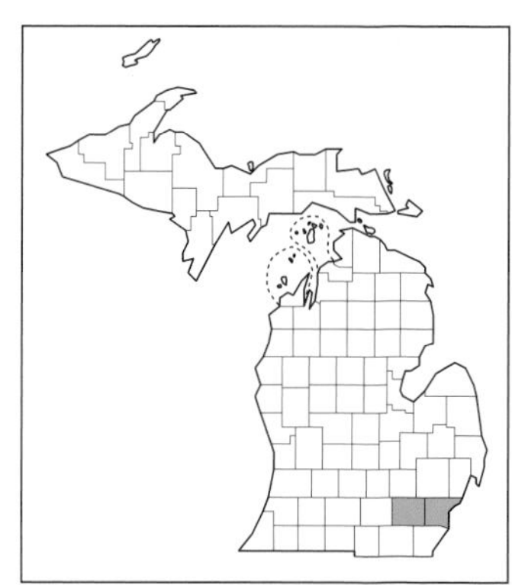

No observations of nectaring activities in Michigan have been reported.

Early stages and host plants: The larva is similar to that of the Cloudless Sulphur.

Sennas are used as the host plant in southern states and the tropics.

Habitat: Likely to be seen in open areas along roads and streams.

Distribution: Two Michigan records: Washtenaw and Wayne counties.

Flight period: August 25 to September 14.

Remarks: This species is a migrant more rare than the Cloudless Sulphur.

Male - Upper

22 Little Sulphur

Eurema lisa

(Boisduval & LeConte)

Adults and food sources: This small yellow sulphur has black outer margins on the wings and a small black discal spot. Undersides are yellow with scattered darker spots. Females are rarely white.

Adults nectar on various flowers, such as asters and goldenrods. They also take moisture from damp roadsides and stream banks.

Early stages and host plants: The caterpillar is reported to be green with one or two white lateral lines.

The favored larval host plant is wild senna; larvae are also reported to use clovers and other legumes.

Habitat: Fields, roadsides and gardens; also Great Lakes coastal areas.

Distribution: Scattered locations throughout the state.

Flight period: June 6 to October 16.

Remarks: This is a frequent southern migrant that may be seen more often in southern counties, especially in late summer.

Male - Upper

Female - Upper

Sleepy Orange

Eurema nicippe (Cramer)

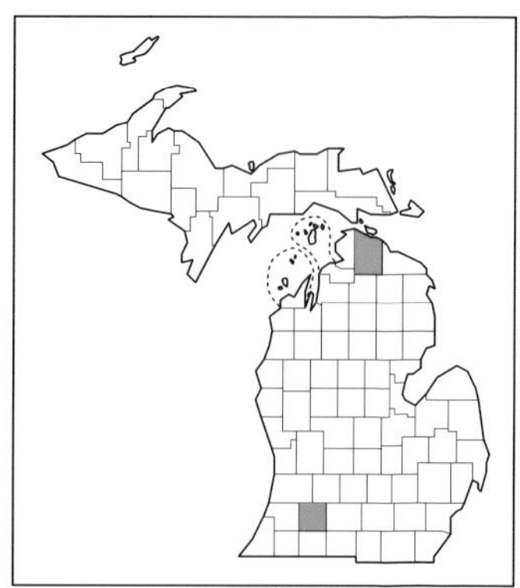

Adults and food sources: This is a small orange sulphur that is slightly larger than the Little Sulphur (No. 22). Both wings have wide, irregular black borders.

Adults are reported to nectar on a wide variety of flowers.

Early stages and host plants: The caterpillar is reported to be green with white lateral lines edged with black.

Wild senna is reported to be the favored host plant.

Habitat: Open areas along roadsides and stream banks.

Distribution: Individual specimens are recorded from Cheboygan (1996) and Kalamazoo (1972) counties.

Flight period: June 20 to August.

Remarks: An infrequent visitor from the South, it may be confused with the larger Orange Sulphur (No. 17).

Male - Upper

Female - Upper

24 Mexican Sulphur

Eurema mexicanum

(Boisduval)

Adults and food sources: The Mexican Sulphur is a small cream-white sulphur with wide black borders sharply indented on the forewing. The hindwing margin is noticeably angular.

Like other sulphurs, it is likely to use a wide variety of nectar sources.

Early stages and host plants: The caterpillar is reported to be green.

The host plant is reported to be one of the wild sennas.

Habitat: Open areas.

Distribution: Livingston and Wayne counties.

Flight period: June 7 to October.

Remarks: This rare southern migrant may occur infrequently in southern counties.

Male - Upper

25 Dainty Sulphur

Nathalis iole Boisduval

Adults and food sources: This is the smallest of the sulphurs. It has elongate, narrow wings that are black and yellow on the upper side. Females have more extensive black areas than males.

Adults use a wide variety of flowers.

Early stages and host plants: The caterpillar is reported to be green with a lateral white and yellow stripe edged with black.

It is reported to use fetid marigold, shepherd's needle and related plants.

Habitat: Dry fields and disturbed areas.

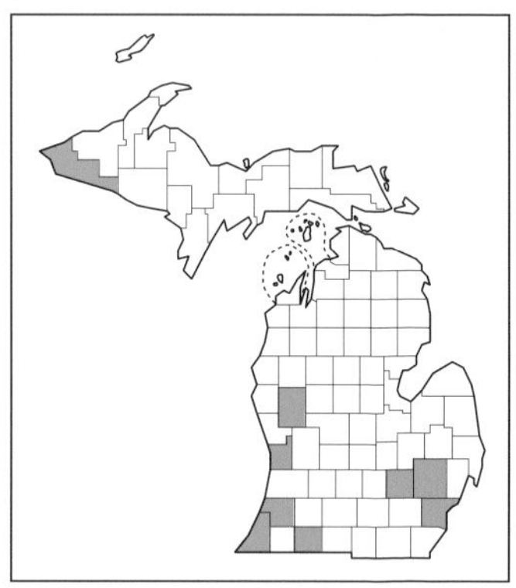

Distribution: Gogebic County and scattered counties in the Lower Peninsula.

Flight period: July 20 to November 14.

Remarks: This is an infrequent southern stray.

Male - Upper

Male - Under

Harvesters, Coppers, Hairstreaks and Blues: *Family Lycaenidae:*

This is a diverse family of small butterflies frequently colored with copper, brown or blue. Some blues are iridescent; some species have fine, hairlike tails, while others have small projections on the hindwing. Most females lay eggs individually on a variety of shrubs, trees and herbs. Many species overwinter in the egg stage, while others overwinter as chrysalids. The caterpillars are small and sluglike with retractable heads; many are green with cream chevrons or stripes. Some eat foliage, but many feed on flowers and developing fruit. The Harvester is carnivorous in the caterpillar stage, feeding on woolly aphids. Many species of lycaenid caterpillars are tended by ants, which obtain a sugary substance from their abdominal glands. They are rewarded for this by being protected from predators and parasites by the ants. The chrysalis is supported by a fine silk girdle usually attached to a leaf or other material near the ground. Some chrysalids emit a barely audible sound when disturbed.

Adults of many species perch on their larval host plant and adjacent plants, and consequently, they are usually not visible until the plant is jarred. This habit may account for the scarcity of some species.

26 Harvester

Feniseca tarquinius

(Fabricius)

Adults and food sources: Wings are distinctly marked with orange and black to dark brown on the upper surface; beneath, they are essentially orange with a few dark spots and faint white markings.

The butterfly never visits flowers but is fond of taking moisture and minerals from bird droppings and damp soils, and honeydew from their woolly aphid hosts.

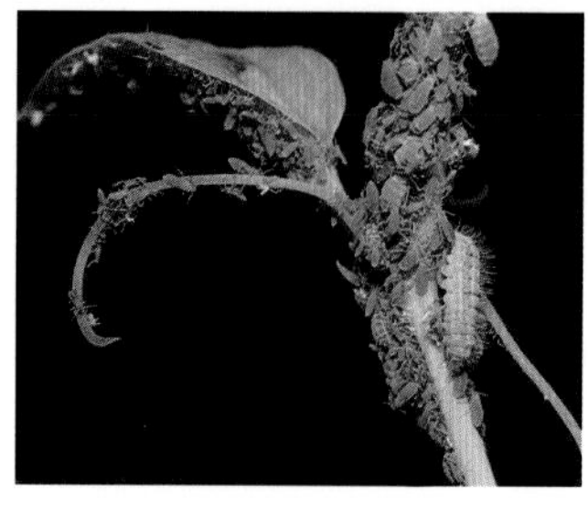

Early stages and host plants: The female lays her single egg in a colony of woolly aphids, which can be found on a wide variety of shrubs, trees and vines. The caterpillar is often found feeding on woolly aphids on tag alder. The caterpillar is greenish brown with fine, white hairs and usually hidden under a clump of aphids.The chrysalis is unique, with dark areas resembling a monkey's face.

Habitat: Deciduous forests, floodplains and alder-bordered stream banks.

Distribution: Throughout Michigan.

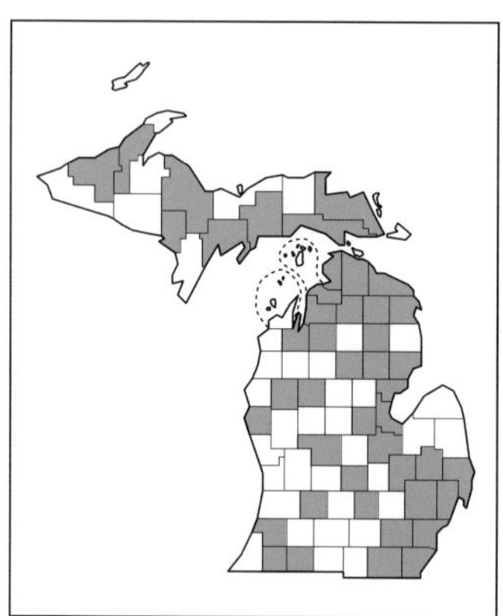

Flight period: At least two broods; May 4 to September 14.

Remarks: Locally uncommon. This is the only carnivorous species of butterfly in North America. The caterpillar requires just three molts and can complete its development in seven to 12 days, largely because of its protein diet. Adults usually are found perching on foliage in small sunlit openings, often near woolly aphid colonies.

Male - Upper

Male - Upper

Female - Under

American Copper

Lycaena phlaeas americana
Harris

Adults and food sources: The upper surface of the forewing is a rich metallic copper with a black border and several spots. The hindwing's upper surface is dark gray with an orange band at the margin. Undersurfaces are lighter with several dark spots.

A wide variety of flowers are used for nectar, such as clover, daisy, butterfly-weed and orange hawkweed.

Early stages and host plants: Caterpillars range from green to rose-red and are covered with short hairs.

Sheep sorrel is the preferred food plant in Michigan.

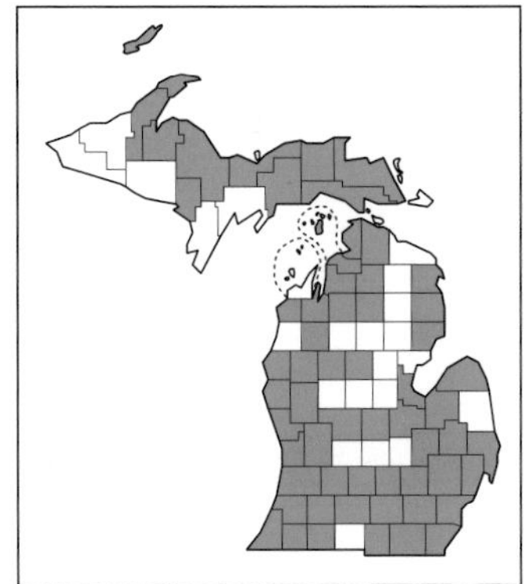

Habitat: Old fields and disturbed areas, including weedy residential lots.

Distribution: Throughout Michigan.

Flight period: Three broods; April 22 to October 6.

Remarks: Sometimes called the Little Copper, this is one of Michigan's most common butterflies. The eastern subspecies found in Michigan (*americana*) is believed to have been introduced from Europe in colonial times, because it more closely resembles European specimens than western North American and Arctic specimens (Opler & Malikul, 1992).

Male - Upper

Female - Upper

Male - Under

28 Bronze Copper

Lycaena hyllus (Cramer)

Adults and food sources: This is Michigan's largest copper. The upper surface of males is iridescent copper-brown with a few dark spots and an orange band on the hindwing. Females are orange-red on the upper surface with black spots. The undersurface of the forewing is light orange; the undersurface of the hindwing is whitish gray. Both wings have several black spots.

Though not an avid flower visitor, it has been seen nectaring on alfalfa, red clover and milkweed.

Early stages and host plants: The caterpillar is yellow-green with a dark dorsal stripe.

Females usually lay individual eggs on one of the water docks and knotweed.

Habitat: Wet meadows, marshes and stream borders with sedges and wild iris.

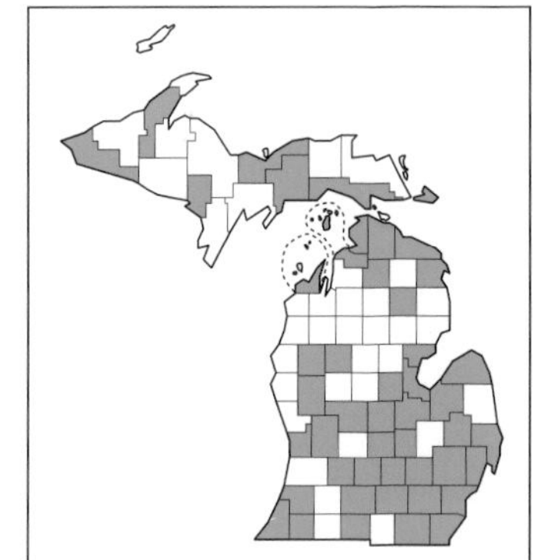

Distribution: Throughout the state but local in its haunts.

Flight period: Two broods; May 15 to October 23.

Remarks: Locally uncommon. Usually seen resting on a sedge or other foliage in wetlands.

Male - Upper

Female - Upper

Male - Under

29 Bog Copper

Lycaena epixanthe michiganensis (Rawson)

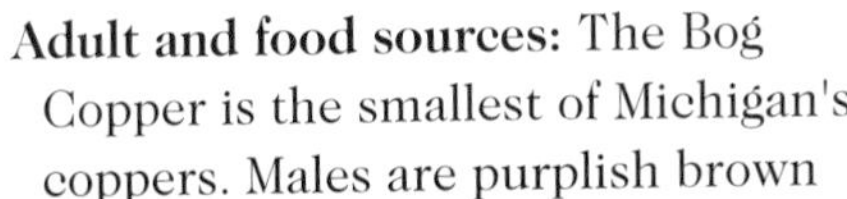

Adult and food sources: The Bog Copper is the smallest of Michigan's coppers. Males are purplish brown and slightly iridescent, with a central spot on the forewing. Females are browner with several spots on each wing. The undersurfaces are largely grayish white, with several spots on the forewing.

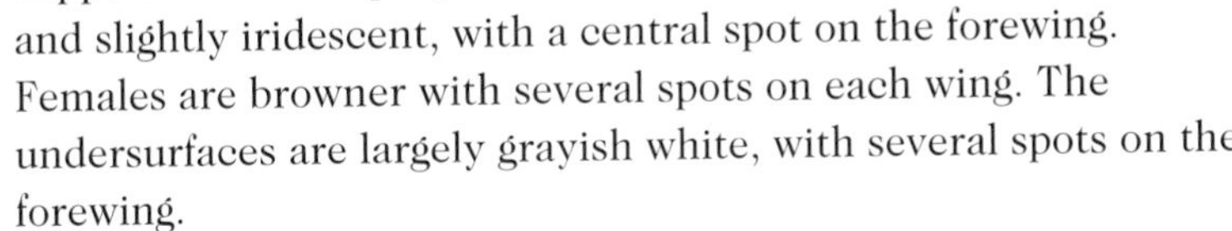

Adults have been found nectaring on cranberry, daisy, bog goldenrod, pearly everlasting and knapweed.

Early stages and host plants: The caterpillar is reported to be bluish green with a dark green dorsal band and oblique dashes, and covered with short white hairs.

Eggs are laid on wild cranberry.

Habitat: Restricted to sphagnum-heath acid bogs.

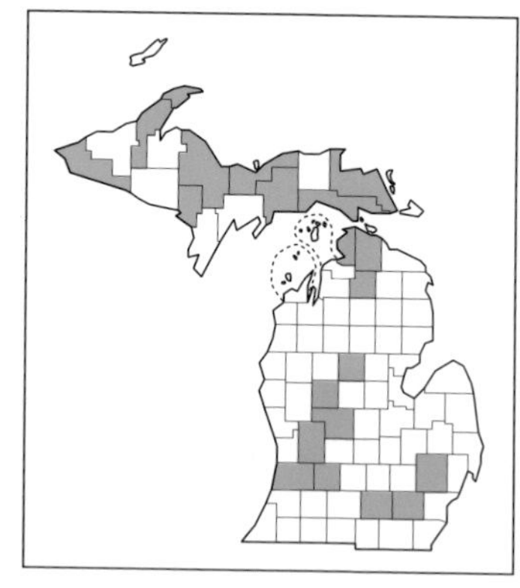

Distribution: Throughout the Upper Peninsula and extending south to Allegan and Washtenaw counties in the Lower Peninsula.

Flight period: Single brood; June 21 to August 21.

Remarks: Locally common. The type locality for the subspecies *michiganensis* is Proud Lake State Recreational Area, Oakland County. This subspecies is found throughout the Great Lakes region and differs from eastern populations, which are essentially light yellow beneath. Flight is low and weak.

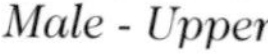

Male - Upper

Female - Upper

Male - Under

30 Dorcas Copper

Lycaena dorcas (W. Kirby)

Adult and food sources: The male is purplish and iridescent on the upper surfaces of both wings. It has a small orange area near the anal angle on the upper surface of the hindwing. Females are largely brown on both wings. Both sexes have several dark spots on the upper surfaces of both wings. The undersurface is orange-brown with black spots.

Adults have been seen nectaring on shrubby cinquefoil and black-eyed Susan.

Early stages and host plants: The caterpillar is light green with a dark green middorsal line and slight traces of white oblique lines.

Eggs are laid on shrubby cinquefoil.

Habitat: Wet meadows, fens, seeps, inland lake margins and some Great Lakes coastal areas.

Distribution: Throughout the state but local in its haunts. Also found on Isle Royale.

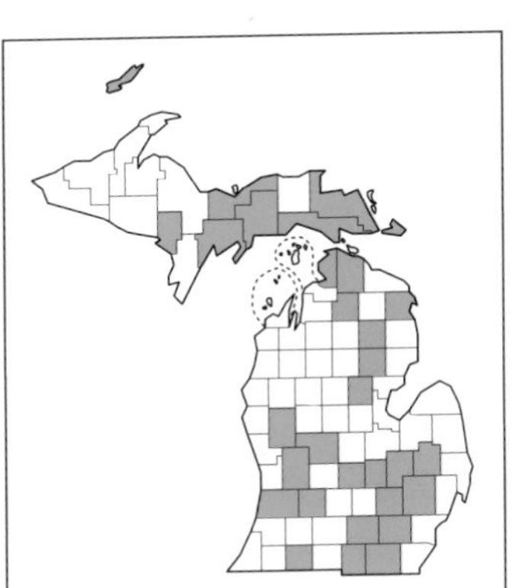

Flight period: Single brood; June 13 to September 21.

Remarks: Locally common. The life history in Michigan was described by Newcomb (1910). Some males may be confused with the Purplish Copper (No. 31), which is slightly larger and more purplish.

Male - Upper

Female - Upper

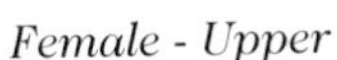

Female - Upper

Male - Under

31 Purplish Copper

Lycaena helloides (Boisduval)

Adults and food sources: Males are purplish and iridescent on the upper surfaces of both wings with an orange band on the hindwing. Females are orange on both wings with extensive brown scaling. Both sexes have several dark spots on the upper surfaces. Beneath, the wings are light orange and gray with distinct dark spots on the forewing.

Adults nectar on goldenrod, New Jersey tea, pepper-grass and white clover.

Early stages and host plants: The caterpillar is green with a number of lateral oblique yellow lines and is covered with short hairs.

Females lay eggs on docks and knotweeds; egg laying is also reported on baby's breath.

Habitat: Roadsides, fields, disturbed areas, sedge marshes and other wetlands.

Distribution: Throughout the Upper Peninsula and widespread in the Lower Peninsula.

Flight period: At least two broods; May 30 to October 17.

Remarks: The species is common in some years. Some males may be confused with Dorcas Copper (No. 30) males, which are smaller.

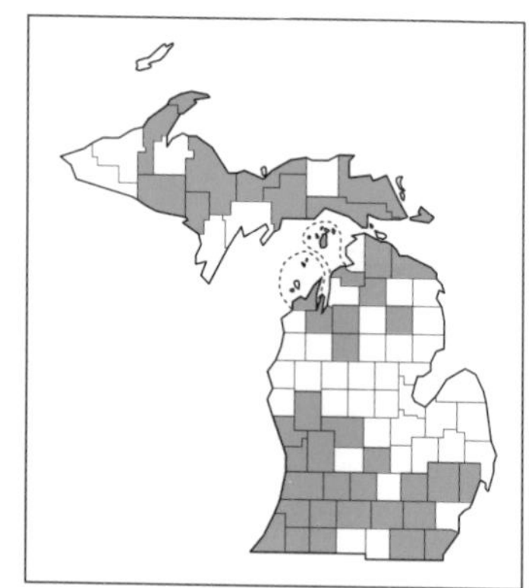

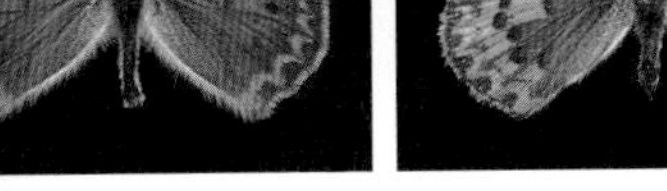

Male - Upper *Female - Upper* *Female - Under*

32 Coral Hairstreak

Satyrium titus (Fabricius)

Adults and food sources: Both sexes are dull brown on upper surfaces and lack tails. The male, as in most hairstreaks, has a small, oval scent-patch near the leading edge of the forewing. Both sexes have a coral band of spots on the undersurface of the hindwings. Females' hindwings are more rounded than males'.

The favorite nectar source is butterfly-weed; blackberry, black-eyed Susan, clovers, dogbane, knapweed, lead-plant, common milkweed, New Jersey tea, spirea and strawberry are also used.

Early stages and host plants: Mature caterpillars are light green with a reddish patch near the head. They hide during the day at the base of the host in litter and are tended by ants.

The preferred host plant in Michigan is wild black cherry. Larvae have also been reported on chokecherry and wild plum.

Habitat: Open areas, forest edges, roadsides and old fields beginning to revert to shrub-forest.

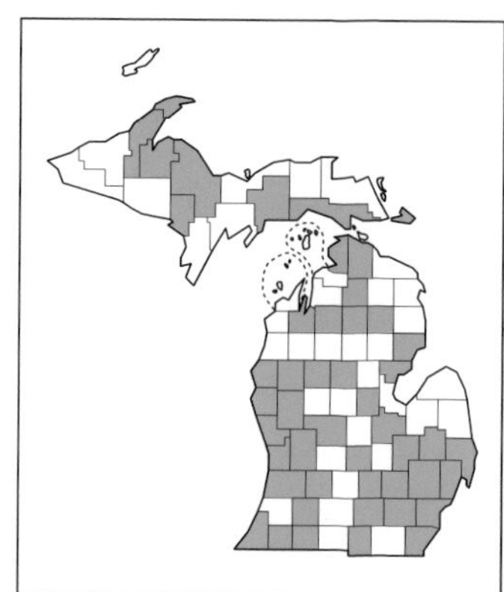

Distribution: Statewide; more common in the Lower Peninsula.

Flight period: Single brood; June 4 to August 26.

Remarks: This is one of Michigan's commonest hairstreaks.

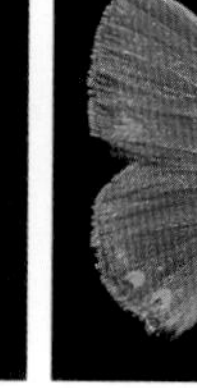

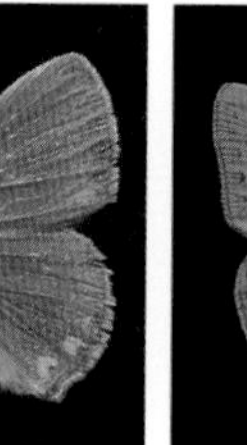

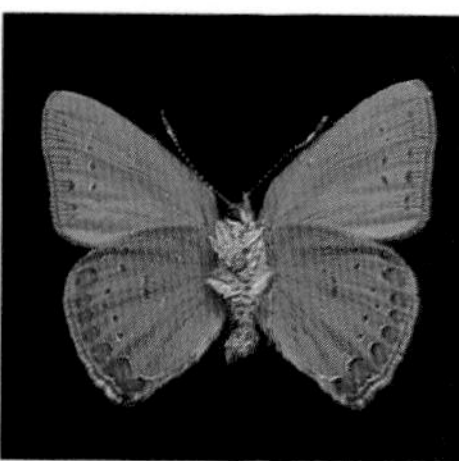

Male - Upper *Female - Upper* *Male - Under*

33 Acadian Hairstreak

Satyrium acadicum
(W.H. Edwards)

Adults and food sources: Adults are brown on upper surfaces with an orange spot near the tail. The undersurfaces are an even gray with small black spots encircled with white and a few orange crescents near the margin of the hindwing. A characteristic blue spot, capped with orange, is located near the tail on the underside.

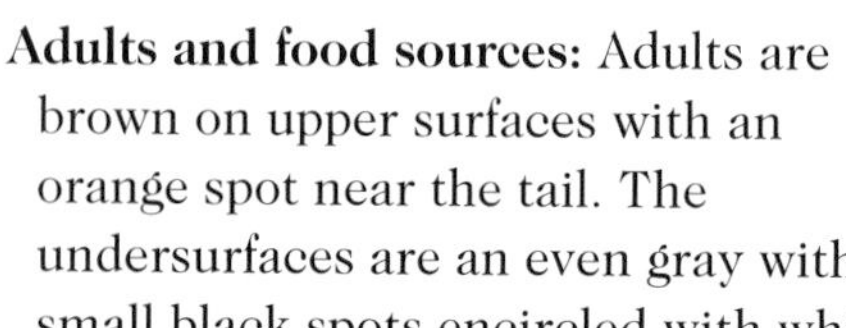

Adults nectar on many flowers found near the host plant, including sweet clover, fleabane, dogbane, common and swamp milkweed, spirea, thistle and joe-pye-weed.

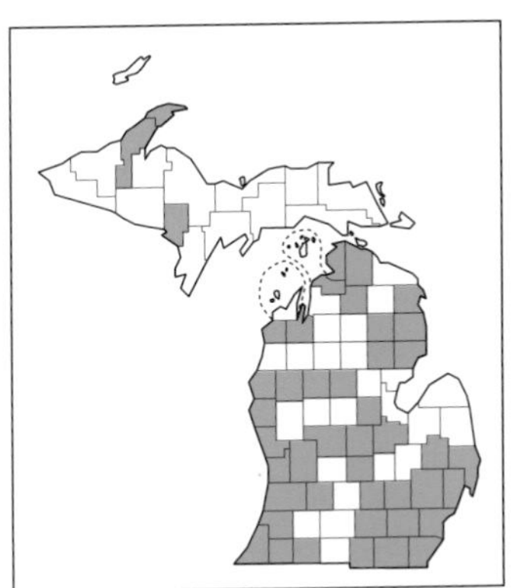

Early stages and host plants: The caterpillar is green with yellow stripes on each side and is tended by ants.

Caterpillar hosts are restricted to willows, such as black and sandbar.

Habitat: Along streams and in wetlands.

Distribution: Throughout the Lower Peninsula and three counties in the Upper Peninsula.

Flight period: Single brood; June 4 to August 14.

Remarks: Locally uncommon. Worn specimens may be confused with Edwards' Hairstreak (No. 34).

Male - Upper

Female - Upper

Female - Under

34 Edwards' Hairstreak

Satyrium edwardsii
(Grote & Robinson)

Adults and food sources: Both sexes are brown without distinguishing marks on the upper surface and with hairlike tails. The undersurface is grayish brown with a series of elongated darker spots outlined with white. Orange crescents and a prominent blue patch (without an orange cap) are located near the tail.

Favorite nectar sources are orange butterfly-weed and New Jersey tea in Michigan. Other flowers are also visited, including sweet clover, lead-plant, vetch and joe-pye-weed.

Early stages and host plants: The mature caterpillar is dark brown with lighter markings. Caterpillars are tended by ants (*Formica integra* Nylander in Montcalm County) and hide in ant nests at the base of the host plants during the day.

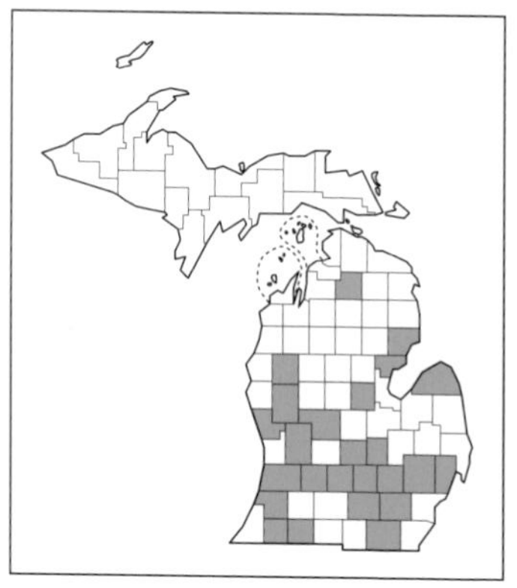

Females lay eggs on black and scarlet oak saplings. Eggs overwinter in crevices and under loose bark around wounds and hatch in early May. Early stages of the caterpillars feed on oak buds; later stages feed on foliage.

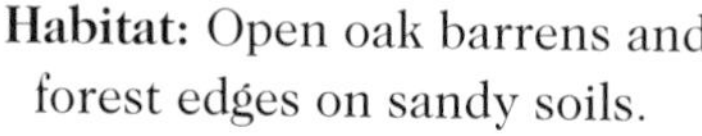

Habitat: Open oak barrens and forest edges on sandy soils.

Distribution: Essentially in southern counties.

Flight period: Single brood; June 14 to August 14.

Remarks: Locally common. Adults frequently perch on sunlit foliage and aggressively pursue other hairstreaks and butterflies that wander into view.

Male - Upper

Female - Upper

Female - Under

35 Banded Hairstreak

Satyrium calanus falacer (Godart)

Adults and food sources: Both sexes are dark brown without distinguishing marks on upper surfaces and have tails. Undersurfaces are brown with a band of broken white lines; a prominent blue patch is adjacent to and nearly as long as a black and reddish crescent near the tail.

Adults nectar on a variety of flowers, especially dogbane and staghorn sumac in southern Michigan. Other flowers visited include sweet clover, fleabane, swamp milkweed and lead-plant.

Early stages and host plants: The caterpillar is usually green with white oblique lines. Some caterpillars are brown.

Eggs are laid on scrub and black oaks and hickories, hatching in spring.

Habitat: Forest openings and edges, old fields and roadsides. Adults perch on sunlit foliage when not nectaring.

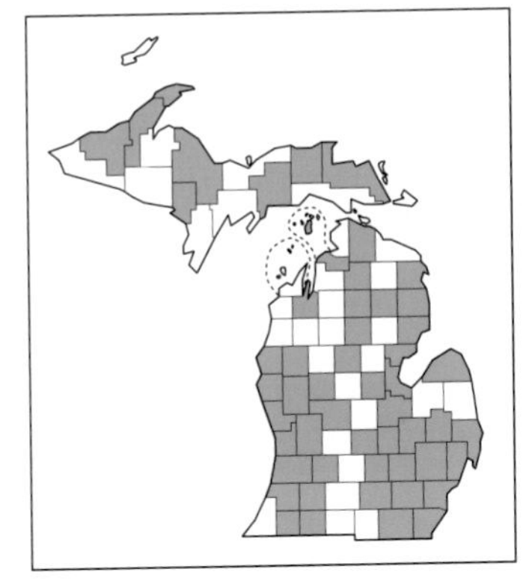

Distribution: Throughout Michigan.

Flight period: Single brood; June 4 to August 25.

Remarks: A common hairstreak. Adults aggressively "dog-fight" with other adults that fly into view. An aberrant form, *heathi* Fletcher, with conspicuous white patches on the undersurface (recorded from Newaygo County), may occasionally be seen. The form *boreale* (Lafontaine), originally described as a distinct species, has been recorded in several southern Michigan

counties. This smaller and darker form, with indistinct markings on the undersurfaces of the wings, needs further study. The nominate subspecies, *S. calanus calanus* (Hübner), inhabits southeastern states and is usually larger with bolder markings on the undersurfaces.

Male - Upper

Female - Upper

Male - Under

36 Hickory Hairstreak

Satyrium caryaevorum (McDunnough)

Adults and food sources: Both sexes look similar to the Banded Hairstreak (No. 35) on the upper surfaces. The undersurface has a broken band of darker ground color edged with white and more offset than in the Banded Hairstreak. A black and orange-capped crescent about half as long as the adjacent distinct blue patch occurs near the tail. This last character will usually separate this hairstreak from the Banded Hairstreak.

Adult nectar sources are similar to those of the Banded Hairstreak.

Early stages and host plants: Caterpillars are light green with two dorsal white lines and lateral whitish oblique lines.

Hickories and walnuts are the preferred hosts; larvae are also reported on oak and ash.

Habitat: Forest openings and edges, old fields and roadsides. Adults perch on sunlit foliage.

Distribution: Southern Lower Peninsula.

Flight period: Single brood; June 18 to August 3.

Remarks: Locally common. Hickory Hairstreaks are frequently seen flying with Banded Hairstreaks and are similarly aggressive.

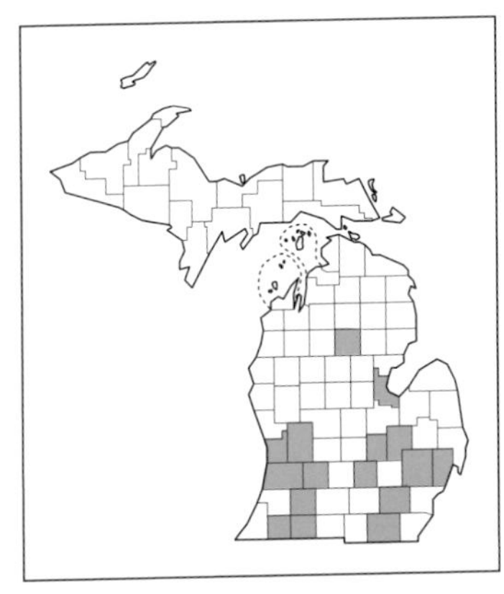

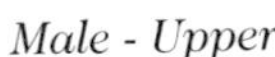

Male - Upper

Female - Upper

Male - Under

37 Striped Hairstreak

Satyrium liparops strigosum (Harris)

Adults and food sources: Both sexes are brown with tails. Undersurfaces have widely spaced broken white lines; a blue patch capped with orange is next to a small black and orange crescent near the tail. The outer margin of the hindwing is slightly indented above the short tail.

Adults nectar on blueberry, white sweet clover, dogbane, goldenrod, lead-plant, common and swamp milkweed, pearly everlasting, staghorn sumac and New Jersey tea.

Early stages and host plants: The caterpillar is bright green with lateral oblique yellowish lines.

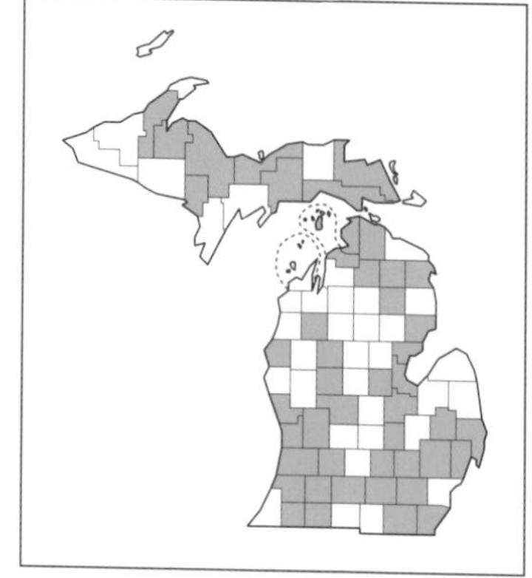

Eggs are laid on blueberry, pin cherry and juneberry in Otsego County and reported elsewhere on New Jersey tea.

Habitat: Forest openings and edges and roadsides in southern counties; oak-pine barrens in northern areas.

Distribution: Throughout Michigan.

Flight period: Single brood; June 25 to August 25.

Remarks: Uncommon. Some northern county specimens have an orange-brownish patch on the forewing. The nominate subspecies, *S. liparops liparops* (LeConte), occurs in southeastern states and is characterized by orange patches on upper wing surfaces.

Male - Upper

Female - Upper

Female - Under

38 Northern Hairstreak

Fixsenia favonius ontario (W.H. Edwards)

Adults and food sources: Upper surfaces are light brown with tails; some have an orange patch on the forewing. Undersurfaces are brown with a broken black line edged with white, a distinct "W" mark near the tail and a blue patch capped with orange.

Adults are reported to nectar on white sweet clover, dogbane, common milkweed and New Jersey tea. The single Michigan specimen was collected on sweet white clover.

Early stages and host plants: The caterpillar is reported to be pale green with a dark green median stripe and lateral oblique green stripes.

Host plants are reported to be oaks.

Habitat: Open woods, forest edges and roadsides.

Distribution: Michigan's only record is from Lenawee County; it may be found elsewhere in the southern counties.

Flight period: Single brood; June 28, 1975.

Remarks: The type location of this subspecies is Port Stanley, Ontario. The Northern Hairstreak is uncommon in adjacent states. It may be confused with some of our other hairstreaks. The nominate subspecies, *F. favonius favonius* J.E. Smith, occurs in southeastern states and has more extensive orange areas on its wings.

Male - Upper

Male - Upper

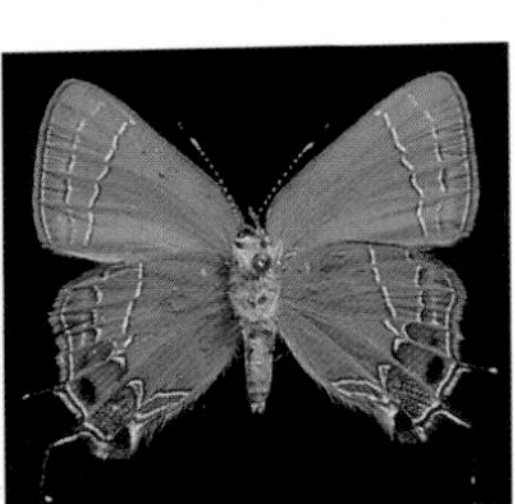

Female - Under

39 Red-banded Hairstreak

Calycopis cecrops (Fabricius)

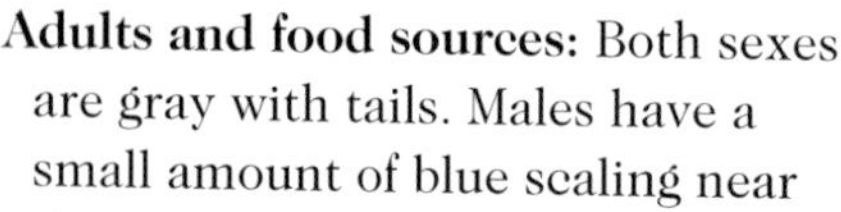

Adults and food sources: Both sexes are gray with tails. Males have a small amount of blue scaling near the base on the upper wing surface; females usually have a large area of blue on upper surfaces. Undersurfaces of both sexes have a distinct red band.

Adults are reported to feed on nectar of cherry, dogbane, common milkweed and New Jersey tea.

Early stages and host plants: The caterpillar is reported to be gray-black and covered with short, fine hairs.

Caterpillars are reported to feed on dwarf sumac, staghorn sumac and oaks. They may also feed on fallen leaves and detritus on the ground.

Habitat: Brushy fields, forest edges and stream banks.

Distribution: Resident status is unknown. One valid record exists from the Pawpaw Lake area in Berrien County. A sighting was also made along the St. Joseph River in St. Joseph County.

Flight period: The above specimen was collected August 6, 1906.

Remarks: It may be easily overlooked or confused with other hairstreaks because of its small size and dull color. It is possible that it may breed in southwestern counties in some years.

Male - Upper

Female - Upper

Male - Under

40 Brown Elfin

Incisalia augustinus (W. Kirby)

Adults and food sources: Both sexes are brown to reddish brown on the upper surfaces and lack tails. The undersurface is reddish brown on the outer portion of the wings and dark brown basally.

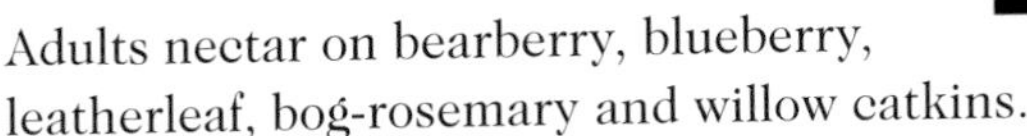

Adults nectar on bearberry, blueberry, leatherleaf, bog-rosemary and willow catkins.

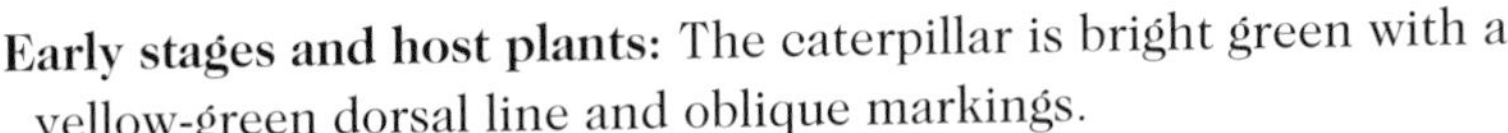

Early stages and host plants: The caterpillar is bright green with a yellow-green dorsal line and oblique markings.

Eggs are laid on bearberry, blueberry and bog laurel. Undoubtedly, other plants in the heath family are also used as hosts.

Habitat: Sphagnum-heath bogs and pine barrens in northern counties. Associated with isolated bogs with highbush blueberry in southern counties.

Distribution: Found in most counties; more common in northern ones.

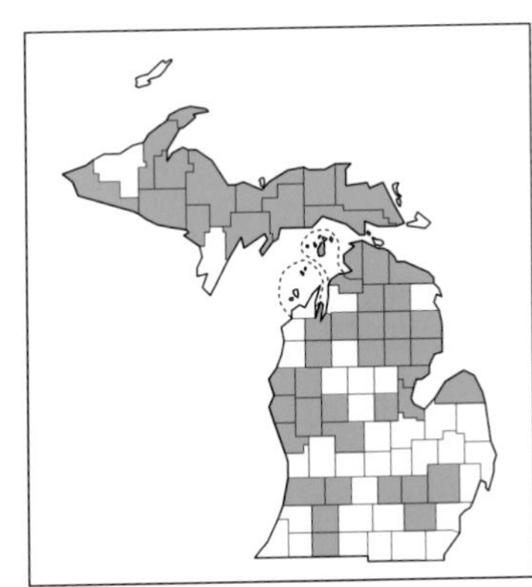

Flight period: Single brood; April 18 to July 16.

Remarks: The Brown Elfin is the most common of Michigan's elfins. It flies low to the ground and is easily overlooked because of its small size and dull color.

Male - Upper

Female - Upper

Female - Under

41 Hoary Elfin

Incisalia polia
Cook & Watson

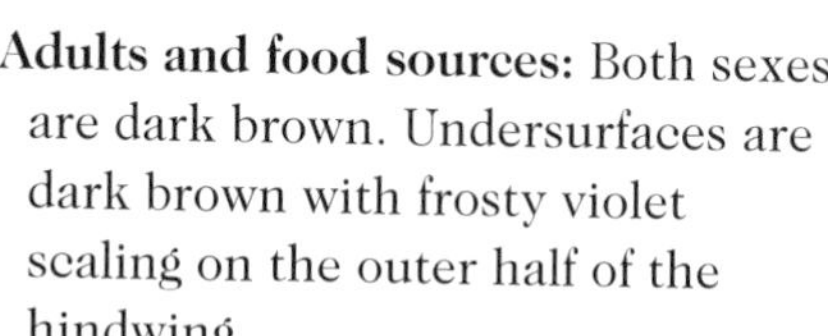

Adults and food sources: Both sexes are dark brown. Undersurfaces are dark brown with frosty violet scaling on the outer half of the hindwing.

Adults nectar on bearberry, blueberry, leatherleaf and wild strawberry.

Early stages and host plants: The caterpillar is green without distinguishing marks.

Females lay eggs on bearberry, the preferred host in Michigan.

Habitat: Oak-pine barrens, especially in northern counties; also along Great Lakes dunes.

Distribution: Throughout the Upper Peninsula, extending into scattered counties of the Lower Peninsula.

Flight period: Single brood; April 3 to June 3.

Remarks: Locally uncommon. The Hoary Elfin flies close to the ground and may be confused with the Brown Elfin (No. 40).

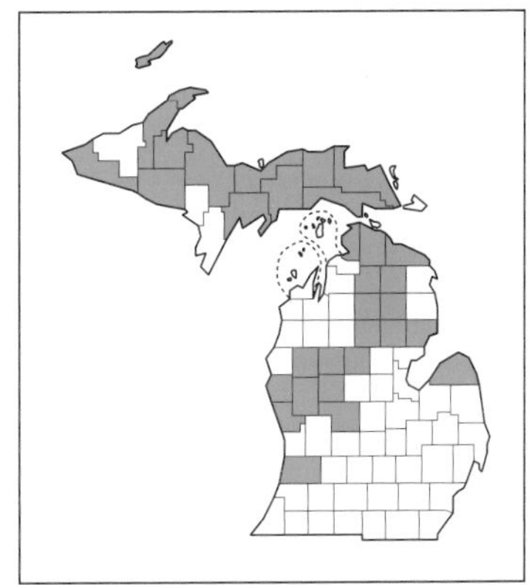

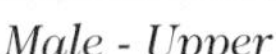

Male - Upper

Female - Upper

Female - Under

42 Frosted Elfin

Incisalia irus (Godart)

Adults and food sources: Both sexes are dark brown, much like the Hoary Elfin (No. 41). Hindwings have short, taillike projections. The undersurface of the forewing has an irregular postmedial line; the outer half of the hindwing is lighter colored than the base and dusted with purplish scales. A distinct black spot is located near the tail.

Few observations have been made of adults nectaring on any flowers other than blueberry.

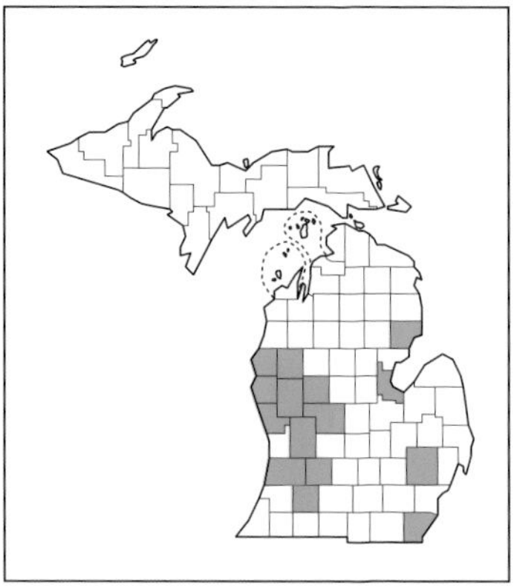

Early stages and host plants: The caterpillar is yellowish green with white lines and dashes and covered with brownish hairs.

The only host plant in Michigan is lupine.

Habitat: Oak savannas, open areas and forest edges in proximity to lupine.

Distribution: Scattered counties in the southern Lower Peninsula extending north along the west side to Mason County and to Iosco County on the east.

Flight period: Single brood; April 25 to June 5.

Remarks: Locally uncommon. The Frosted Elfin is listed by the Michigan Natural Features Inventory as a threatened species. It is easily overlooked; adults fly close to the ground, alighting on dead leaves and twigs.

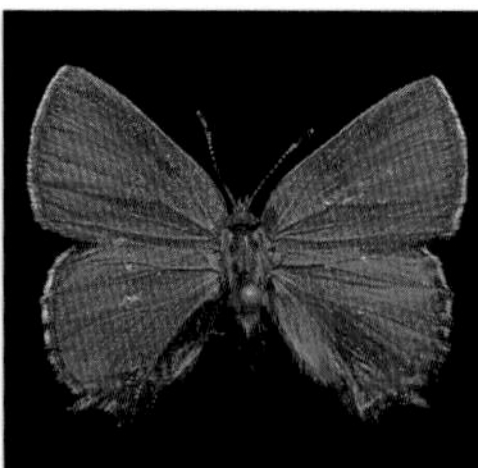

Male - Upper *Female - Upper* *Female - Under*

43 Henry's Elfin

Incisalia henrici
(Grote & Robinson)

Adults and food sources: Both sexes are orange-brown with a prominent tail on the hindwing. The male lacks the scent patch on the upper surface of the forewing. Undersurfaces are yellowish brown on the outer half of the wings; the hindwing has a distinct outer extension of the basal dark brown area. Fresh specimens may have some green scaling on the undersurface of the hindwing.

Adults have been observed feeding on nectar of bearberry and chokecherry in Michigan.

Early stages and host plants: Caterpillars are light green with lighter lateral lines and a distinct serrated profile.

Caterpillars are found on maple-leaved viburnum in Michigan. They are also reported to feed on holly, huckleberry and redbud. Adults have been observed near wild raisin and Michigan holly in northern counties — these may also be host plants.

Habitat: Open oak-pine barrens, forest openings and edges, and swamp borders.

Distribution: Scattered locations throughout most of Michigan.

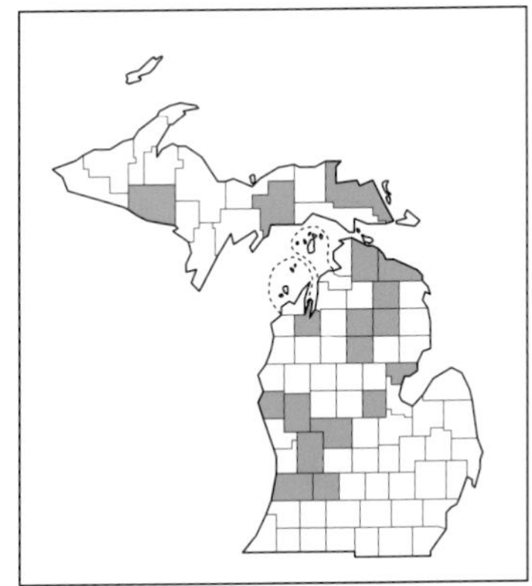

Flight period: Single brood; May 5 to June 6.

Remarks: Locally uncommon. Listed by the Michigan Natural Features Inventory as a species of special concern.

Male - Upper

Female - Upper

Female - Under

44 Eastern Pine Elfin

Incisalia niphon clarki
Freeman

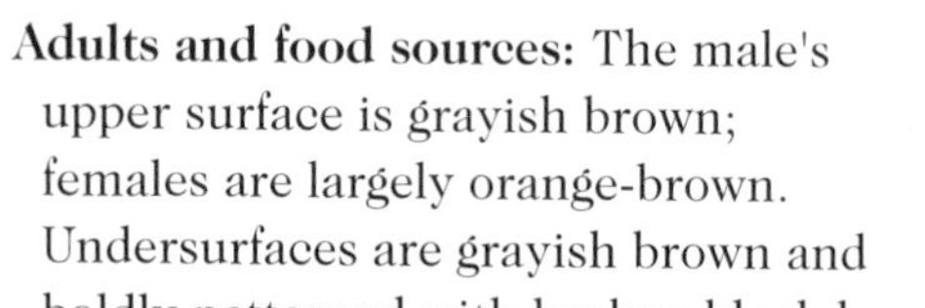

Adults and food sources: The male's upper surface is grayish brown; females are largely orange-brown. Undersurfaces are grayish brown and boldly patterned with broken black bands edged with white.

Adults feed on nectar of bearberry, blueberry, chokecherry, bog laurel, lilac, New Jersey tea, pussy-toes and birdfoot violet. They may also take moisture and nutrients from trails and roadsides.

Early stages and host plants: The caterpillar is dark green with two cream stripes, mimicking the colors of pine needles.

Females lay eggs on lateral buds and developing needles of jack and white pine in Michigan.

Habitat: Open pine barrens, forest edges and roadsides.

Distribution: Throughout the Upper Peninsula and in most Lower Peninsula counties.

Flight period: Single brood; April 18 to July 11.

Remarks: A common elfin in jack pine barrens. The Pine Elfin may be confused with Western Pine Elfin (No. 45) in the Upper Peninsula, where both fly in the same habitat. The northern subspecies found in Michigan and throughout the Great Lakes region differs from the nominate subspecies, *I. niphon niphon* (Hübner), by having lighter colors and less contrasting markings.

Male - Upper

Female - Upper

Female - Under

45 Western Pine Elfin

Incisalia eryphon (Boisduval)

Adults and food sources: The upper surface of the male is similar to that of the Pine Elfin (No. 44). Females have more orange on the upper surface than Pine Elfin females. Undersurfaces are reddish brown with a distinctly jagged dark band near the edge of the hindwing.

Nectar choices are unknown at this time but probably similar to those of the Pine Elfin.

Early stages and host plants: The caterpillar is very similar to that of the Pine Elfin.

Host plants are reported to be hard pines. Michigan specimens have been associated with white pine, a soft pine, the suspected host.

Habitat: Coniferous forest edges and openings, along roads and trails bordered with white pine.

Distribution: Throughout the Upper Peninsula.

Flight period: Single brood; May 15 to July 3.

Remarks: Locally uncommon. Its habitat and distribution in Michigan are still poorly known.

Male - Upper

Female - Upper

Female - Under

46 White-M Hairstreak

Parrhasius m-album (Boisduval & LeConte)

Adults and food sources: The upper surface is iridescent blue with a black border and tails. The undersurface is grayish brown with a black line edged with white that forms a distinct M near the tail and a small white spot near the leading edge of the hindwing.

Adults are reported to nectar on common milkweed, goldenrod, sumac and other flowers.

Early stages and host plants: The caterpillar is dark green with dark dorsal and oblique stripes.

Oaks are reported to be the host; the host plant in Michigan is unknown.

Habitat: Open woods, forest edges, roadsides and brushy fields near oaks.

Distribution: Known only from Muskegon County.

Flight period: Probably two broods; August 12, 1964.

Remarks: This distinctive hairstreak may occasionally stray into southern counties. It has been recorded from Door County, Wisconsin, and Point Pelee, Ontario.

Male - Upper

Male - Under

47 Gray Hairstreak

Strymon melinus humuli (Harris)

Adults and food sources: The upper surface is gray with orange spots near the tails. The undersurface is lighter gray; the hindwing has two orange and black spots near the tail and a fine broken line of black and white.

Adults nectar on goldenrod, blazing-star, milkweed, wild strawberry and vetch. They're also reported on white sweet clover, dogbane, mints and other flowers.

Early stages and host plants: Caterpillars vary from green to reddish brown with oblique markings.

Females lay eggs on an assortment of plants; usually plants in the pea and mallow familes are selected.

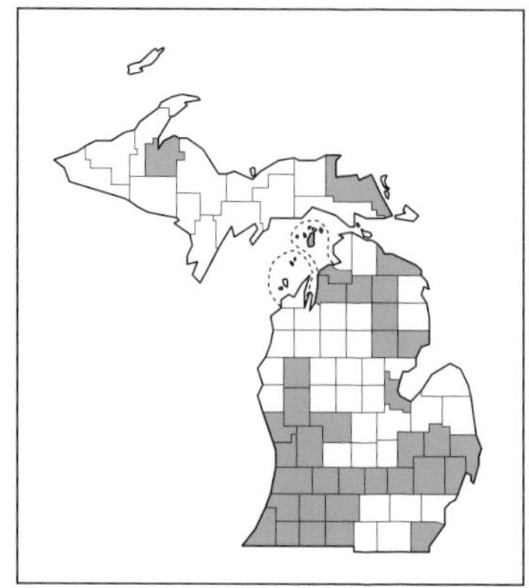

Habitat: Open areas such as cultivated legumes, residential gardens, weedy fields and disturbed areas in oak-pine barrens.

Distribution: Throughout most of the Lower Peninsula and a few counties in the Upper Peninsula.

Flight period: Two broods; April 23 to October 12.

Remarks: Common. This is the least particular of Michigan hairstreaks in selecting nectar sources and host plants and habitat. The larger nominate species, *S. melinus melinus* (Hübner), is found in the Gulf states.

Male - Upper *Female - Upper*

Female - Under *Female - Under*

48 Early Hairstreak

Erora laetus (W.H. Edwards)

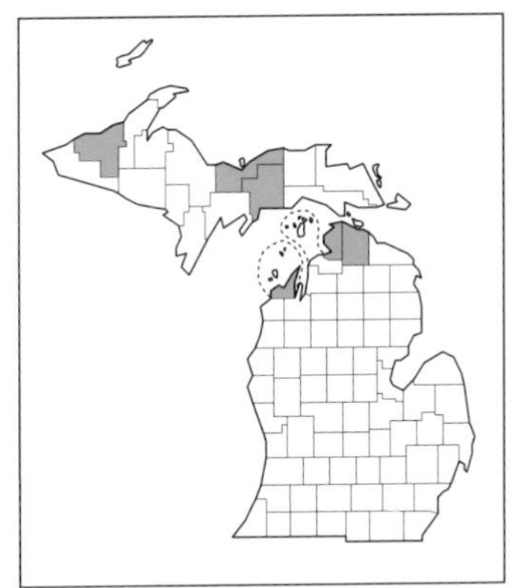

Adults and food sources: The upper surface is blackish gray. The male has a small area of blue on the hindwing, but the female has an extensive blue area. The undersurface is gray-green with a series of tiny orange spots.

There are few Michigan observations of adults nectaring on any plants except common milkweed and wild strawberry. Adults may also be found taking moisture and nutrients from sandy forest trails.

Early stages and host plants: Caterpillars range from green to reddish brown with darker patches.

The only reported host plants are beech and beaked hazelnut. Most Michigan records occur in proximity to beech forests.

Habitat: Openings, edges and sun-dappled trails in northern hardwoods containing beech.

Distribution: Scattered counties in the Upper Peninsula and the northern Lower Peninsula.

Flight period: Two broods; May 14 to July 21.

Remarks: This is a scarce hairstreak that reportedly spends much of its time in the forest canopy, making it difficult to see and collect. It's listed by the Michigan Natural Features Inventory as a special concern species.

Male - Upper

Female - Upper

Male - Under

49 Reakirt's Blue

Hemiargus isola (Reakirt)

Adults and food sources: This is a tailless blue with a prominent black spot near the lower outer edge of the hindwing; females have less blue scaling. The undersurface is light gray; the forewing has five distinct black spots.

One Michigan specimen has been observed nectaring on clover. Like other blues, this butterfly probably nectars on a variety of flowers.

Early stages and host plants: The life history has not been reported.

Host plants are reported to be many in the pea family.

Habitat: Prairies, open fields and roadsides.

Distribution: Two specimens have been recorded from Allegan and Washtenaw counties. It has also been reported from Eaton and Montcalm counties.

Flight period: Probably one brood; July 8-18.

Remarks: This is a southwestern species that may occasionally stray into the southern counties and breed there. It's easily confused with the Eastern Tailed Blue (No. 50) in flight.

Male - Upper

Female - Upper

Male - Under

50 Eastern Tailed Blue

Everes comyntas (Godart)

Adults and food sources: This species and the Western Tailed Blue (No. 51) are the only Michigan blues with tails. The upper surface of males is iridescent blue; females are dark brown, with two small orange spots near the tail. Spring females have blue on the inner portion of the wings. Undersurfaces of both sexes are gray-white with small black markings and two orange spots near the tail.

Adults feed on nectar of aster, sweet white clover, white clover, dogbane, fleabane, goldenrod, wild strawberry and butterfly-weed.

Early stages and host plants: The caterpillar is dark green with a brown dorsal stripe and oblique lateral stripes and is covered with short hairs.

Host plants include a variety of pea family plants.

Habitat: Prairies, old fields, pastures and disturbed areas with a variety of legumes.

Distribution: Throughout Michigan, except Isle Royale.

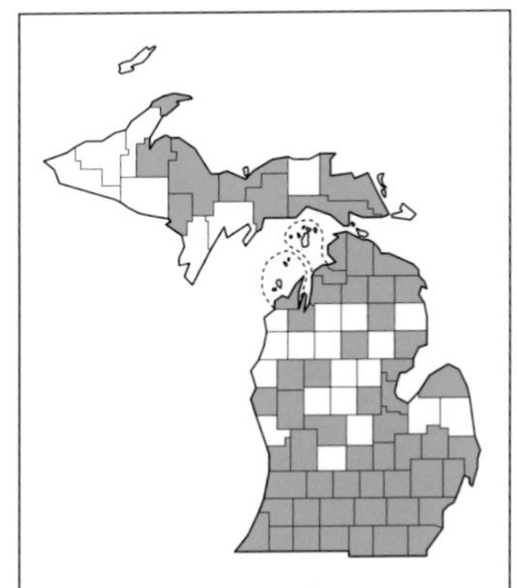

Flight period: Three broods; April 23 to October 16.

Remarks: This common Michigan butterfly may be confused with the Western Tailed Blue in the Upper Peninsula.

Male - Upper *Female - Upper*

Female - Upper *Male - Under*

51 Western Tailed Blue

Everes amyntula (Boisduval)

Adults and food sources: This butterfly is slightly larger than the Eastern Tailed Blue (No. 50); females are darker than males. Undersurfaces are whitish with indistinct black markings and a faint orange spot near the tail.

No Michigan observations of nectaring adults have been made; they probably use some of the flowers visited by the Eastern Tailed Blue.

Early stages and host plants: Caterpillars are green to yellow-green with reddish marks.

Host plants are reported to be several legumes; caterpillars feed on flowers and young seed pods. Females have been observed laying eggs on flower heads of pale vetchling on Isle Royale.

Habitat: Open aspen-fir woods on Isle Royale. It's reported to favor openings in Canadian zone forests.

Distribution: Recorded from Mackinac County and Isle Royale. Probably found elsewhere in the Upper Peninsula.

Flight period: Single brood; May 28 to July 25.

Remarks: Uncommon. It may easily be confused with the Eastern Tailed Blue. Adults fly higher above the ground than Eastern Tailed Blues.

Male - Upper

Female - Upper

Female - Under

52 Spring Azure

Celastrina ladon (Cramer)

Adults and food sources: Both sexes are iridescent blue on the upper surfaces with a checkered margin; females have a black border on the forewing and a thin black border on the hindwing. Under magnification, the upper surfaces of males have long, overlapping scales that overlay the blue color-producing scales. Undersurfaces are light gray with small black spots; the hindwing occasionally has a wide dark margin and central dark patch.

Adults seldom nectar but usually take moisture and nutrients from puddles and damp areas.

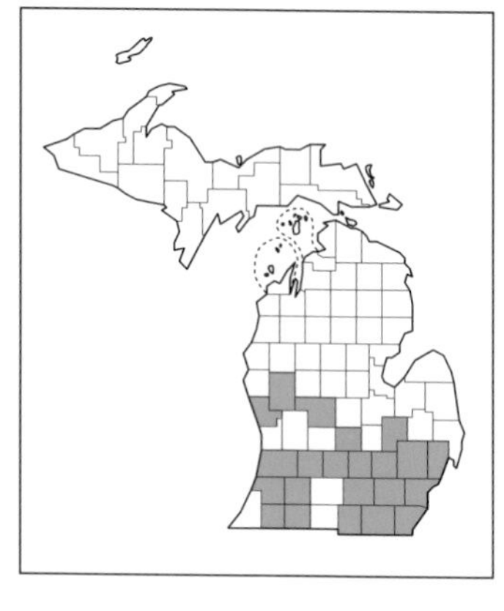

Early stages and host plants: The caterpillar is light green to pinkish with greenish, oblique lateral stripes and is attended by ants.

Eggs are laid among the flower buds of maple-leaved viburnum and flowering dogwood.

Habitat: Forest openings and edges and along trails in forests.

Distribution: The southern half of the Lower Peninsula.

Flight period: Single brood; April 2 to May 27.

Remarks: Common. It may be easily confused in nature with the Northern Spring Azure (No. 54) and can be found along sunlit trails in early spring.

Male - Upper

Female - Upper

Male - Under

Female - Under

53 Summer Azure

Celastrina neglecta (W.H. Edwards)

Adults and food sources: The upper surface of the male's forewing is bright blue; the hindwing is whitish blue with a slightly bluer margin. The upper surface of the female's forewing is bluish white with a wide black border; the hindwing is bluish white with a blackish edge on the inner edge. The fringe of both sexes is white without black checkering. Undersurfaces are grayish white with small black spots.

Adults nectar on dogbane, common milkweed, staghorn sumac, spirea, New Jersey tea and a variety of other flowers.

Early stages and host plants: The caterpillar is similar to that of the Spring Azure (No. 52).

Eggs are laid on flower heads of plants including composites, dogwood, legumes, mints, spirea and sumac.

Habitat: Forest openings, edges, brushy fields, along roads and streamsides.

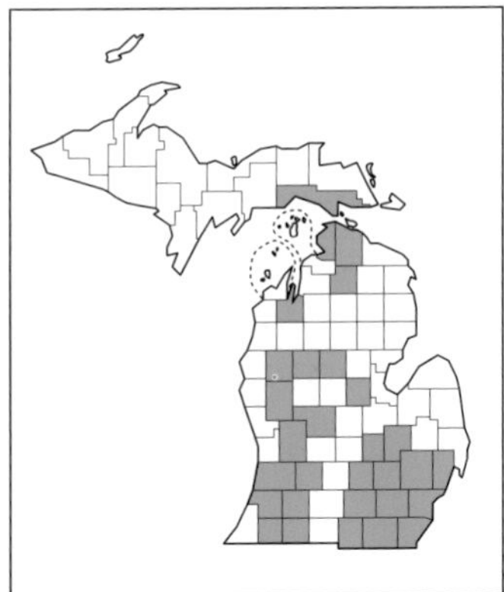

Distribution: Southern counties of the Lower Peninsula, extending to scattered northern counties, including Mackinac County.

Flight period: At least two broods; June 15 to October 5.

Remarks: Common. The flight dates are the best way to distinguish this blue from other azures, especially in late summer.

Male - Upper *Female - Upper*

Male - Under *Female - Under*

54 Northern Spring Azure

Celastrina lucia (W. Kirby)

Adults and food sources: The upper surfaces of both sexes are iridescent blue with a black checkered fringe on the hindwing; females have a black border on the forewing. The undersurface of the hindwing is dingy gray with black spots, frequently with dark borders and a dark central patch. Under magnification, the upper surfaces of males have shorter scales than those of the Spring Azure arranged in alternating rows of blue scales and white androconia scales, which gives a more brillant effect than the scales on the Spring Azure (No. 52).

Adults seldom nectar but frequently take moisture and nutrients from puddles and damp spots along trails.

Early stages and host plants: The caterpillar is similar to that of the Spring Azure.

Females lay eggs on flower heads of wild black cherry, chokecherry, blueberry and Labrador tea.

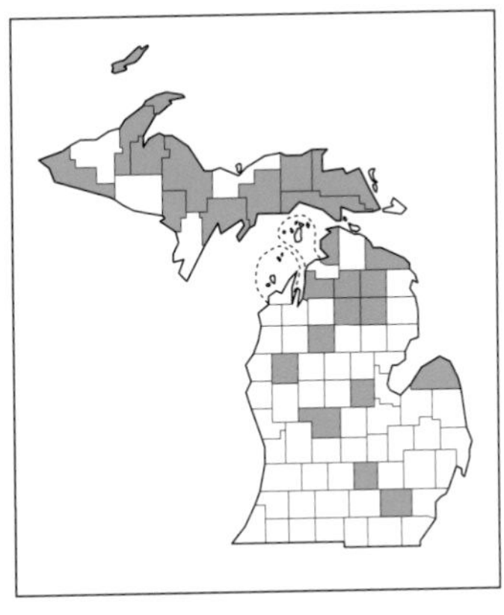

Habitat: Forest openings and edges and along forest trails.

Distribution: Throughout the Upper Peninsula, including Isle Royale, and extending south in the Lower Peninsula to Washtenaw County, overlapping the range of the Spring Azure.

Flight period: Single brood; April 18 to June 30.

Remarks: Common. It is easily confused in nature with the Spring Azure where the two populations overlap.

Male - Upper *Female - Upper*

Male - Under *Male - Under*

55 Silvery Blue

Glaucopsysche lygdamus couperi Grote

Adults and food sources: Upper surfaces of males are bright, iridescent silvery-blue with black borders; females are duller blue with indistinct wide black borders. The undersurfaces of both sexes are gray with distinct white-rimmed black spots. Some southern specimens have larger spots.

Adults nectar on blueberry, chokecherry, dandelion and strawberry.

Early stages and host plants: The caterpillar is green to purplish with a dark dorsal stripe and oblique white stripes and is attended by various species of ants.

Eggs are laid on alfalfa, sweet clover, vetchling and vetch.

Habitat: Open areas, brushy fields and forest openings in oak barrens.

Distribution: Throughout Michigan.

Flight period: Single brood; April 27 to July 1.

Remarks: Locally common. The Silvery Blue may easily be confused with some of Michigan' s other blues. Some southern Michigan specimens, with large spots on the undersurface, resemble the more southern subspecies, *G. lygdamus lygdamus* (Doubleday).

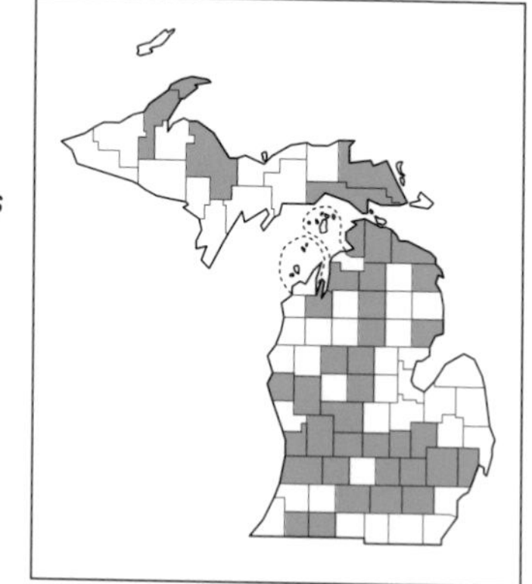

Male - Upper *Male - Under*

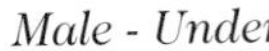

Male - Under *Female - Upper*

56 Northern Blue

Lycaeides idas nabokovi Masters

Adults and food sources: The upper surfaces of males are violet-blue. The blue on females is much reduced by blackish outer areas and several black spots on the lower edge of the hindwing. Undersurfaces of both sexes are whitish gray with numerous black spots; the lower edge of the hindwing has small iridescent silver spots capped with light orange. The fringe of the hindwing underneath has a black line broken into small spots at the ends of the veins.

Few observations of adults nectaring have been made; those were on red clover and orange hawkweed.

Early stages and host plants: No caterpillar description has been reported for Michigan; it's probably very similar to the Karner Blue caterpillar.

Females lay eggs on dwarf bilberry in Michigan.

Habitat: Openings in pine barrens and on rock outcroppings.

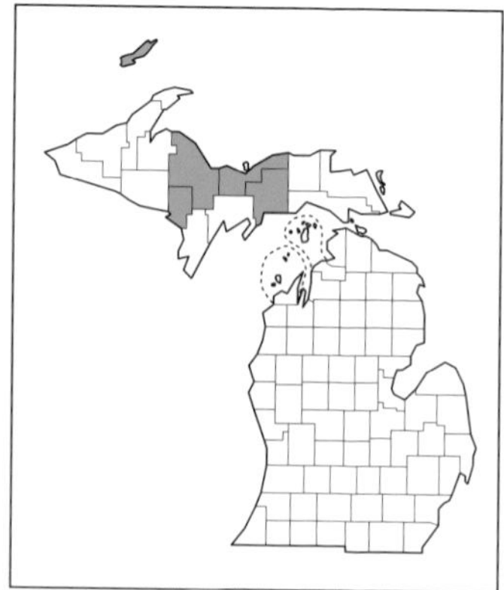

Distribution: Known from four counties in the Upper Peninsula: Alger, Dickinson, Marquette and Schoolcraft. Also found on Isle Royale. This subspecies is also known from parts of Minnesota, Wisconsin, Manitoba and Ontario.

Flight period: Single brood; June 3 to July 24.

Remarks: Uncommon. Location will serve to separate this species from the Karner Blue (No. 57). The Northern Blue is listed as a threatened species by the Michigan Natural Features Inventory.

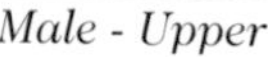

Male - Upper

Female - Upper

Male - Under

57 Karner Blue

Lycaeides melissa samuelis Nabokov

Adults and food sources: Upper surfaces of males are dark blue. The blue on females is much reduced by a blackish outer area; the margin of the hindwing has a partial orange band bordering several black spots. Undersurfaces are whitish gray with numerous black spots; the hindwing has several small iridescent silver spots capped with orange. The fringe has a continuous black line.

Adults nectar on blackberry, butterfly-weed, orange hawkweed, dotted monarda, downy phlox, New Jersey tea and St. John's-wort.

Early stages and host plants: The caterpillar is light green with fine hairs and is tended by ants.

The host plant is lupine.

Habitat: Openings and edges in oak barrens and oak savannas.

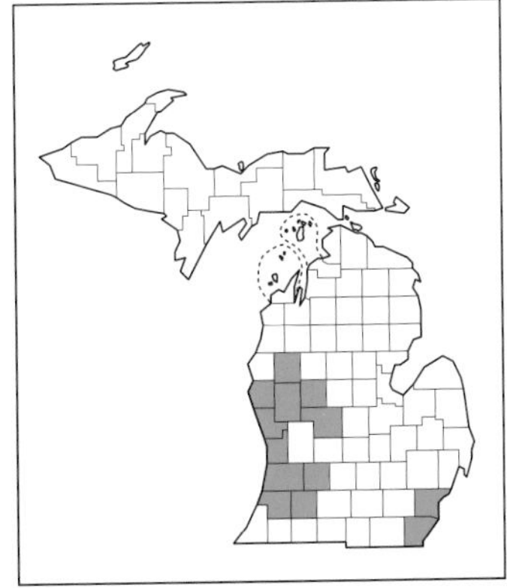

Distribution: Southern counties extending north to Lake County.

Flight period: Two broods; May 24 to August 26.

Remarks: Locally common. The subspecies *samuelis*, which occurs from New York to Minnesota, differs from the more western

nominate species by the rounder forewing apex; smoother, more grayish color beneath; and female orange submarginal lunules restricted to the hindwing. It's currently listed as endangered by the U.S. Fish and Wildlife Service and the Michigan Natural Features Inventory.

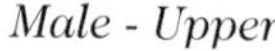
Male - Upper

Female - Upper

Female - Under

58

Greenish Blue

Plebejus saepiolus amica (W.H. Edwards)

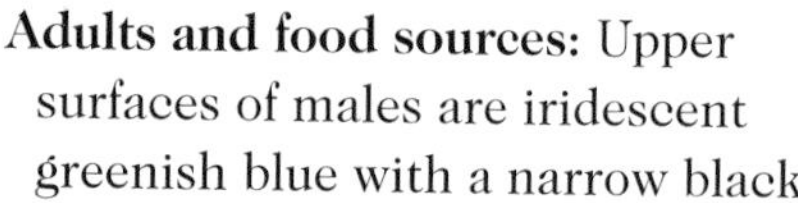

Adults and food sources: Upper surfaces of males are iridescent greenish blue with a narrow black border. Females are brown to reddish brown with blue scaling at the bases of the wings. Undersurfaces are whitish gray with small black spots and some bluish scaling at the bases of the wings.

Adults are recorded nectaring on alsike clover and orange hawkweed.

Early stages and host plants: The caterpillar is green or reddish.

The females lay eggs on alsike clover, the only known host in Michigan.

Habitat: Old fields, forest openings and roadsides in the Canadian zone.

Distribution: Throughout the Upper Peninsula and on Isle Royale, and extending into northern counties in the Lower Peninsula.

Flight period: Single brood; May 31 to July 30.

Remarks: Locally common. It often flies with the Northern Blue (No. 56) in some areas and may be confused with it in flight. The Michigan subspecies has smaller spots on the undersurfaces than the western nominate subspecies, *P. saepiolus saepiolus* (Boisduval).

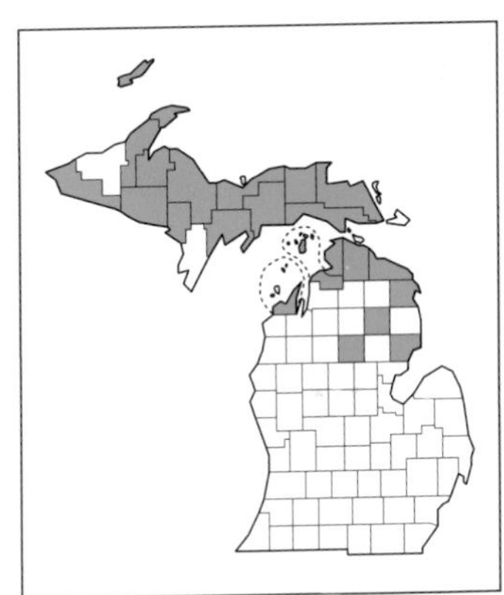

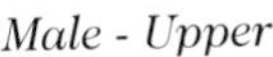

Male - Upper

Female - Upper

Male - Under

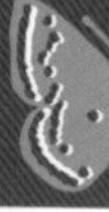

Metalmarks: ***Family Riodinidae:*** This family of small butterflies has only one species found in Michigan; only three species are found east of the Mississippi River. Upper surfaces are reddish brown with many small black and metallic spots; undersurfaces are bright orange with small black and metallic spots. Adults behave like moths in flight and typically alight on the underside of foliage. Eggs are laid on plants in the composite family; Michigan females lay eggs on swamp thistle. Caterpillars are sluglike and covered with long, whitish hairs; they overwinter in leaf debris. Chrysalids are attached by a silk button and girdle to a lower leaf surface or other substrate.

59 Swamp Metalmark

Calephelis mutica McAlpine

Adults and food sources: Upper surfaces are red-brown with small black spots and two rows of metallic spots. Undersurfaces are bright orange with small black and metallic spots. Females' wings are more rounded than males'.

Adults have been observed nectaring on shrubby cinquefoil, black-eyed Susan and swamp thistle.

Early stages and host plants: The caterpillar is green with black dots and covered with long, white hairs and resembles a tiger moth caterpillar.

Females lay eggs on swamp thistle. The caterpillar overwinters and feeds on the undersurface of thistle leaves in spring, causing the upper tissue to dry and leaving white, transparent-looking patches.

Habitat: Marshes, wet meadows, openings in tamarack-poison sumac fens and shrubby cinquefoil seeps.

Distribution: Scattered counties in the southern half of the Lower Peninsula.

Flight period: Single brood; June 30 to August 25.

Remarks: In flight, adults behave like moths, usually alighting with wings spread on the underside of leaves.

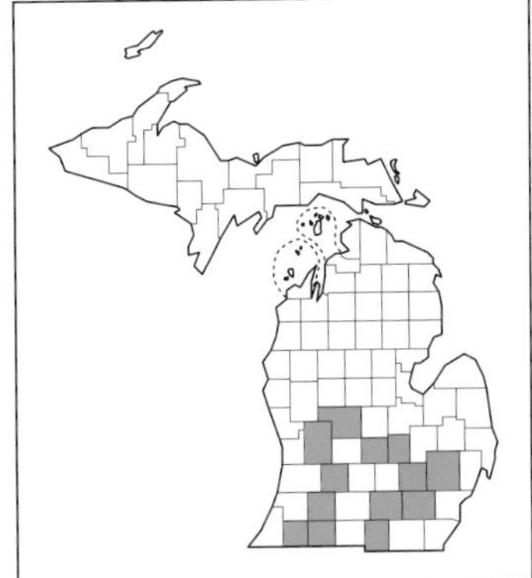

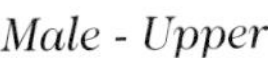

Male - Upper

Female - Upper

Male - Under

Brushfoots: *Family Nymphalidae:* This is a large family of small to large butterflies of various colors (frequently orange and brown), patterns and wing shapes. Included in this family are the snouts, longwings, fritillaries, checkerspots, crescents, anglewings, tortoise shells, ladies, admirals, and leaf and emperor butterflies. Many seek flowers, while others prefer plant sap or rotting fruit and other decaying organic matter for nutrients. The males' forelegs are reduced to brushlike appendages—hence the "brushfoot" name. Eggs are laid singly or in clusters on a wide variety of plants, including thistle, hops and several tree species. Caterpillars of many species feed colonially in early stages and are covered with spines or have spiny tubercles on their heads. The dark-colored caterpillars of many fritillaries feed at night. Some species hibernate as adults; others overwinter as early stage caterpillars or as chrysalids. Some adults, such as anglewings and tortoise shells, are among the longest lived butterflies, living 6 months or more. Chrysalids of most species hang from a silk mat attached to a twig or other surface.

60 Snout Butterfly

Libytheana carinenta bachmanii (Kirtland)

Adults and food sources: Upper surfaces are dark brown with orange patches; the forewing is squared off, with white spots. The palpi are extended to resemble a beak. Undersurfaces are either mottled or uniform gray.

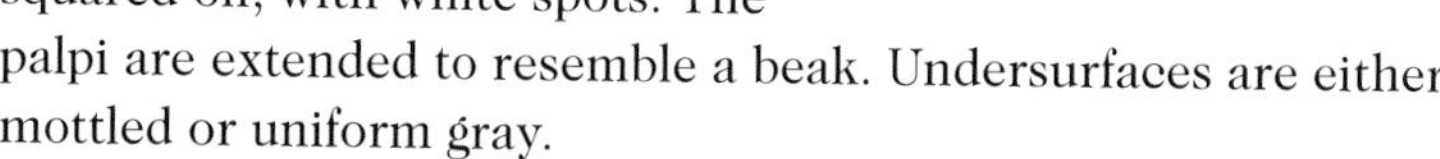

Adults nectar on wild carrot, white sweet clover, goldenrod, staghorn sumac and hops.

Early stages and host plants: The caterpillar is dark green with yellow dorsal and lateral stripes. The head area is swollen like that of a sphinx moth caterpillar and has two black tubercles.

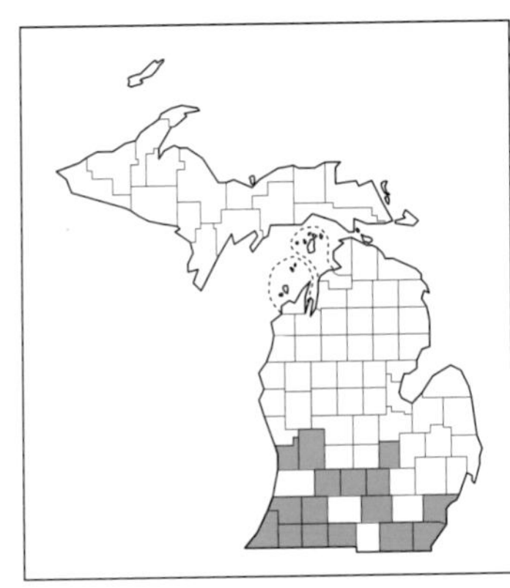

Hackberry is the only host in Michigan.

Habitat: Floodplain forest openings and edges, streamsides and brushy wetlands.

Distribution: Scattered counties in the southern half of the Lower Peninsula.

Flight period: Probably two broods; June 10 to October 5.

Remarks: Adults rest head-down on vegetation. This southern migrant occurs infrequently in southern counties along streams. The nominate subspecies, *L. carinenta carinenta* (Cramer), occurs in South America.

Female - Upper

Male - Under

61 Gulf Fritillary

Agraulis vanillae (Linnaeus)

Adults and food sources: Upper surfaces are bright orange with a few black spots and three black-rimmed white spots on the forewing. Undersurfaces have distinctive iridescent, elongated silver spots on the hindwing.

Adults are reported to favor lantana as a nectar source in southern states.

Early stages and host plants: The caterpillar is glossy black with dorsal and lateral red stripes and is covered with black spines.

Passion vine is reported to be the only host plant.

Habitat: Open fields, roadsides, brushy areas and open woods.

Distribution: Recorded from Ingham County; also sighted in Gratiot and Washtenaw counties.

Flight period: July 28, 1992.

Remarks: This southern migrant may occur rarely in southern counties.

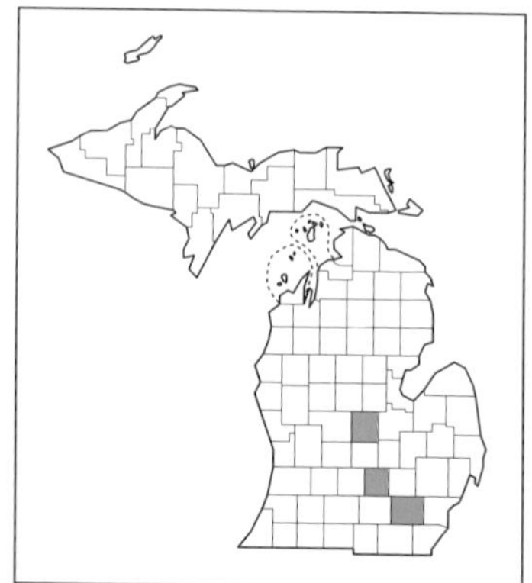

Male - Upper

Female - Under

62

Variegated Fritillary

Euptoieta claudia (Cramer)

Adults and food sources: Upper surfaces are light orange with black spots and bars; the hindwing margin is slightly scalloped. Undersurfaces are lighter colored, marked similarly to upper surfaces but without silver spots.

Adults have been observed nectaring on alfalfa, red clover, purple loosestrife, butterfly-weed, joe-pye-weed and Labrador tea.

Early stages and host plants: The caterpillar is reddish orange with rows of alternating black and white patches and covered with black spines.

Hosts are reported to be a variety of plants, including may-apple, purslane and passion vine. Females have been observed laying eggs on pansy.

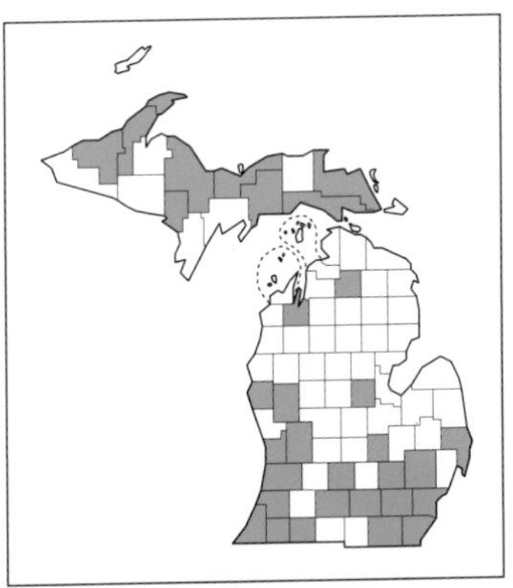

Habitat: Meadows, disturbed areas, pastures, streamsides and bogs.

Distribution: Scattered Lower and Upper Peninsula counties.

Flight period: Probably two broods; May 13 to October 31.

Remarks: This butterfly varies in abundance from year to year. Most records are from southern Michigan counties in late summer.

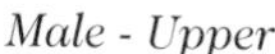

Male - Upper

Female - Under

63 Great Spangled Fritillary

Speyeria cybele cybele (Fabricius)

Adults and food sources: Upper surfaces are two-tone orange and brownish orange with heavy black markings. Undersurfaces are similarly colored except for a wide, yellowish submarginal band and iridescent silver spots on the hindwing.

Adults nectar on a wide variety of flowers, including bergamot, red clover, daisy, dogbane, knapweed, common milkweed, staghorn sumac, black-eyed Susan, New Jersey tea, thistle and vetch.

Early stages and host plants: The caterpillar is velvety black with black spines arising from red-yellow bases and a pair of gray dots between each pair of spines.

Females lay eggs on various violet species; some eggs are deposited on debris near violets. Caterpillars hatch in fall and overwinter without feeding until spring.

Habitat: Forest openings and edges, roadsides, old fields and meadows.

Distribution: Most counties of the Lower Peninsula.

Flight period: Single brood; June 4 to September 17.

Remarks: This is our most common large fritillary. Oddly marked individuals, with coalescing black markings, infrequently occur. Males emerge several days before females, chararcteristic of species in this genus.

Male - Upper

Female - Upper

Female - Under

63a Krautwurm's Fritillary

Speyeria cybele krautwurmi (Holland)

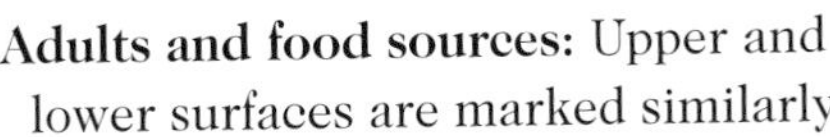

Adults and food sources: Upper and lower surfaces are marked similarly to those of the Great Spangled Fritillary (No. 63). Males are slightly smaller and females are distinctly pale fulvous, contrasting with a dark basal area.

Adults nectar on knapweed, thistle and joe-pye-weed.

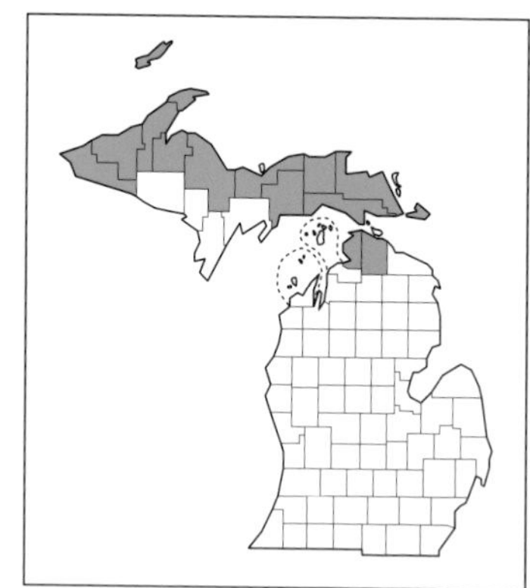

Early stages and host plants: Similar to those of the Great Spangled Fritillary.

Habitat: Forest openings and edges, forest roads and trails, and old fields.

Distribution: Throughout the Upper Peninsula, including Isle Royale, and into the northern counties of the Lower Peninsula.

Flight period: Single brood; June 24 to August 26.

Remarks: Common. The type locality of this subspecies is Mackinac County, at Les Cheneaux.

Male - Upper

Female - Upper

64 Aphrodite Fritillary

Speyeria aphrodite (Fabricius)

Adults and food sources: Upper surfaces are bright orange with black spots and bars. Females are more reddish orange than males. Undersurfaces are similar to the upper surface, except for a narrow, pale submarginal band and iridescent silver spots on the hindwing; the ground color on the hindwing is reddish brown.

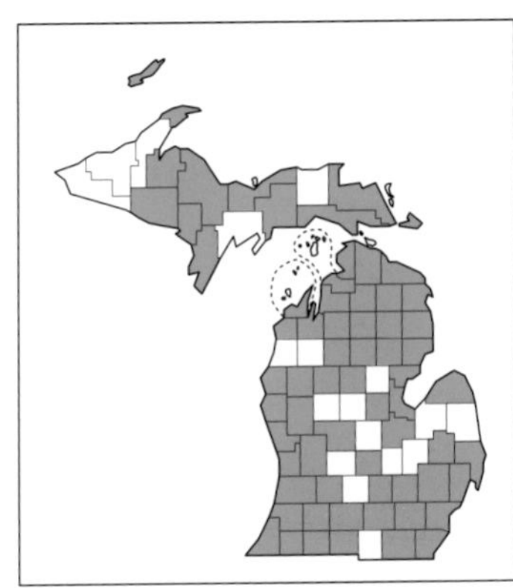

Adults nectar on orange hawkweed, knapweed, common milkweed and blazing-star.

Early stages and host plants: The caterpillar is similar to that of the Great Spangled Fritillary (No. 63) but with brownish spines.

Various violet species are the larval hosts.

Habitat: Oak-pine barrens, upland fields, prairies and roadsides.

Distribution: Throughout Michigan, including Isle Royale.

Flight period: Single brood; June 13 to September 23.

Remarks: Common. The form *alcestis* (Edwards), without the pale submarginal band on the undersurface of the hindwing, occurs occasionally in southern counties.

Male - Upper

Female - Upper

Male - Under

65 Regal Fritillary

Speyeria idalia (Drury)

Adults and food sources: The upper surface of the forewing is reddish orange with black and white spots. The hindwing is black with white spots in females and reddish submarginal spots in males. The undersurface of the hindwing is blackish gray with white spots (not metallic silver).

Adults have been observed nectaring on alfalfa, common milkweed, blazing-star and butterfly-weed.

Early stages and host plants: The caterpillar is velvety black with yellowish orange blotches and is covered with orange-based silver spines tipped with black.

Various species of violets are used as larval hosts.

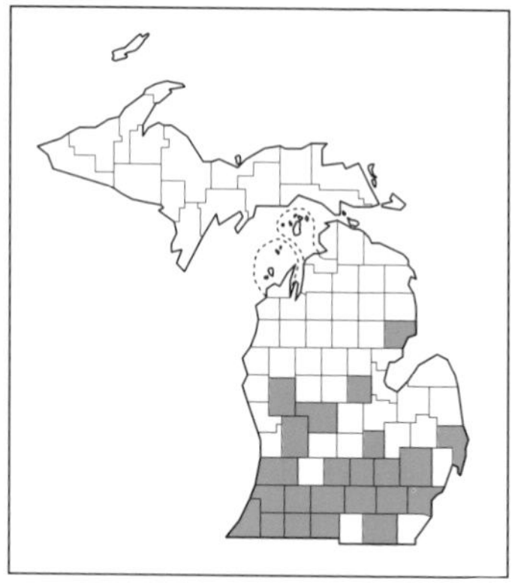

Habitat: Prairies, meadows, old fields, and floodplain forest openings and edges.

Distribution: Scattered counties in the southern portion of the Lower Peninsula.

Flight period: Single brood; June 22 to September 7.

Remarks: This species has always been scarce in Michigan; it has declined throughout much of its range in northern states. It is currently listed as endangered by the Michigan Natural Features Inventory.

Male - Upper

Female - Upper

Female - Under

66 Atlantis Fritillary

Speyeria atlantis (W.H. Edwards)

Adults and food sources: Upper surfaces are orange with black spots and bars and black borders. The undersurface of the hindwing is purplish brown with a narrow, yellowish submarginal band and iridescent silver spots.

Adults nectar on pearly everlasting, fireweed, fleabane, orange and yellow hawkweed, knapweed and New Jersey tea. They have been observed feeding on coyote feces.

Early stages and host plants: The caterpillar is yellow-green with a black dorsal line and is covered with gray spines.

Various violet species are used as larval hosts.

Habitat: Canadian zone forest openings and edges, old fields and roadsides.

Distribution: Throughout the Upper Peninsula, including Isle Royale, and scattered counties in the Lower Peninsula, south to Washtenaw County.

Flight period: Single brood; June 12 to September 10.

Remarks: Very common in the Upper Peninsula on trail and roadside flowers.

Male - Upper

Female - Upper

Female - Under

67 Bog Fritillary

Boloria eunomia dawsoni (Barnes & McDunnough)

Adults and food sources: Upper surfaces are orange with heavy black spots and bars, frequently dusted with black scaling.The undersurface of the forewing is lighter orange with smaller spots and bars; the hindwing has a series of non-metallic white spots, including submarginal black-outlined white spots.

Adults have been observed nectaring on bog laurel and Labrador tea in sphagnum-heath bogs. Probably other heaths are also used.

Early stages and host plants: The caterpillar is red-brown with reddish spines; the butterfly overwinters in this stage.

Females have been observed laying eggs on wild cranberry. They are also reported to use alpine smartweed, violets and willow as hosts.

Habitat: Restricted to open sphagnum-heath bogs in Michigan.

Distribution: Scattered counties in the Upper Peninsula. It is a holarctic species; the Great Lakes region subspecies is known as *dawsoni*.

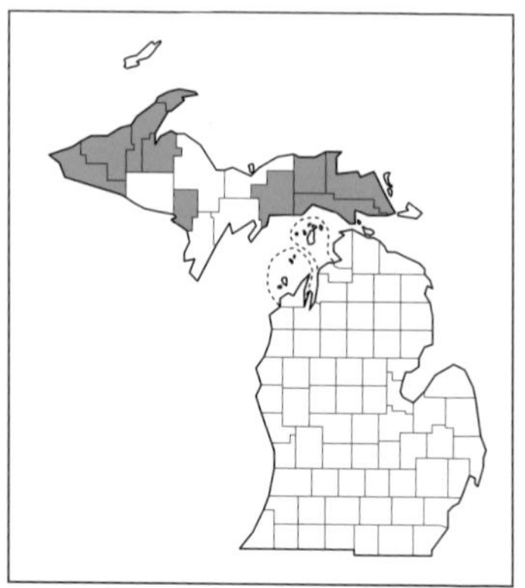

Flight period: Single brood; May 27 to July 2.

Remarks: Locally common in some years. This subspecies has a very short flight period, two weeks or less, in any bog. Males are very aggressive with one another or other butterflies and engage in aerial "dogfights".

Male - Upper

Female - Upper

Male - Under

68

Silver-bordered Fritillary

Boloria selene myrina (Cramer)

Adults and food sources: Upper surfaces are orange with black markings that are lighter than those of the Bog Fritillary (No. 67). The undersurface of the hindwing is marked similarly except for iridescent silver spots.

Adults nectar on aster, boneset, pearly everlasting, goldenrod, knapweed, wild iris, Labrador tea and thistle.

Early stages and host plants: The caterpillar is dark gray with darker blotches and pale yellow spines and two long, black thoracic spines.

Hosts are reported to be various violet species.

Habitat: Bogs, wet meadows and sedge marshes.

Distribution: Most Lower Peninsula counties. There is some overlapping with the Bog Silver-bordered Fritillary (No. 68a), the more northern subspecies.

Flight period: Two broods; May 4 to September 29.

Remarks: It is as common as the Meadow Fritillary (No. 69) in Michigan.

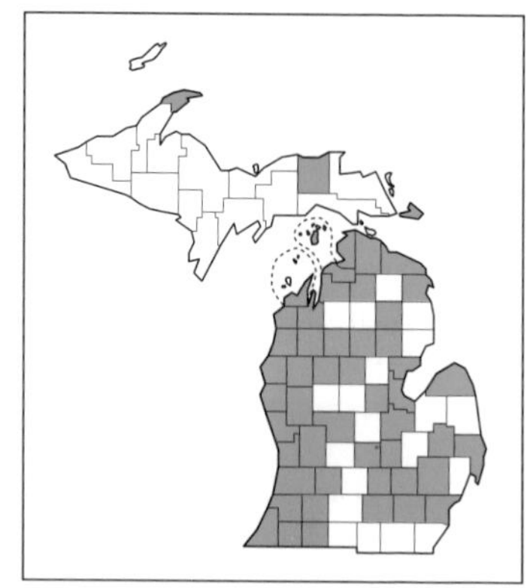

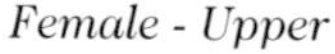
Female - Upper

Female - Under

68a Bog Silver-bordered Fritillary

Boloria selene atrocostalis (Huard)

Adults and food sources: Upper surfaces are similar to those of the Silver-bordered Fritillary (No. 68) except for heavy black scaling on
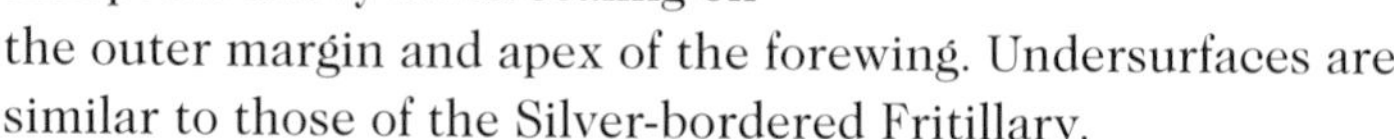
the outer margin and apex of the forewing. Undersurfaces are similar to those of the Silver-bordered Fritillary.

Adults have been observed nectaring on red clover, goldenrod and Labrador tea.

Early stages and host plants: Similar to those of the Silver-bordered Fritillary.

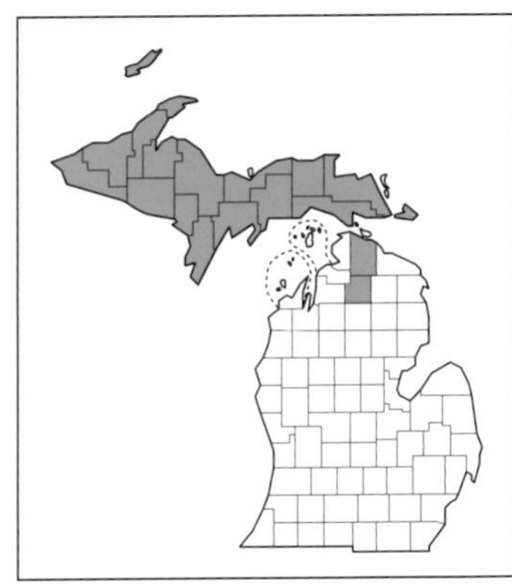

Habitat: Bogs and adjacent trails and roadsides.

Distribution: Throughout the Upper Peninsula, including Isle Royale, and extending into the northern counties of the Lower Peninsula, where it overlaps with the Silver-bordered Fritillary.

Flight period: Two broods; May 15 to August 30.

Remarks: Locally common. This is essentially a bog-restricted subspecies. It is easily confused with the Bog Fritillary (No. 67) in flight.

Male - Upper

69 Meadow Fritillary

Boloria bellona (Fabricius)

Adults and food sources: Upper surfaces are orange with many black spots and bars, which is typical of all large and small fritillaries. The upper portion of the forewing is squared. The undersurface of the hindwing is without black markings and has purplish scaling on the outer portion.

Adults nectar on red clover, dandelion, daisy, black-eyed Susan and bog-rosemary.

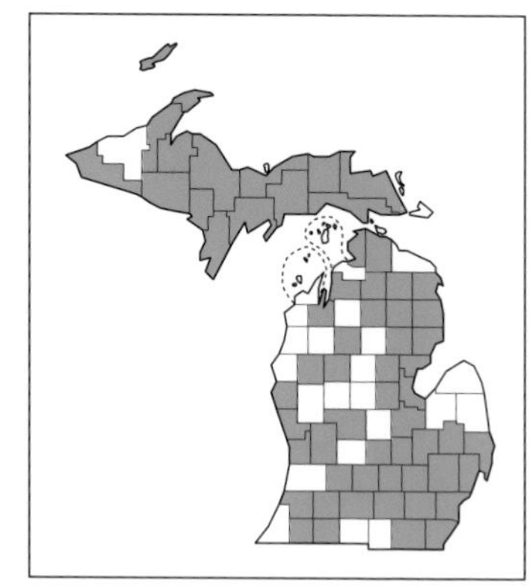

Early stages and host plants: The caterpillar is shiny green with yellowish brown spines.

Various violet species are reported to be larval hosts.

Habitat: Moist meadows, pastures, old fields and clearings being invaded by violets.

Distribution: Throughout Michigan, including Isle Royale.

Flight period: Two broods; April 30 to October 6.

Remarks: Locally common. Northern Michigan specimens tend to be darker in color and markings.

Male - Upper

Female - Upper

Male - Under

70 Frigga Fritillary

Boloria frigga saga
(Staudinger)

Adults and food sources: Upper surfaces are two-tone — the outer portion is orange and the basal area is dark orange-brown. The forewing apex is rounded. Undersurfaces of the hindwing are similar to those of the Meadow Fritillary (No. 69) except for more light areas, especially the off-white basal patch.

Though it is not an avid flower visitor, adults have been observed nectaring on bog laurel and bog-rosemary.

Early stages and host plants: The caterpillar is black with purplish lateral lines and is covered with black spines.

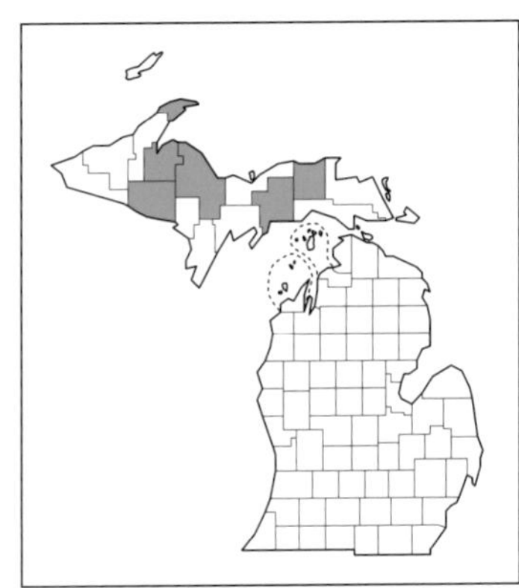

Females have been observed laying eggs on wild cranberry, bog laurel and bog-rosemary in Michigan. Caterpillars have been reared in captivity on dwarf birch.

Habitat: Sphagnum-heath bogs with dwarf birch.

Distribution: Scattered counties in the Upper Peninsula.

Flight period: Single brood; May 15 to June 29.

Remarks: Locally uncommon. A bog-restricted species; usually seen flying in the wettest areas. Our population may represent a new subspecies upon further study. Currently listed as a special concern species by the Michigan Natural Features Inventory.

Male - Upper

Female - Upper

Female - Under

71 Freija Fritillary

Boloria freija
(Thunberg)

Adults and food sources: Upper surfaces are orange with black markings as in other small fritillaries; basal areas are noticeably darker. The undersurface of the hindwing has a median zigzag black line and arrowhead-shaped white spots.

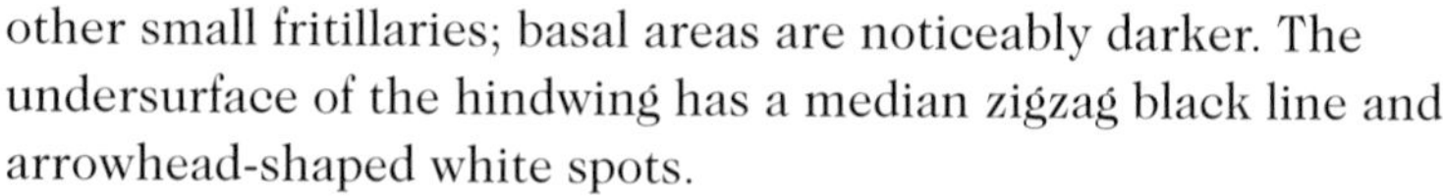

Though it's not an avid flower visitor, adults have been observed nectaring on leatherleaf and bog-rosemary.

Early stages and host plants: The caterpillar is blackish brown with black spines.

Michigan females have been observed laying eggs on wild cranberry, and larvae have been reared on this plant in captivity.

Habitat: Sphagnum-heath bogs with an abundance of leatherleaf. Also collected on the uplands in Porcupine Mountains State Park.

Distribution: Scattered counties in the Upper Peninsula.

Flight period: Single brood; May 8 to June 5.

Remarks: Locally uncommon. This is the fastest flying and smallest of our small fritillaries. The species is believed to overwinter as a chrysalis. Our population probably represents an undescribed subspecies and needs further research.

This species is currently listed as a special concern species by the Michigan Natural Features Inventory.

Male - Upper

Female - Upper

Female - Under

72 Gorgone Checkerspot

Chlosyne gorgone carlota (Reakirt)

Adults and food sources: Upper surfaces have alternating bands of dark brown and orange areas. The undersurface of the hindwing has a zigzag pattern of brown and orange areas.

Adults are reported to nectar on various species of yellow-flowered composites, fleabane, common milkweed and white sweet clover.

Early stages and host plants: The caterpillar is yellow with black stripes and is covered with black spines.

Reported host plants include sunflowers; females have been observed selecting *Helianthus petiolaris* Nutt. in Sand Hills State Forest, Mason County, Ill., for egg laying.

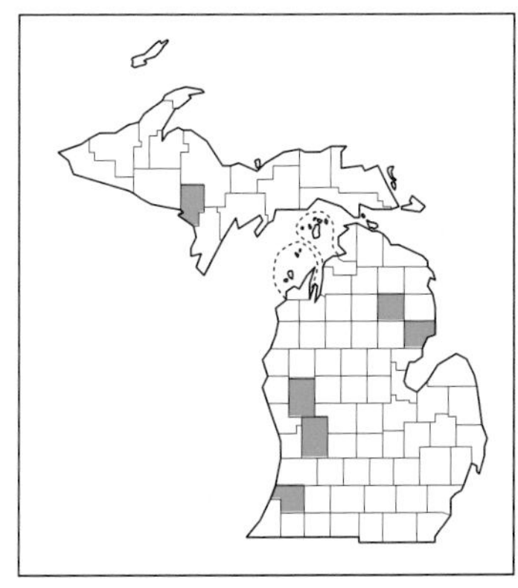

Habitat: Prairies, old fields, oak-pine barrens and streamsides.

Distribution: Dickinson County in the Upper Peninsula and five counties in the Lower Peninsula.

Flight period: Probably two broods in the Lower Peninsula; May 26 to August 7.

Remarks: The last Michigan record of this butterfly was from Van Buren County in 1958 (Fleming). This species may be confused with other checkerspots and crescents; that may explain why it has not been reported recently. It's currently listed as a special concern species by the Michigan Natural Features Inventory.

Male - Upper

Female - Under

73 Silvery Checkerspot

Chlosyne nycteis (Doubleday & Hewitson)

Adults and food sources: The upper surface is similar to that of the smaller Gorgone Checkerspot (No. 72) except for some white-centered submarginal spots. The undersurface is paler than the upper surface. The hindwing has a silvery marginal crescent.

Adults nectar on fleabane, common milkweed, staghorn sumac, vetch and butterfly-weed.

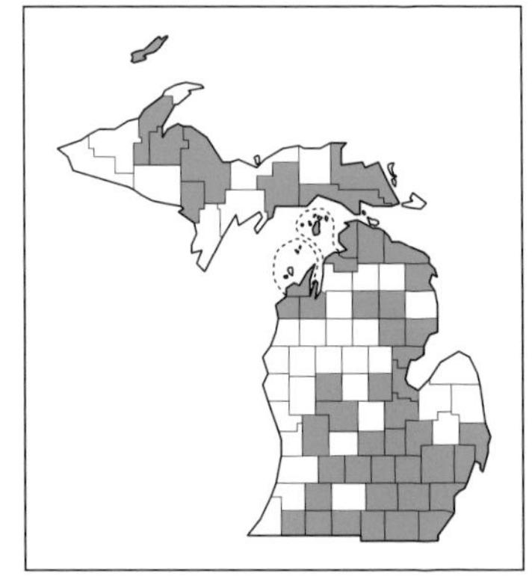

Early stages and host plants: The caterpillar is brownish black with broken yellow lateral stripes and white dots and is covered with black spines.

Females lay eggs on several species of composites, including aster, sunflower and wing-stem.

Habitat: Floodplain forest openings, meadows, marshes and roadsides.

Distribution: Throughout Michigan, including Isle Royale.

Flight period: Two broods; May 26 to September 5.

Remarks: Locally common. It is easily confused with Gorgone and Harris' Checkerspots (Nos. 72 and 74) in flight.

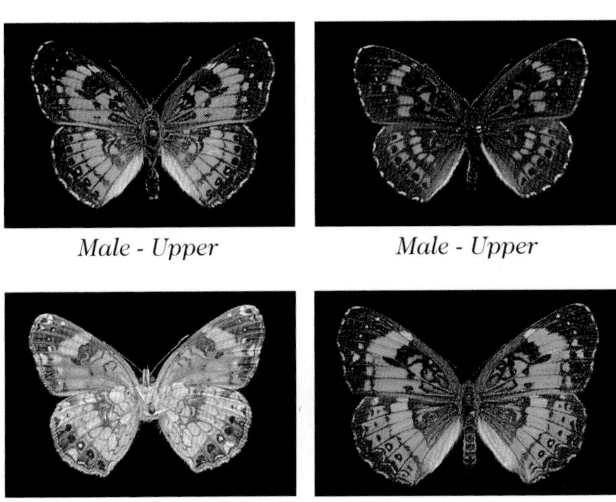

Male - Upper *Male - Upper*

Male - Under *Female - Upper*

74 Harris' Checkerspot

Chlosyne harrisii (Scudder)

Adults and food sources: Upper surfaces are similar to those of the Silvery Checkerspot except borders are wider. Undersurfaces' ground color is orange to reddish tan; the hindwing has three bands of white spots and crescents.

Though it's not an avid flower visitor, adults nectar on dogbane and vetch. Adults also take moisture and nutrients from damp soils.

Early stages and host plants: The caterpillar is reddish orange with a black dorsal stripe and two transverse stripes and is covered with black spines.

The only known host plant is flat-topped white aster.

Habitat: Marsh edges, moist pastures, meadows, wet ditches and roadsides.

Distribution: Scattered counties throughout Michigan.

Flight period: Single brood; May 31 to July 30.

Remarks: Locally uncommon. It is easily confused with other checkerspots.

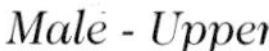

Male - Upper

Male - Under

Female - Upper

75

Pearl Crescent

Phyciodes tharos (Drury)

Adults and food sources: Upper surface orange areas in males are separated by fine black lines. The undersurface of the hindwing has crisp brown lines and a dark marginal patch contrasting with the orange ground color and usually with a distinct pearl crescent. Females are more mottled on the undersurface of the hindwing; spring and fall specimens are mottled gray. Males have black antennal clubs.

Adults nectar on a wide variety of flowers, including blackberry, butterfly-weed, dogbane, goldenrod and joe-pye-weed.

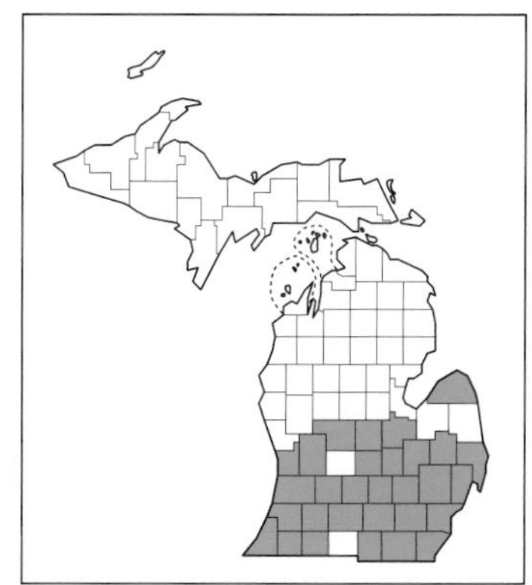

Early stages and host plants: The caterpillar is dark brown with brown spines. The head has white patches.

Females lay eggs on a variety of asters.

Habitat: Forest openings and edges, meadows, pastures, old fields and roadsides.

Distribution: Throughout the southern half of the Lower Peninsula.

Flight period: At least two broods; May 13 to October 8.

Remarks: This is one of Michigan's commonest butterflies. It's easily confused with our other crescents.

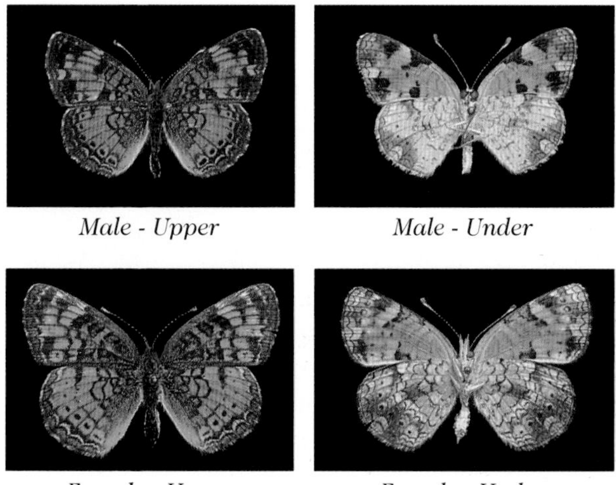

Male - Upper *Male - Under*

Female - Upper *Female - Under*

76 Northern Pearl Crescent

Phyciodes selenis
(W. Kirby)

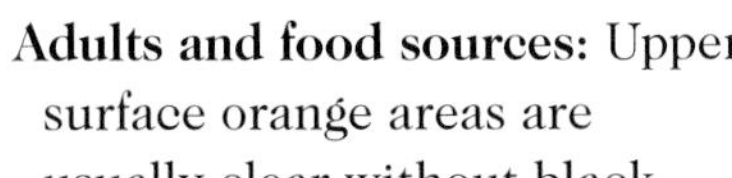

Adults and food sources: Upper surface orange areas are usually clear without black veins, and the postmedial orange band is often contrastingly lighter. On the undersurface of the hindwing, brown lines and a dark marginal patch are lighter than in the Pearl Crescent (No. 75), and there is a distinct pearl crescent-shaped marking. The female is similar to the Pearl Crescent. The male's antennal club is orange.

Adults nectar on many flowers visited by the Pearl Crescent, and they frequently take moisture and nutrients from damp soils.

Early stages and host plants: The caterpillar is dark brown with pinkish gray spines.

Host plants are unknown in Michigan, but they are probably similar to those of the Pearl Crescent.

Habitat: Forest openings and edges, old fields, streamsides and roadsides.

Distribution: Throughout the Upper Peninsula, including Isle Royale, and extending into the Lower Peninsula, south to Wayne County.

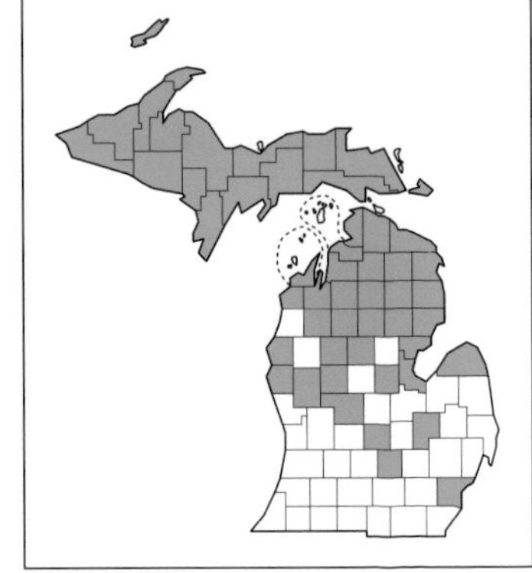

Flight period: Single brood, flying between the first two broods of the Pearl Crescent; June 3 to August 3.

Remarks: Very common. Not every specimen, especially females, can be identified on the basis of appearance alone. It's easily confused with the Pearl Crescent where populations overlap. The Northern Pearl Crescent is slightly larger.

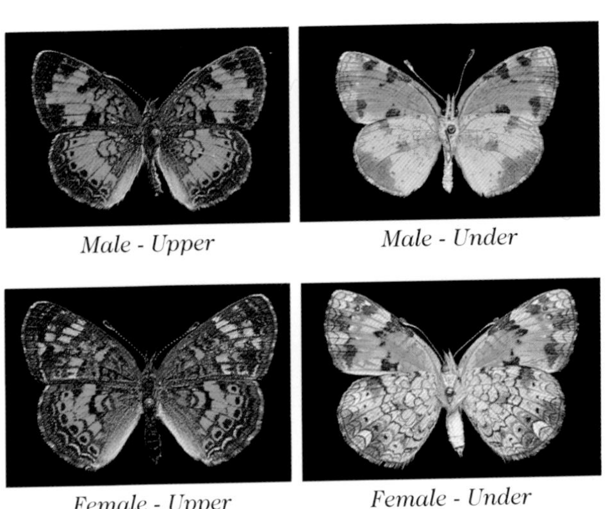

Male - Upper *Male - Under*

Female - Upper *Female - Under*

77 Tawny Crescent

Phyciodes batesii (Reakirt)

Adults and food sources: Upper surfaces of the male are orange with heavier black markings than on other crescents; the postmedial band is contrastingly lighter orange. The undersurface of the male's hindwing is yellowish tan with light brown markings and several dark marginal spots. The male's antennal club is black and white. The undersurface of the female is more mottled, similar to other crescents.

Adults have been observed nectaring on blackberry, daisy and orange hawkweed, and seen on streambanks and roadsides taking moisture and nutrients from damp soils.

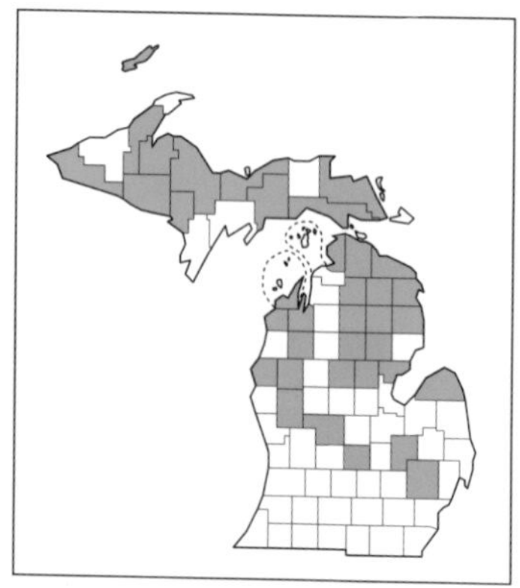

Early stages and host plants: The caterpillar is brown with a pinkish tinge and a pale dorsal stripe; early stages are incompletely known.

Females lay eggs on wavy-leaved aster.

Habitat: Meadows, pastures, old fields, streambanks and roadsides, especially in the Canadian life zone.

Distribution: Throughout the Upper Peninsula, including Isle Royale, and scattered counties in the Lower Peninsula.

Flight period: Single brood, flying between the first broods of the Pearl Crescent (No. 75); May 3 to July 31. A partial second brood may occur.

Remarks: It is more common in northern counties. Currently listed as a special concern species by the Michigan Natural Features Inventory. Easily confused with other crescents.

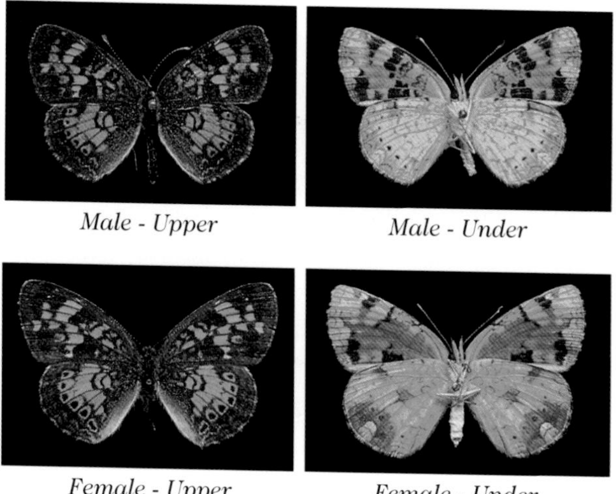

Male - Upper *Male - Under*

Female - Upper *Female - Under*

78 Baltimore

Euphydryas phaeton
(Drury)

Adults and food sources: Upper surfaces are black with cream-white spots on the outer half and a marginal row of orange spots. They usually have two orange spots on the inner half of the forewing. Undersurfaces are boldly marked with white and orange spots.

Adults feed on nectar from shrubby cinquefoil, dogbane, common and swamp milkweed, and black-eyed Susan.

Early stages and host plants: Caterpillars are orange-red, striped with black and covered with black spines.

Early stages overwinter in silken nests on the host plant.

Females lay eggs on one of the figwort family of plants, usually false foxglove or turtlehead in Michigan. A variety of plants are eaten in spring, including honeysuckle, plantain and willow.

Habitat: Brushy swamps, marshes, wet meadows and oak-pine barrens.

Distribution: Throughout Michigan.

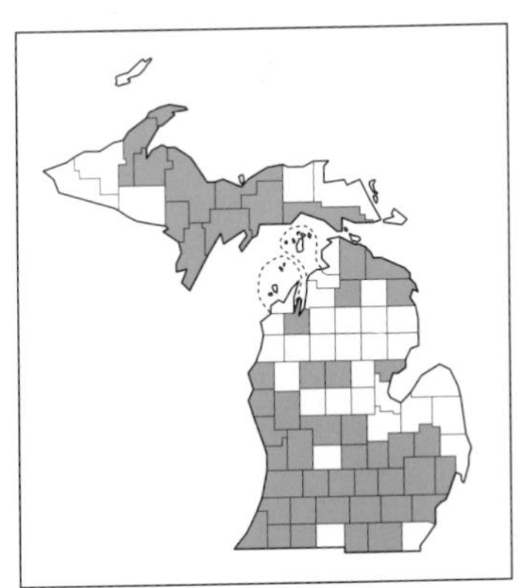

Flight period: Single brood; May 27 to August 7.

Remarks: Locally common. More study is needed on taxonomic differences between wetland and upland populations.

Male - Upper

Male - Under

Female - Upper

79 Question Mark

Polygonia interrogationis (Fabricius)

Adults and food sources: The upper surface of the forewing in summer and winter forms is orange with black spots. The hindwing of the summer form is largely black with short tails; the hindwing of the winter form is orange and black with longer violet-tipped tails. The undersurface of the hindwing has the characteristic silver question mark.

Adults rarely nectar on flowers but have been observed on aster, common milkweed and bog-rosemary; most seek tree sap and rotted fruit and take moisture and nutrients from damp soils.

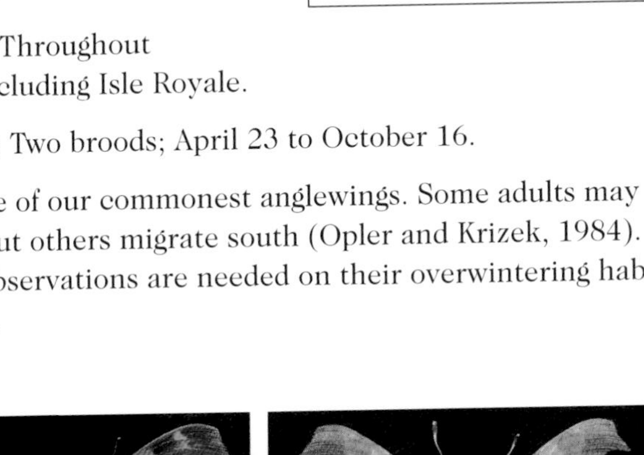

Early stages and host plants: The caterpillar varies from black to yellow with yellowish to red lines and is covered with yellow to reddish and black spines.

Eggs are laid on elm, nettle, hackberry and hops.

Habitat: Forest openings, edges and trails, roadsides and streamsides.

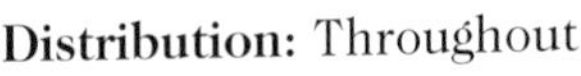

Distribution: Throughout Michigan, including Isle Royale.

Flight period: Two broods; April 23 to October 16.

Remarks: One of our commonest anglewings. Some adults may hibernate, but others migrate south (Opler and Krizek, 1984). More field observations are needed on their overwintering habits in Michigan.

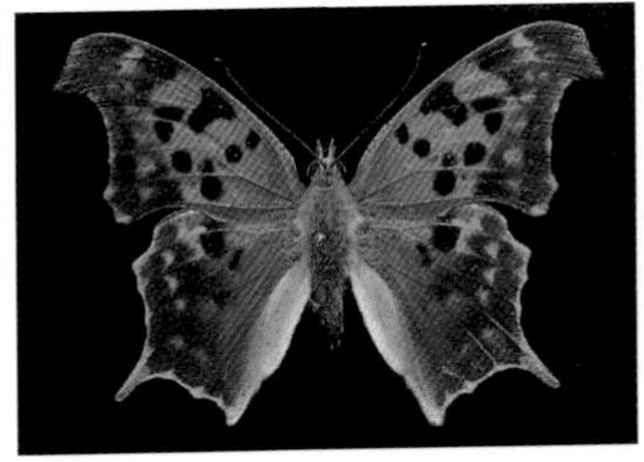

Male - Upper (Winter form)

Male - Under

Female - Upper (Summer form)

(80) Comma or Hop Merchant

Polygonia comma (Harris)

Adults and food sources: The upper surfaces of summer and winter forms are similar to those of the Question Mark (No. 79), but these are smaller butterflies with more irregular wing margins and shorter tails. The margin of the hindwing is edged with violet and with orange spots. The undersurface of the hindwing has the distinctive silver comma mark.

It rarely nectars on flowers but has been observed on common milkweed. Commas usually feed on tree sap, rotted fruit and decaying organic matter, and take moisture and nutrients from damp soils.

Early stages and host plants: Caterpillars vary from black to greenish brown and white and are covered with black to white spines.

Eggs are laid on elm, nettle and hops.

Habitat: Forest openings, edges and trails, swamps and streamsides.

Distribution: Throughout Michigan, including Isle Royale.

Flight period: Two broods; March 22 to October 15.

Remarks: Common. Adults hibernate and will appear during winter thaws. They are easily attracted to artificial bait.

Male - Upper (Winter form)

Male - Upper (Summer form)

Male - Under

81 Satyr Anglewing

Polygonia satyrus (W.H. Edwards)

Adults and food sources: Upper surfaces are similar to those of the Comma, but the outer margin of the hindwing is lighter with larger yellow spots that usually form a solid band. The undersurface is golden brown to purplish brown with darker bands; it has a silver comma.

No observations of adults nectaring on flowers have been made in Michigan; adults seek moisture and nutrients from damp soils, tree sap and carrion.

Early stages and host plants: The caterpillar is black with a wide greenish white dorsal band and lateral lines and is covered with black and greenish white spines.

The host plants are reported to be nettles.

Habitat: Forest openings, edges, along streams, pine barrens and roadsides.

Distribution: Scattered counties in the Upper Peninsula.

Flight period: Two broods; May 4 to September 27.

Remarks: Uncommon. These butterflies are attracted to artificial bait. They're usually seen along sunny forest trails in Canadian zones, as are other anglewings. It hibernates as an adult.

Male - Upper *Female - Under*

82 Green Comma

Polygonia faunus (W.H. Edwards)

Adults and food sources: Upper surfaces are very similar to those of the Comma except for more jagged wing margins. The undersurfaces of both wings have two rows of small green spots, and there's a small silver comma on the hindwing. Males are mottled gray; females are an even grayish brown.

A few nectaring observations on dandelion have been made. Adults prefer tree sap and take moisture and nutrients from damp soils.

Early stages and host plants: The caterpillar is yellow-brown to red with a dorsal greenish white band and lateral broken orange bands. Spines are white and brown.

Eggs are laid on various plants, including alder, birch, blueberry, gooseberry and willow.

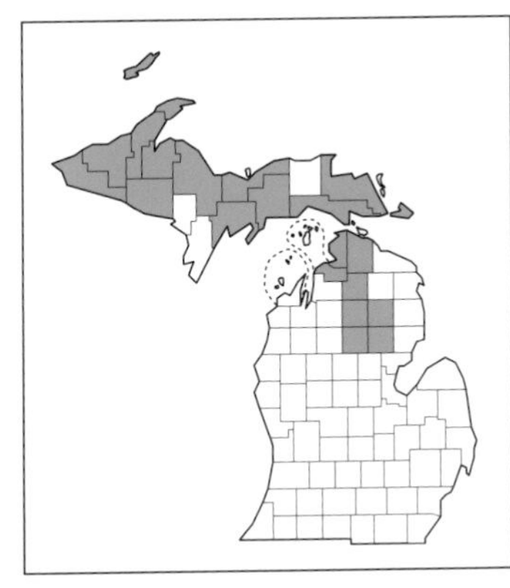

Habitat: Usually in coniferous forests and trails in Canadian zones.

Distribution: Throughout the Upper Peninsula, including Isle Royale, and in the northern half of the Lower Peninsula.

Flight period: One brood; April 26 to September 20.

Remarks: More numerous than the Satyr Anglewing (No. 80). It is attracted to artificial bait and usually seen along sunny forest trails in Canadian zones, as are other anglewings. It hibernates as an adult.

Male - Upper

Male - Under

Female - Under

83 Hoary Comma

Polygonia gracilis (Grote & Robinson)

Adult and food sources: Upper surfaces are patterned like those of other anglewings but have heavier dark markings. Undersurfaces are gray-brown with the outer half distinctly hoary white to silvery gray. A silver comma, blunt at the ends, is present on the hindwing.

No observations of nectaring have been made in Michigan; adults prefer tree sap and moisture and nutrients from damp soils.

Early stages and host plants: The caterpillar is predominantly black and marked with white; spines are black marked with white.

Host plants are reported to be currant and gooseberry.

Habitat: Boreal forest openings and edges, stream margins and trails.

Distribution: Scattered counties in the Upper Peninsula.

Flight period: Single brood; July 23-31.

Remarks: Scarce in Canadian zone conifers. Habits are similar to those of the Green Comma (No. 82). Adults can be collected in a bait trap. It's currently listed as a special concern species by the Michigan Natural Features Inventory. A worn specimen previously identified as *P. zephrus* (W.H. Edwards) (now considered a western subspecies of *gracilis*) is included with the Michigan *gracilis* records.

Male - Upper

Male - Under

Gray Comma

Polygonia progne (Cramer)

Adults and food sources: Upper surfaces are patterned like those of other anglewings. The hindwing is mahogany-red in the center to blackish on the border. Undersurfaces are striated gray without the whitish outer portion of the Hoary Comma (No. 83); the silver comma tapers at the ends.

Adults seldom feed on nectar but have been observed on common milkweed. Adults prefer tree sap and rotting fruit, and taking moisture and nutrients from damp soils.

Early stages and host plants: The caterpillar is yellowish brown with dark blotches and lines and black or yellow spines.

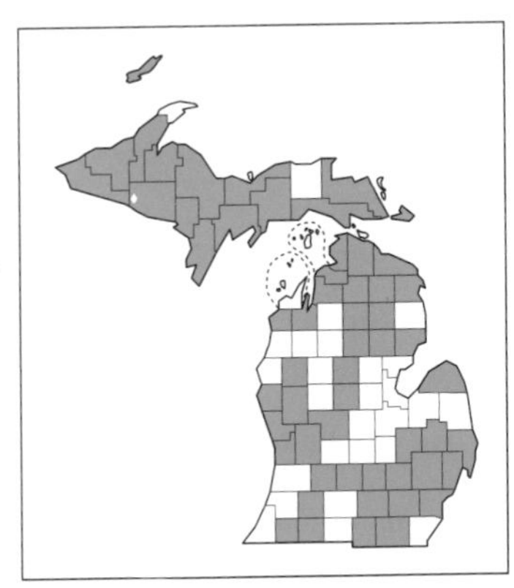

Eggs are laid on wild gooseberry in Michigan.

Habitat: Forests, swamps, pine barrens and trails.

Distribution: Throughout Michigan, including Isle Royale.

Flight period: Two broods; April 9 to October 11.

Remarks: Common. Habits are similar to those of other anglewings. Adults are easily attracted to artificial bait.

Male - Upper

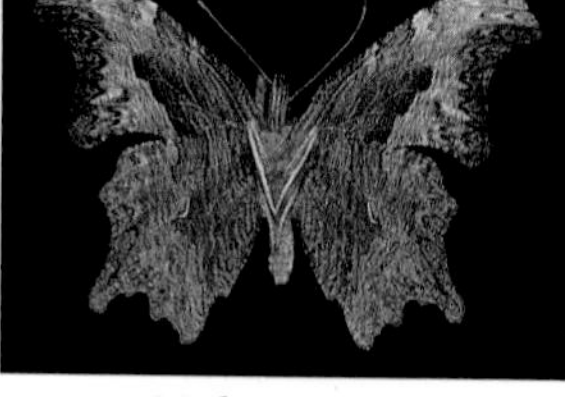

Male - Under

85 Compton Tortoise Shell

Nymphalis vau-album j-album (Boisduval & LeConte)

Adults and food sources: This medium-sized to large butterfly has a mix of black, brown, orange, white and yellow on upper surfaces with jagged margins and a small tail projection on the hindwing. Undersurfaces are a mix of mottled light and dark brown, with a distinct white J-shaped mark on the hindwing.

Adults seldom take nectar from flowers; one has been observed on knapweed. Adults are fond of tree sap and rotting fruit, and they take moisture and nutrients from damp soils.

Early stages and host plants: The caterpillar is light green with black spines.

Eggs are laid on aspen, birch and willow.

Habitat: Forest openings, edges and trails, especially in northern counties.

Distribution: Throughout Michigan, including Isle Royale.

Flight period: Single brood; March 19 to November 20.

Remarks: More common in northern counties. Adults hibernate in hollow logs and outbuildings and may appear during winter thaws. They're attracted to artificial bait. The nominate subspecies, *N. vau-album vau-album* (Denis & Schiffermuller), occurs in Europe.

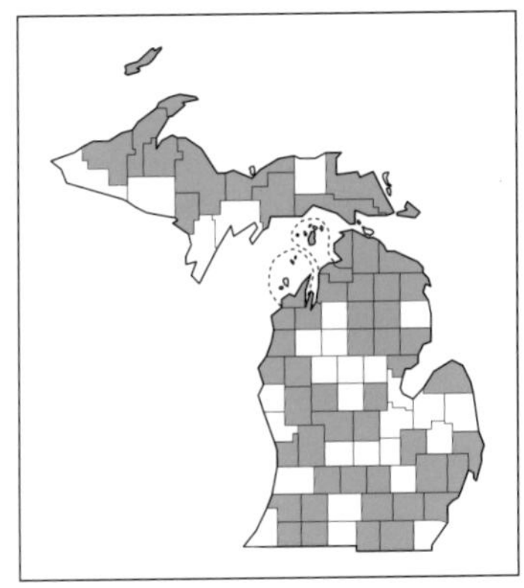

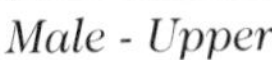

Male - Upper

Male - Under

86 California Tortoise Shell

Nymphalis californica (Boisduval)

Adults and food sources: The upper surface resembles that of the Compton Tortoise Shell (No. 85) except that the wings have more orange-brown and wider black margins. The undersurface is brownish with darker lines and blotches and without a white discal comma.

No observation of adults feeding has been made in Michigan; like other tortoise shells, these probably feed on tree sap and take moisture and nutrients from damp soils.

Early stages and host plants: The caterpillar is reported to be black to reddish black with white dots and whitish lateral bands and orange or black spines.

Wild-lilac is the reported host plant in western states.

Habitat: Forest openings and edges and roadsides. May swarm and spread from the west to many other areas.

Distribution: Essentially a western species that was recorded in Emmet and Mason counties in 1945.

Flight period: September 4-6, 1945.

Remarks: The Michigan records are stray migrants; specimens have also been recorded from Wisconsin and Pennsylvania (Ebner, 1970).

Male - Upper

87 Mourning Cloak

Nymphalis antiopa
(Linnaeus)

Adults and food sources: Upper surfaces are purplish black with wide yellow margins edged with iridescent blue spots; the hindwing has a tail-like projection. Undersurfaces are dark brown and barklike with yellowish margins.

Adults seldom visit flowers; one observation has been made on common milkweed. Adults prefer tree sap and overripe fruit and take moisture and nutrients from damp soils.

Early stages and host plants: The caterpillar is black with small white marks and red dots and is covered with black spines. Larvae feed communally on foliage.

Eggs are laid in clusters. The preferred host in Michigan is willow; it's also reported to use aspen, birch, elm and hackberry.

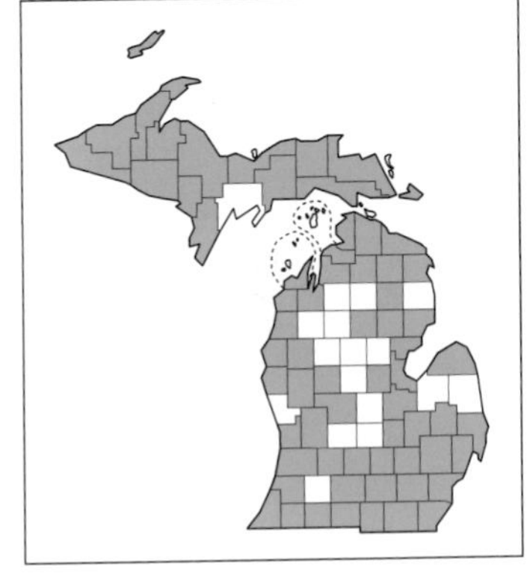

Habitat: Forest openings, edges, swamps, meadows, stream margins and roadsides; also rural and urban areas.

Distribution: Throughout Michigan, including Isle Royale.

Flight period: Usually two broods; March 21 to November 1.

Remarks: Common. Adults hibernate in hollow logs and woodpiles and may fly during winter thaws. The Mourning Cloak is one of the first butterflies seen in spring. It is attracted to artificial bait.

Male - Upper

88 Milbert's Tortoise Shell

Nymphalis milberti
(Godart)

Adults and food sources: This is the smallest of Michigan's tortoise shells. Upper surfaces have a yellowish orange submarginal band and a black basal area. A marginal band is black with blue spots. Undersurfaces have a blackish outer half and darker inner area.

Adults feed on nectar from a variety of flowers, including alfalfa, black-eyed Susan, boneset, daisy, dandelion, dogbane, goldenrod, knapweed, vetch, joe-pye-weed and willow catkins. They also feed on tree sap and rotted fruit.

Early stages and host plants: The caterpillar is black with tiny white spots and a broken, greenish yellow stripe and is covered with black spines. Early stages feed collectively within a leaf shelter. Clusters of eggs are laid exclusively on nettles.

Habitat: Swamp and marsh edges, meadows, wet pastures, stream margins and roadside ditches.

Distribution: Throughout Michigan, including Isle Royale.

Flight period: At least two broods; March 22 to November 17.

Remarks: Common. Adults hibernate in hollow logs, barns and outbuildings.

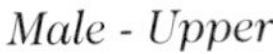

Male - Upper

Female - Upper

89 American Painted Lady

Vanessa virginiensis (Drury)

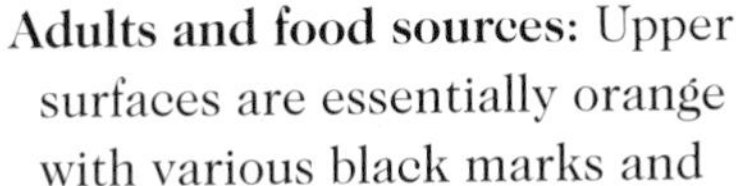

Adults and food sources: Upper surfaces are essentially orange with various black marks and a few white spots near the apex of the forewing. The undersurface of the hindwing has two large, black-ringed blue spots, which easily distinguish it from the Painted Lady (No. 90), which has four smaller eyespots.

Adults take nectar from aster, red clover, chokecherry, dogbane, orange hawkweed, lilac, common milkweed, bog-rosemary and Labrador tea.

Early stages and host plants: The caterpillar has alternating black and orange-yellow bands with small, white dots and is covered with blackish spines.

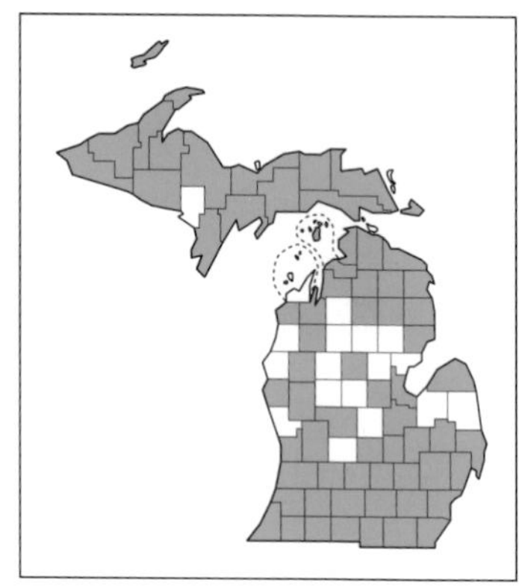

Eggs are usually laid on pearly everlasting and pussy-toes in Michigan; burdock and cudweed are also used.

Habitat: Old fields, prairies, meadows, disturbed areas and roadsides.

Distribution: Throughout the state, including Isle Royale.

Flight period: Usually two broods; April 30 to October 26.

Remarks: Common. No definite information is available on hibernating habits; adults probably cannot survive Michigan winters. Adult numbers fluctuate from year to year.

Male - Upper

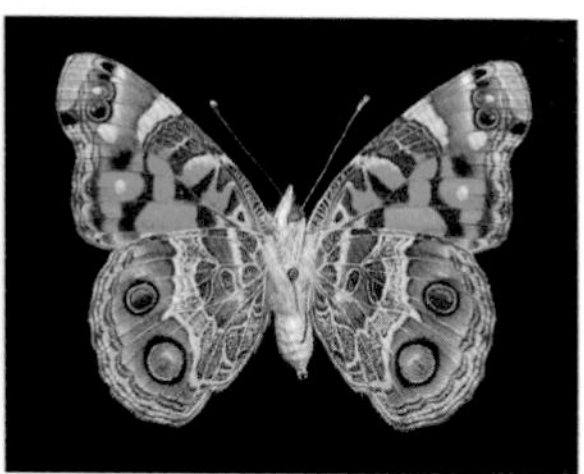

Female - Under

90 Painted Lady

Vanessa cardui (Linnaeus)

Adults and food sources: Upper surfaces are similar to those of the American Painted Lady (No. 89), but the ground color is more pinkish orange. Undersurfaces are similar except for four small, indistinct submarginal eyespots. The summer form is larger and brighter.

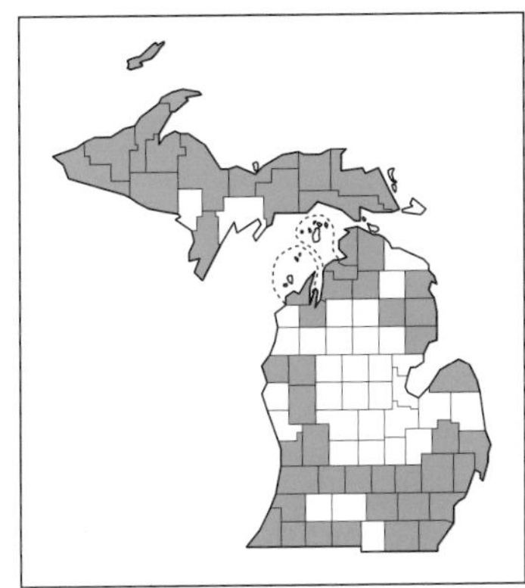

Adults nectar on blackberry, buttonbush, catnip, ironweed, knapweed, lupine, Labrador tea, blazing-star and joe-pye-weed.

Early stages and host plants: The caterpillar is yellowish green mottled with black and covered with black spines. Caterpillars live solitarily within loose webbing on the host plant.

Eggs are usually laid on thistle and burdock in Michigan; other plants are also chosen, such as asters, hollyhock and common mallow.

Habitat: Old fields, meadows, disturbed areas, pastures and roadsides.

Distribution: Throughout Michigan, including Isle Royale.

Flight period: Usually two broods; May 16 to October 16.

Remarks: No definite information is available on hibernating habits; adults probably cannot survive Michigan winters. Adult numbers fluctuate greatly from year to year. This is a cosmopolitan butterfly widely distributed throughout the world.

Male - Upper

Female - Under

91 Red Admiral

Vanessa atalanta rubria (Fruhstorfer)

Adults and food sources: Upper surfaces are black with distinctive red bands and a few white apical spots. Undersurfaces are similar on the forewing; the hindwing is mottled and lacks the red band.

Adults nectar on red clover, bog laurel, lilac, common milkweed, blazing-star, bog-rosemary, staghorn sumac, teasel and joe-pye-weed. They also feed on tree sap and rotted fruit.

Early stages and host plants: The caterpillar is blackish to yellowish green with black and yellow stripes and is covered with blackish spines.

Eggs are laid on nettles in Michigan.

Habitat: Swamp openings and edges, marshes, meadows, disturbed areas, and rural and urban gardens and parks.

Distribution: Throughout Michigan, including Isle Royale.

Flight period: Two broods; April 23 to October 29.

Remarks: Common. No definite information is available on hibernating habits; adults probably cannot survive Michigan winters. Adult numbers fluctuate from year to year. They are attracted to artificial bait. The nominate subspecies, *V. atalanta atalanta* (Linnaeus), occurs in Europe and is very similar to the Michigan subspecies.

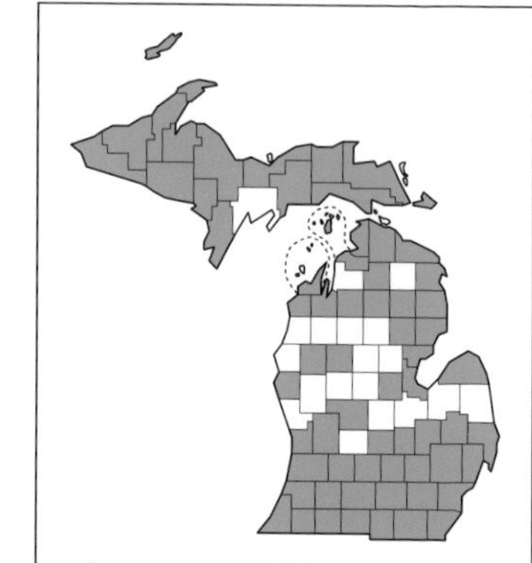

Male - Upper

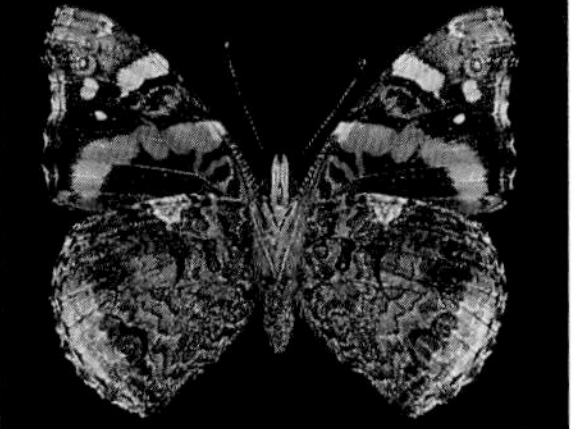

Male - Under

Buckeye

Junonia coenia (Hübner)

Adults and food sources: Upper surfaces are distinctive, with one eyespot on the forewing and two on the hindwing. The undersurface of the forewing is similar; the hindwing is light brown with two small submarginal spots.

Adults have been observed nectaring on asters, red clover and hooded ladies' tresses; they also visit dogbane, knapweed and peppermint.

Early stages and host plants: The caterpillar is blackish with broken yellow lines and is covered with bluish black spines. The head is orange and black.

Eggs are laid on false foxglove, plantain, wild snapdragon and toadflax.

Habitat: Old fields, pastures, meadows, disturbed areas, coastal dunes and roadsides.

Distribution: Throughout Michigan, including Isle Royale.

Flight period: Two broods; June 1 to October 22.

Remarks: Generally considered to be a more southern species that migrates into northern states. No definite information is available on hibernating habits; adults probably cannot survive Michigan winters. Adult numbers fluctuate from year to year.

Male - Upper

Female - Upper

Male - Under

93 White Admiral

Limenitis arthemis arthemis
(Drury)

Adults and food sources: Upper surfaces are black with a distinctive white band; the hindwing has a submarginal row of orange spots. Undersurfaces are similar except the ground color is gray to orange-gray with orange spots near the bases of the wings.

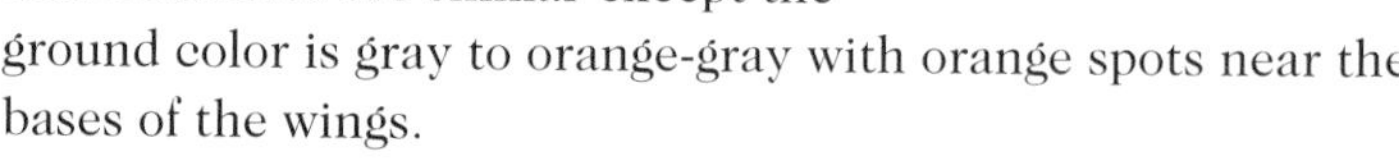

Adults infrequently visit flowers except for common milkweed and joe-pye-weed; they frequently take moisture and nutrients from damp soils, bird feces and other organic matter.

Early stages and host plants: The caterpillar is mottled brown or green with a whitish saddle patch and lateral line and clubbed thoracic horns. Young caterpillars overwinter in a hibernaculum on the host plant.

Eggs are laid on birch and aspen; females may also select juneberry and hawthorn.

Habitat: Northern forest openings, edges, trails and roadsides.

Distribution: Throughout the Upper Peninsula, including Isle Royale, and the northern counties of the Lower Peninsula, and south to Cass County.

Flight period: Two broods; May 21 to September 20.

Remarks: Common. Hybrids with the Red-spotted Purple (No. 93a) frequently occur around the Straits of Mackinac. Some hybrids have no or only slight traces of the white band on upper surfaces. The White Admiral is attracted to artificial bait.

Male - Upper

Male - Upper (Hybrid)

Male - Under

93a Red-spotted Purple

Limenitis arthemis astyanax (Fabricius)

Adults and food sources: Upper surfaces are black with purplish blue on the outer portion of the hindwing. Undersurfaces are similar to those of the White Admiral (No. 93) except they lack the white band.

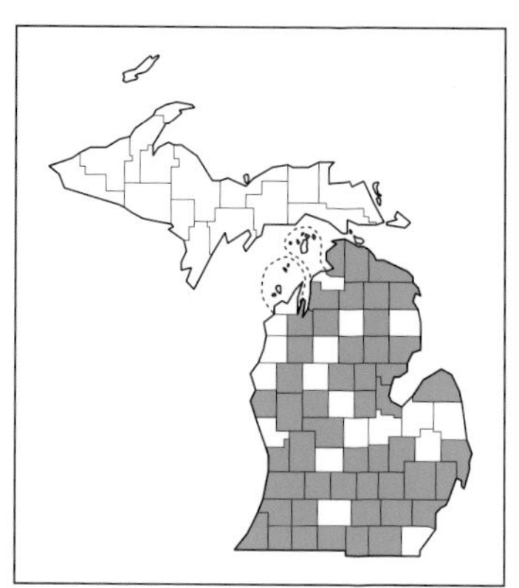

Adults are seldom observed nectaring except on dogbane and staghorn sumac; they frequently take moisture and nutrients from damp soils, dung, carrion and tree sap.

Early stages and host plants: The caterpillar is similar to that of the White Admiral except for more slender horns and a body with more warts. The young caterpillar overwinters in a hibernaculum on the host plant.

Eggs are usually laid on wild black cherry; females may also select other cherries and aspen.

Habitat: Forest openings and edges, old fields, trails and roadsides.

Distribution: Most of the Lower Peninsula; a slight overlap with the White Admiral.

Flight period: Two broods; June 1 to September 14.

Remarks: Common. Hybrids with the White Admiral occur; rare hybrids with the Viceroy (No. 94) also occur. Adults are attracted to artificial bait.

Male - Upper

Female - Upper

Male - Under

Viceroy

Limenitis archippus (Cramer)

Adults and food sources: The upper surface is orange with black veins and margins; the hindwing has a curved black line across the wing. Undersurfaces are similar but lighter.

Adults feed on nectar from a variety of flowers, including aster, blackberry, bouncing Bet, goldenrod, thistle and joe-pye-weed; they also take moisture and nutrients from damp soils, carrion and dung.

Early stages and host plants: The caterpillar is olive-green with blotches of white and a few small black areas and a pair of spiny thoracic horns. The young caterpillar overwinters in a hibernaculum on the host plant.

Eggs are laid only on willows, frequently on sandbar willow in wetlands.

Habitat: Marshes, meadows, stream and lake margins, roadside ditches.

Distribution: Throughout Michigan, except Isle Royale.

Flight period: Usually two broods; May 25 to October 5.

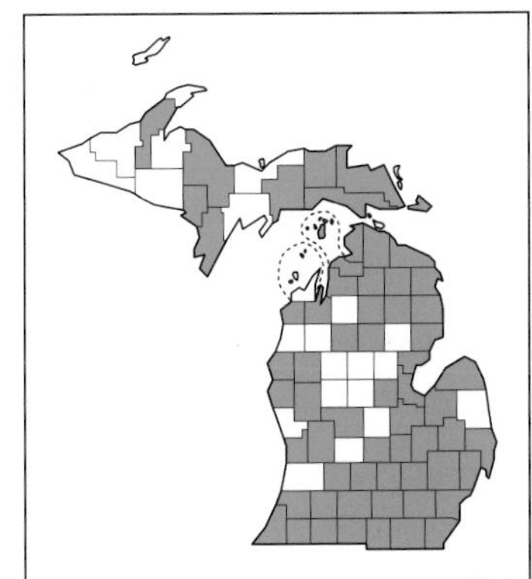

Remarks: Common. In flight, the Viceroy can be mistaken for the Monarch (No. 110), which it mimics. The black line across the upper surface of the hindwing easily separates it from the Monarch. Adults are attracted to artificial bait.

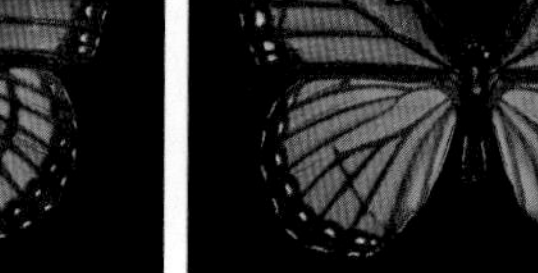

Male - Upper *Female - Upper*

95 Goatweed Butterfly

Anaea andria Scudder

Adults and food sources: Upper surfaces are reddish orange with a hooked forewing tip and a short tail on the hindwing. The female is more orange and has an irregular, pale orange submarginal band. Undersurfaces are an even grayish brown.

Adults feed on rotting fruit, tree sap, bird droppings and dung.

Early stages and host plants: The caterpillar is gray-green with small, warty tubercles; tubercles on the head are orange. The caterpillar rests in a folded leaf shelter.

Females are reported to lay eggs on goatweed, which is not found in Michigan.

Habitat: Forest openings and edges and along streams.

Distribution: Specimens are recorded from Ottawa, Van Buren and Washtenaw counties.

Flight period: May 8 to October 17.

Remarks: This is a casual stray into southern Michigan counties. It is easily attracted to artificial bait.

Male - Upper

Female - Upper

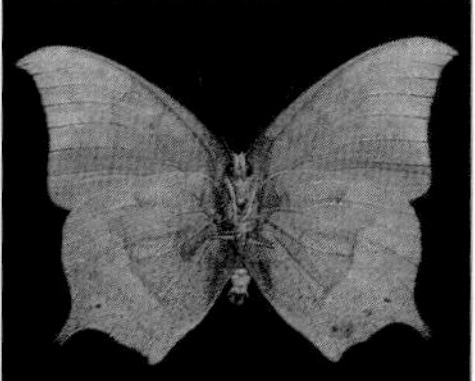
Male - Under

96 Hackberry Butterfly

Asterocampa celtis
(Boisduval & LeConte)

Adults and food sources: Upper surfaces are grayish brown with white spots in a blackish area near the forewing apex and a distinct black oval spot in the submarginal area of the forewing. Several submarginal black spots occur on the hindwing. Undersurfaces are lighter gray but similarly marked. The female is slightly larger with more rounded wings.

Adults almost never nectar on flowers but have been observed on staghorn sumac and bladdernut. They prefer tree sap, rotting fruit and dung; they also take moisture and nutrients from damp soils.

Early stages and host plants: The caterpillar is yellowish green and tapered at both ends, with a forked tail; the head has a pair of spiny, forked horns. The caterpillar overwinters under dead leaves.

Hackberry is the only known host plant in Michigan.

Habitat: Swamp openings and edges and along streams; also urban areas planted with the host plant.

Distribution: The southern third of the Lower Peninsula.

Flight period: Two broods; June 17 to September 4.

Remarks: Locally common. Males are very pugnacious with others of their kind and other butterflies. Adults frequently fly and rest high in trees. They are easily attracted to artificial bait.

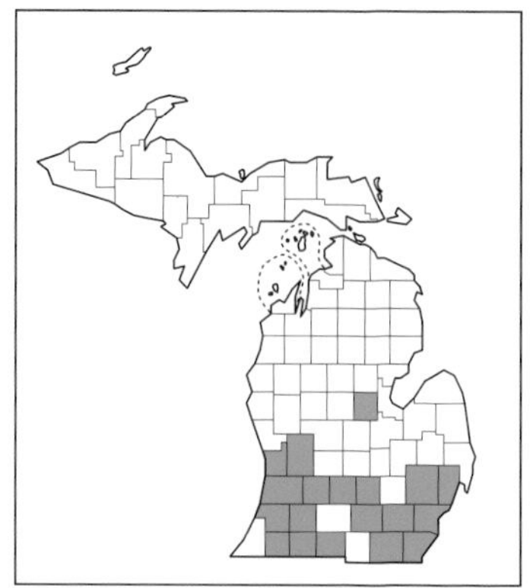

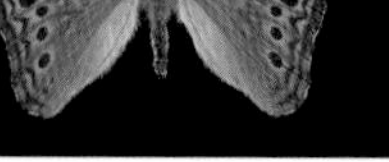

Male - Upper

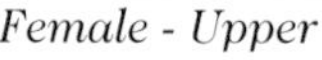

Female - Upper

Male - Under

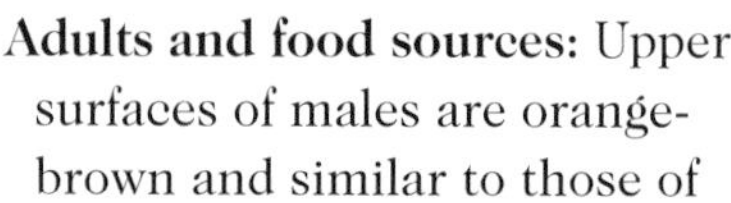

97 Tawny Emperor

Asterocampa clyton
(Boisduval & LeConte)

Adults and food sources: Upper surfaces of males are orange-brown and similar to those of the Hackberry Butterfly (No. 96); the forewing lacks the submarginal black oval spot. The female is much larger, lighter orange-brown and marked like the male. Undersurfaces are grayish brown.

Adults seldom nectar on flowers but have been observed on bergamot and wild carrot. They prefer tree sap, rotting fruit and dung; they also take moisture and nutrients from damp soils.

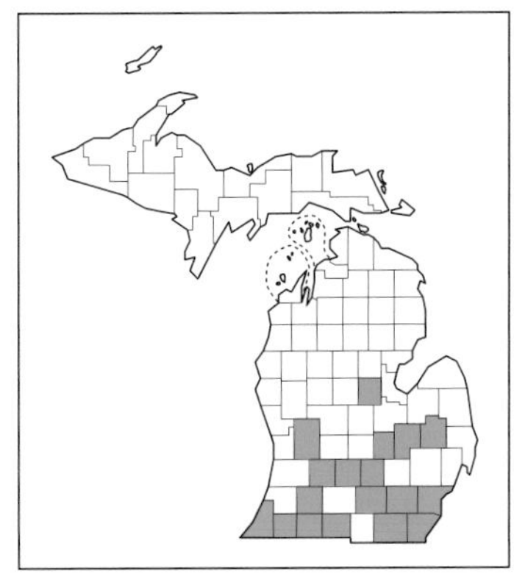

Early stages and host plants: The caterpillar is yellowish green with a dark green dorsal stripe; the head has a pair of branched, spiny horns. The caterpillar over-winters under dead leaves.

Hackberry is the only host plant in Michigan.

Habitat: Swamp openings and edges and along streams.

Distribution: The southern third of the Lower Peninsula.

Flight period: One brood; June 20 to August 31.

Remarks: Locally common. Habits are similar to those of the Hackberry Butterfly. Adults are easily attracted to artificial bait.

Male - Upper

Male - Upper

Male - Under

Female - Upper

Satyrs, Wood Nymphs and Arctics:

Family Satyridae: This family contains medium-sized brown butterflies. Many have one or more eyespots on the upper and undersurfaces of the wings. Most have a forewing costal vein swollen at the base. Adults have four functional legs; the first pair is merely a brushlike appendage, a character that some authorities use to place these butterflies in the family Nymphalidae. Most species are weak flyers that inhabit open forest and brushy areas. A few species nectar on flowers while others prefer tree sap, rotting fruit or dung. Grasses and sedges are favored host plants. Caterpillars are generally green with a forked posterior. Most species overwinter as caterpillars. A few species require two years to complete their development. Chrysalids either hang from a silk button attached to some material or form in ground debris.

98 Northern Pearly Eye

Enodia anthedon A.H. Clark

Adults and food sources: Upper surfaces are light brown with three prominent dark spots on the forewing and five dark spots on the hindwing. Undersurfaces are lighter brown with a row of smaller dark spots, usually with a central white dot.

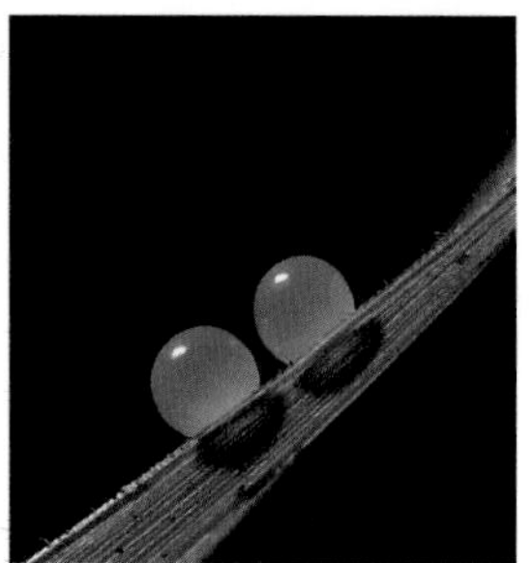

Adults have not been observed on flowers but prefer tree sap and come to artificial bait.

Early stages and host plants: The caterpillar is yellowish green with yellow and green stripes; the head has a pair of red-tipped horns.

Females are reported to lay eggs on various species of grass, including bottlebrush grass.

Habitat: Deciduous forests, swamps and edges, and along streams.

Distribution: Throughout Michigan.

Flight period: Usually single-brooded; June 18 to September 3.

Remarks: Locally common. It is frequently found resting on tree trunks in forests.

Male - Upper

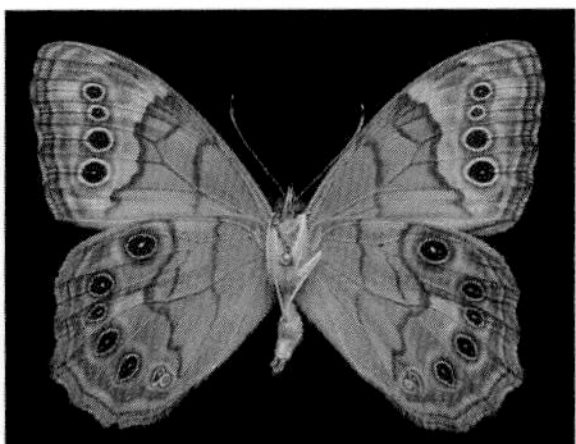

Male - Under

99 Creole Pearly Eye

Enodia creole (Skinner)

Adults and food sources: Upper surfaces are similar to those of the Northern Pearly Eye (No. 98), but the apex of the wing is extended. The male has areas of raised, dark scent scales on the forewing. Undersurfaces are similar to those of the Northern Pearly Eye.

Adults are reported to prefer tree sap.

Early stages and host plants: The caterpillar is reported to be similar to that of the Northern Pearly Eye.

Eggs are laid on switch cane, which is not found in Michigan.

Habitat: Moist forests, swamps.

Distribution: One specimen in the U.S. National Museum was collected by Bruce in Michigan, but no specific location was given. It has been recorded from northern Indiana (Shull, 1987).

Flight period: No date is given on the Michigan specimen. It is double-brooded in southern states, usually June to September.

Remarks: There is considerable doubt about the validity of this record (Irwin, 1970). The host plant does not range into Michigan, and the species is not known to stray far from its habitat. It is possible that it is an accidental stray, possibly aided by prolonged southern winds.

Male - Upper

Female - Upper

100 Eyed Brown

Satyrodes eurydice (Johansson)

Adults and food sources: Upper surfaces are light brown with submarginal rows of small dark spots. Undersurfaces are lighter brown to orange-brown with ringed dark spots, each with a white central dot; each wing has a distinct zigzag line across it.

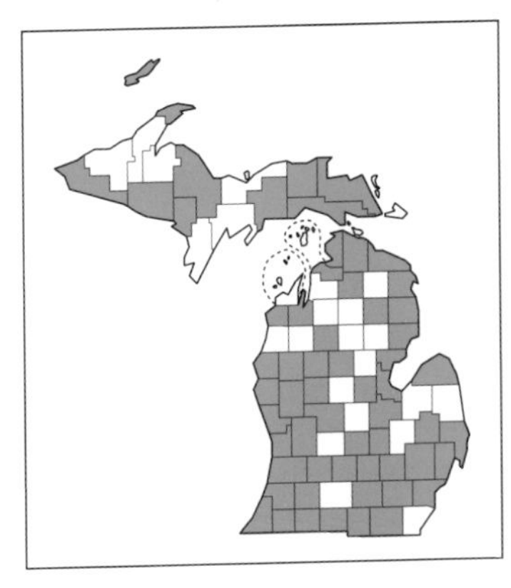

Adults are reported to nectar occasionally on swamp milkweed and joe-pye-weed; they may prefer plant sap and bird droppings.

Early stages and host plants: The caterpillar is yellowish green with reddish lateral stripes and a pair of reddish horns on the head.

Single eggs are laid on a variety of sedges.

Habitat: Open sedge marshes, meadows and edges.

Distribution: Throughout Michigan, including Isle Royale.

Flight period: Single brood; May 30 to August 24.

Remarks: Locally common. Some females are extremely pale. Some Upper Peninsula populations resemble subspecies *fumosa* Leussler and should be further studied.

Male - Upper

Dark male - Upper

Female - Upper

Male - Under

101 Appalachian Eyed Brown

Satyrodes appalachia leeuwi (Gatrelle & Arbogast)

Adults and food sources: Upper surfaces are grayish brown with small, dark submarginal spots. Undersurfaces are lighter than the upper and have submarginal ringed spots with white dots; the pattern is similar to the Eyed Brown (No. 100) but has a sinuous line across each wing (it's a zigzag line in the Eyed Brown).

Adults feed on tree sap and probably bird droppings; they are easily attracted to artificial bait.

Early stages and host plants: The caterpillar is similar to that of the Eyed Brown.

Females lay eggs on wide-leaf sedge.

Habitat: Fens, moist forests, swamps and shrub swamps with an understory of sedges.

Distribution: Most Lower Peninsula counties and Dickinson County in the Upper Peninsula.

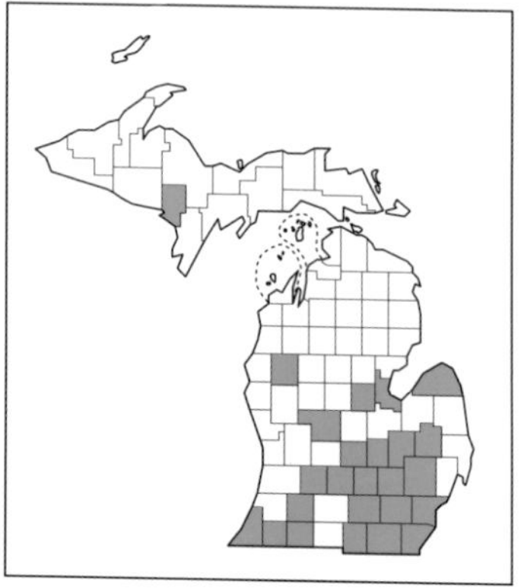

Flight period: Single brood; June 14 to August 15.

Remarks: Locally common. This species was unrecognized from Michigan until 1970 (Carde *et al.*), when it was shown to be distinct from the Eyed Brown. The northern subspecies *leeuwi* is darker than southern *S. appalachia appalachia* (R.L. Chermock) and ranges across the northern states to Minnesota. The type locality is the Wakelee Fen, Cass County, Mich.

Male - Upper *Female - Upper* *Male - Under*

102 Mitchell's Satyr

Neonympha mitchellii French

Adults and food sources: Upper surfaces are brown without markings; the female is slightly larger than the male. The undersurface of the hindwing has a submarginal row of yellow-ringed black spots, each with silvery scales. Both wings have two reddish marginal bands.

No observations of adults feeding have been made in Michigan. Plant sap or bird droppings may be acceptable.

Early stages and host plants: The caterpillar is green with white stripes.

Natural host plants are unknown; caterpillars are reared in captivity on a variety of sedges.

Habitat: Tamarack-poison sumac fens and open swamps.

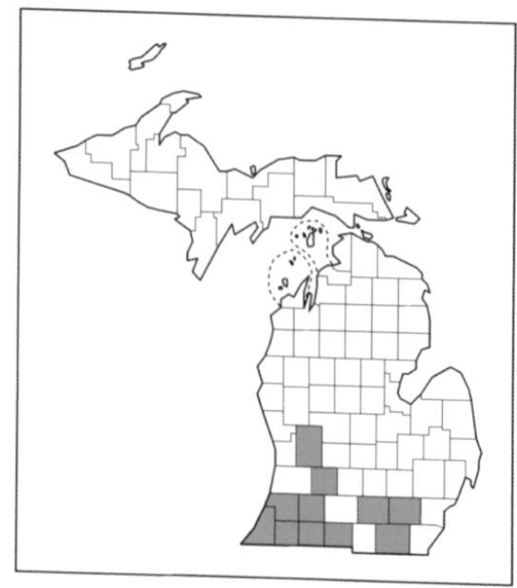

Distribution: Several counties in southern and southwestern Michigan.

Flight period: Single brood; June 21 to July 24.

Remarks: This species was discovered in the Wakelee Fen, Cass County, in 1889. It's currently listed as a federal and state endangered species. Information on distribution in Michigan is still incomplete. It flies weakly and low among brush and sedges and is easily overlooked.

Male - Upper *Female - Upper* *Female - Under*

103 Little Wood Satyr

Megisto cymela (Cramer)

Adults and food sources: The upper surfaces of the forewing are brown with two yellow-ringed black eyespots; the hindwing has one such eyespot. Undersurfaces are lighter brown with more prominent yellow-ringed black eyespots with silvery scales.

Adults have been observed nectaring on common milkweed and staghorn sumac; they probably also take plant sap and bird droppings, as do other satyrs.

Early stages and host plants: The caterpillar is pale brown tinged with green and has a median black stripe and brown patches. It's covered with fine hairs and small tubercles.

Eggs are laid on various species of grasses.

Habitat: Deciduous forests, openings, edges, oak-pine barrens, fens and brushy old fields.

Distribution: Statewide, except Isle Royale.

Flight period: Usually single-brooded; May 3 to August 16.

Remarks: Some populations exhibit characteristics and habits that suggest two species; more research is needed. This is one of Michigan's commonest butterflies. It flies with Mitchell's Satyr (No. 102) in some fens in southwestern Michigan and may cause some confusion in reporting these species.

Male - Upper

Female - Upper

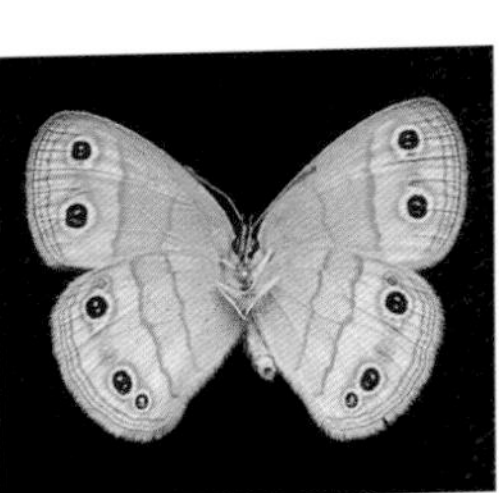

Male - Under

104 Inornate Ringlet

Coenonympha tullia inornata
W.H. Edwards

Adults and food sources: Upper surfaces are orange to ochre-brown without markings. The undersurface of the forewing is orange-brown and grayish green; the hindwing is grayish green, usually without spots and with an incomplete whitish line.

Adults nectar on alsike clover and yellow hawkweed; they have also been reported on fleabane, ironweed and mint.

Early stages and host plants: The caterpillar is dark green with paler lateral stripes.

Eggs are laid on various grasses; caterpillars in captivity can be reared on rush.

Habitat: Open northern forests, grassy old fields, meadows and roadsides.

Distribution: Throughout the Upper Peninsula and into the northern Lower Peninsula; a recent record from St. Clair County.

Flight period: Single brood, with partial second brood; June 4 to August 2.

Remarks: Common. This is one of the few avid flower visitors among the satyrines. A holarctic species recognized by several subspecies in the northern states and Canada; our subspecies, *inornata*, occurs throughout the Great Lakes region and eastern Canada. More research is needed on the Michigan populations.

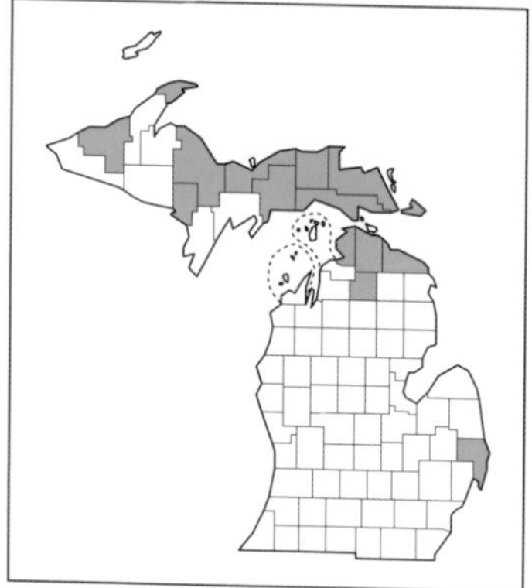

Male - Upper

Female - Upper

Female - Under

105

Wood Nymph

Cercyonis pegala nephele
(W. Kirby)

Adults and food sources: In northern populations, the upper surfaces are dark brown, usually with two prominent black eyespots with tiny white centers on the forewing. Some southern Michigan populations have a dull to bright yellow patch surrounding the black eyespots. Undersurfaces of forewings and hindwings have two prominent, yellow-ringed black eyespots with white centers.

Adults nectar on aster, bergamot, knapweed, goldenrod, common milkweed, blazing-star, joe-pye-weed and blue vervain. They are attracted to artificial bait.

Early stages and host plants: The caterpillar is green, becoming paler at the rear, with pale stripes and a reddish forked tail.

Eggs are laid on various grasses.

Habitat: Prairies, meadows, brushy fields, disturbed areas and roadsides.

Distribution: Throughout the state, including Isle Royale.

Flight period: Single brood; June 11 to September 22.

Remarks: Common. Southern Michigan populations with the yellow patch on the forewing are regarded as the subspecies *C. pegala alope* (Fabricius) by some taxonomists.

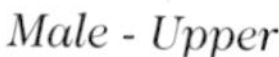

Male - Upper

Female - Upper

Male - Under

"Alope" Forms

Male - Upper

Female - Upper

Male - Under

106 Red-disked Alpine

Erebia discoidalis
(W. Kirby)

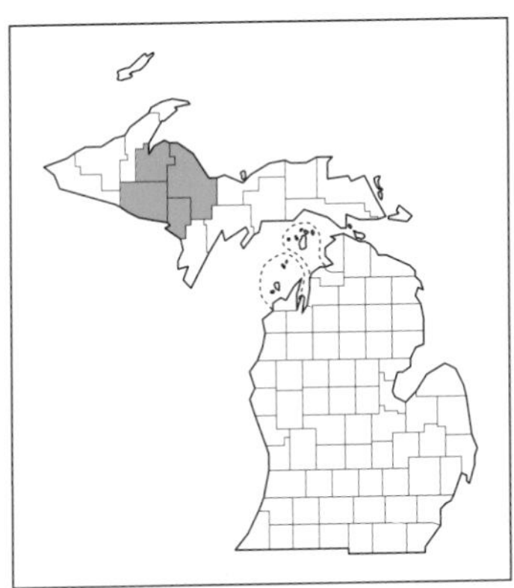

Adults and food sources: Upper surfaces are dark brown with a large dull reddish patch on the forewing. Undersurface edges are frosted with bluish gray but without distinct markings. Sexes are similar.

Like other satyrines, these butterflies are probably attracted to plant sap and moisture in damp soils. Adults have been attracted to a bait trap.

Early stages and host plants: Early stages are green with lighter lines.

Caterpillars can be reared on cotton-grass sedge in captivity; the natural host plant is unknown.

Habitat: Large sphagnum bogs with abundant cotton-grass and grassy meadows.

Distribution: Baraga, Dickinson, Iron and Marquette counties in the Upper Peninsula.

Flight period: Single brood; May 5 to June 3.

Remarks: Uncommon. Adults are usually active before noon and in late afternoon, shunning the midday sun. Distribution and life history in Michigan still need research. It's listed as a species of special concern by the Michigan Natural Features Inventory.

Male - Upper

Male - Under

107 Macoun's Arctic

Oeneis macounii (W.H. Edwards)

Adults and food sources: Upper surfaces are orange-brown with narrow black margins; the forewing usually has two black eyespots, and the hindwing has one smaller eyespot. The undersurface of the forewing is essentially orange-brown with two eyespots; the hindwing is mottled blackish brown, usually with a tiny eyespot.

Adults have been observed nectaring on mountain maple and bastard-toadflax on Isle Royale; one was attracted to a bait trap.

Early stages and host plants: The caterpillar is greenish to brown with lateral brownish stripes. Two seasons are required for full larval development.

The natural host plant is unknown, but caterpillars can be reared on various grasses in captivity.

Habitat: Open jack pine forest, mixed hardwood openings, edges and brushy rocky ridges.

Distribution: Throughout most of Isle Royale and on the larger satellite islands.

Flight period: Single brood in even-numbered years; June 16 to July 2.

Remarks: It may also occur in elevated areas in Keweenaw, Houghton and Ontonagon counties. More research is needed on distribution and life history in Michigan. It is currently listed as a species of special concern by the Michigan Natural Features Inventory.

Male - Upper

Female - Upper

Female - Under

108 Chryxus Arctic

Oeneis chryxus strigulosa McDunnough

Adults and food sources: Similar to Macoun's Arctic but smaller. Upper surfaces are orange-brown; the inner portion of the male's forewing has a dark area of scent scales. The undersurface of the hindwing is mottled with black striations and whitish veins and usually has a small eyespot.

Females have been observed nectaring on exotic cherry and wild strawberry in Otsego County.

Early stages and host plants: The caterpillar is brownish with darker and lighter lateral stripes; a late stage overwinters.

Eggs are laid on Pennsylvania sedge in Michigan.

Habitat: Open jack pine barrens, dry grassy openings and open brushy ridges.

Distribution: Scattered counties in the Upper Peninsula, including Isle Royale, and the northern half of the Lower Peninsula to Montcalm and Muskegon counties.

Flight period: Single brood; May 4 to June 21.

Remarks: Locally common. The subspecies *strigulosa* refers to isolated populations found in eastern Canada and northern Michigan and Wisconsin. It is smaller and more orange than the western nominate subspecies, *O. chryxus chryxus* (Doubleday& Hewitson). A kingbird was observed preying on flushed adults in Newaygo County.

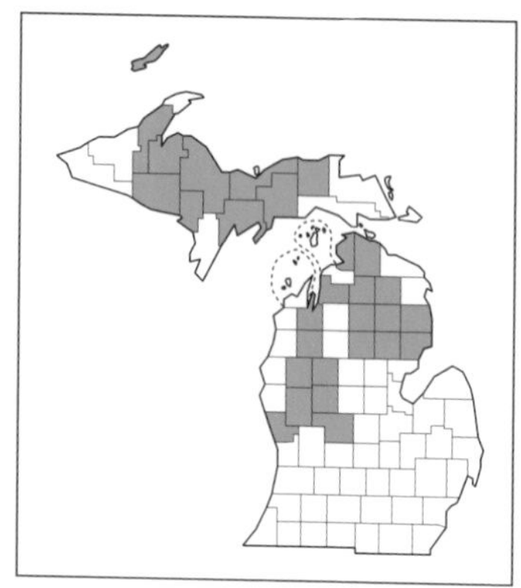

Male - Upper

Female - Upper

Male - Under

109 Jutta Arctic

Oeneis jutta ascerta Masters & Sorenson

Adults and food sources: Upper surfaces are grayish brown with yellowish submarginal patches and usually one to three black spots on the forewing and one on the hindwing. The undersurface of the hindwing is mottled blackish brown with scattered gray scaling.

Adults have been observed nectaring on Labrador tea in Wisconsin; no observations of nectaring or other food choices have been made in Michigan.

Early stages and host plants: The caterpillar is pale green with brownish lateral lines. Two seasons are required for full larval development.

Eggs are laid on cotton-grass in Michigan.

Habitat: Black spruce-tamarack-sphagnum bog openings and edges.

Distribution: Throughout the Upper Peninsula.

Flight period: Single brood in odd-numbered years; May 20 to July 4.

Remarks: Locally common. Adults frequently rest on trunks of spruce and tamarack. A female was observed laying an egg on live spruce and dead tamarack branches in a Michigan bog. The subspecies *ascerta* is found throughout the Great Lakes region; the nominate subspecies, *O. jutta jutta* (Hübner), occurs in northern Europe.

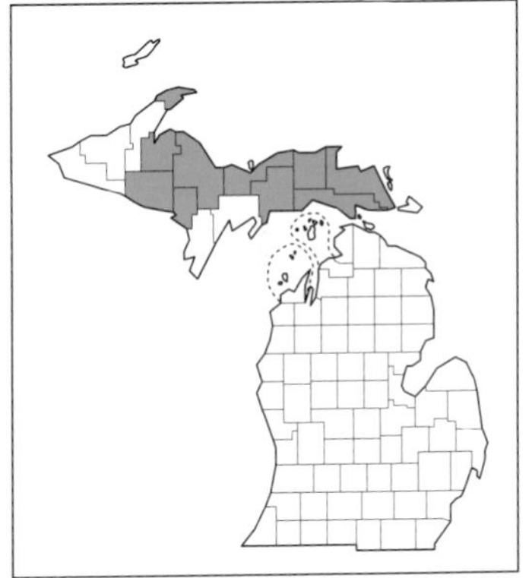

Male - Upper

Female - Upper

Male - Under

Milkweed Butterflies: *Family Danaidae:*

The milkweed butterflies are medium to large species, most of which live in tropical areas. Michigan has recorded two species; the Monarch is the better known. Males have a distinctive scent patch on the hindwing. Females lay eggs on milkweed plants such as the common milkweed in our area. Caterpillars usually ingest a cardiac glycoside contained within these plants, which is later sequestered within adults. This makes both the caterpillar and the adult distasteful to predators. The Monarch is well known for its migrations to Mexico in the fall and the return migration in the spring. Caterpillars are alternately banded and possess fleshy filaments near the head. The chrysalis, usually bright green, hangs down from various structures.

110 Monarch

Danaus plexippus
(Linnaeus)

Adults and food sources: This large orange butterfly has black veins on both wings and a black margin with small white spots on each wing. The male has a distinctive black scent patch on its hindwing near the inner margin. The female's veins are wider; otherwise it's similar to the male. The undersides are similarly marked but are lighter orange.

Favorite nectar plants include several milkweeds, with common milkweed the favorite. Adults also nectar on dogbane, goldenrod, knapweed, ironweed, garden marigold, blazing-star, Labrador tea, thistle and joe-pye-weed.

Early stages and host plants: The caterpillar is banded black, yellow and white; the head is black and white striped. Three pair of fleshy black filaments are located near the head.

Preferred hosts are several milkweeds. Common milkweed is usually the plant used in Michigan; occasionally swamp milkweed is used.

Habitat: Old fields, meadows, prairies, disturbed areas and roadsides.

Distribution: Throughout Michigan, including Isle Royale.

Flight period: Usually two broods; May 10 to October 23.

Remarks: The Monarch is the model for the Batesian mimic Viceroy (No. 94), which is usually not distasteful to predators. Michigan Monarchs begin their migration to the south in August and September and may assemble in large numbers in the afternoon on foliage along Great Lakes shorelines during this period. Presumably these Monarchs terminate their journey in the mountains of central Mexico (Opler & Krizek, 1984). Some early spring adults are worn, suggesting a long flight. There is still some question whether these individuals are the progeny of females that migrated north from overwintering areas in Mexico.

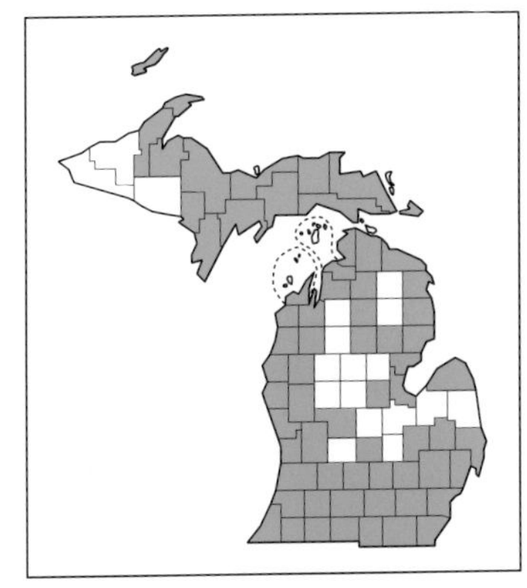

Male - Upper

Female - Upper

111 Queen

Danaus gilippus berenice (Cramer)

Adults and food sources: Upper surfaces of both sexes are deep chestnut-brown with small white apical spots and black margins. The underside of the hindwing has black veins and a black margin with a double row of white spots. The male has a black scent patch on the upper surface of the hindwing.

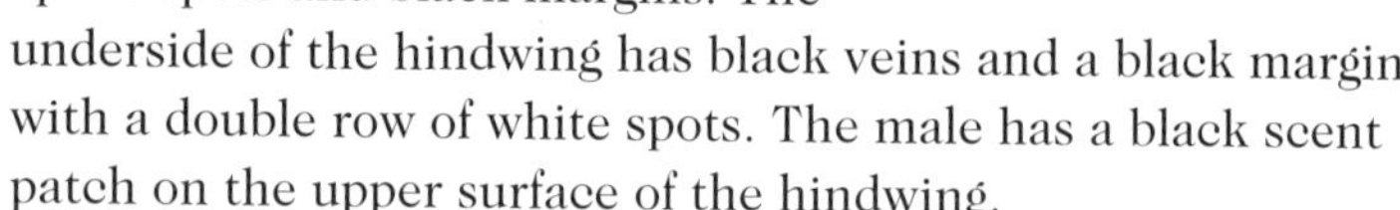

Adults are reported to nectar on milkweed plants.

Early stages and host plants: The caterpillar is brown-white with bands of brown and yellow and a lateral yellowish green stripe. Three pairs of black fleshy filaments are located near the head.

Females are reported to lay eggs on various milkweeds.

Habitat: Open fields, pastures, gardens, disturbed areas and roadsides.

Distribution: Recorded from Oakland and Saginaw counties in the Lower Peninsula.

Male - Upper

Flight period: August 28, 1995, and September 15, 1991.

Remarks: A female was collected in an open field south of Saginaw; a specimen was photographed by R.W. Holzman in his Royal Oak yard. The Queen is a rare accidental southern stray; there are few reports from other northern states.

Skippers: *Family Hesperiidae:* Skippers are a group of small to medium-sized, usually dull-colored butterflies that have a fast and darting flight. They have large bodies with powerful wing muscles and relatively wide heads and large eyes. Unlike other butterflies, nearly all have hooklike projections at the ends of their clubbed antennae. Males of many species have a brand or stigma of dark specialized scent scales on the forewing; some males have such scales in costal folds on the forewing. All have six fully developed legs. Most skippers lay eggs on a wide assortment of grasses and sedges, but some use legumes and other shrubs and trees as host plants. Caterpillars are usually greenish to brownish, some with fine, short hairs; nearly all have a collarlike constriction just back of the head. Many make a nest by folding over a piece of leaf or binding two or more leaves together. Some overwinter as mature larvae in flimsy cocoons constructed within litter or fresh or dried leaves.

112 Silver-spotted Skipper

Epargyreus clarus (Cramer)

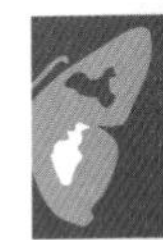

Adults and food sources: Michigan's largest skipper has dark brown upper surfaces with semitransparent yellowish spots on the forewing. The undersurface of the hindwing has the characteristic large silver spot. The hindwing also has a slight taillike projection.

Adults are fond of a large variety of flowers, including alfalfa, blackberry, bergamot, dogbane, honeysuckle, wild iris, knapweed, purple loosestrife, staghorn sumac, black-eyed Susan, blazing-star, New Jersey tea, vetch and joe-pye-weed.

Early stages and host plants: The caterpillar is yellow with greenish cross-lines and a brown head with two large orange spots. The mature caterpillar hides during the day in a nest of leaves held together with silk.

Eggs are laid on several plants in the pea family, including black and honey locust, hog peanut and wisteria.

Habitat: Open forest and brushy fields, disturbed areas, and along streams and roadsides.

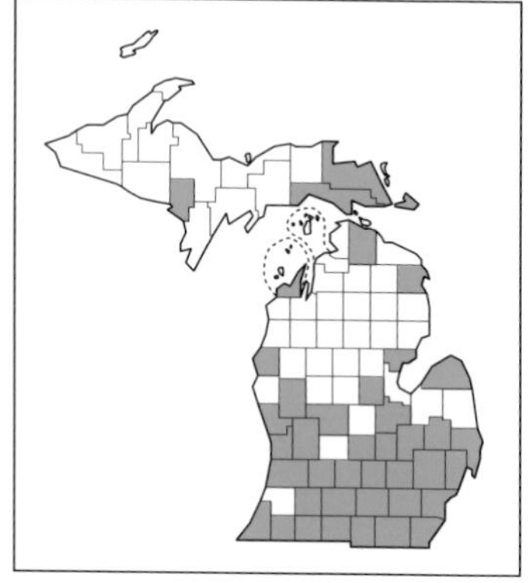

Distribution: Mainly the southern half of the Lower Peninsula, and three counties in the Upper Peninsula.

Flight period: Two broods; May 15 to September 28.

Remarks: Common. Adults perch several feet above the ground; they engage in frequent aerial encounters with other males and other insects.

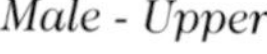

Male - Upper

Male - Under

(113) Long-tailed Skipper

Urbanus proteus (Linnaeus)

Adults and food sources: This is our only skipper with distinctive long tails. Upper wing surfaces have an iridescent greenish sheen. Scattered white spots occur on the forewing.

It is reported to nectar on a wide variety of flowers, including composites.

Early stages and host plants: The caterpillar is yellowish green with a dorsal black stripe and yellow to reddish stripes on the sides.

Females are reported to lay eggs on several legumes, including beggar's-ticks and wisteria.

Habitat: Forest edges, brushy fields, disturbed areas, roadsides and gardens.

Distribution: One record from Wayne County.

Flight period: Throughout the year in the South.

Remarks: The only Michigan specimens were accidental strays. The late Dr. W.W. Newcomb (1913) reported specimens collected on Belle Isle in the Detroit River sometime before 1913. It has since been reported from Columbus, Ohio, and Point Pelee, Ontario, Canada.

Male - Upper

114 Hoary Edge

Achalarus lyciades (Geyer)

Adults and food sources: Upper surfaces are dark brown with an irregular, semitransparent yellowish patch on the forewing. The undersurface of the hindwing has the characteristic whitish patch.

Adults have been observed nectaring on blackberry, blueberry, red clover and vetchling; they're reported on dogbane, common milkweed and New Jersey tea.

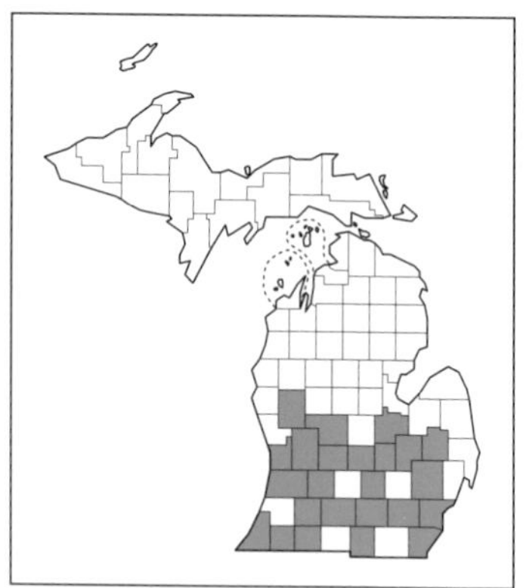

Early stages and host plants: The caterpillar is dark green with a darker dorsal line and orange lateral stripes and is covered with many yellow-orange dots.

Females usually lay eggs on beggar's-ticks in Michigan; other legumes may also be selected.

Habitat: Open forests and edges, brushy fields and roadsides.

Distribution: The southern half of the Lower Peninsula.

Flight period: Single brood; May 30 to August 15.

Remarks: Uncommon. Males perch on tall dead weeds and aggressively chase other butterflies, frequently returning to the same perch.

Male - Upper

Male - Under

115 Southern Cloudy Wing

Thorybes bathyllus (J.E. Smith)

Adults and food sources: Upper surfaces are brown with semitransparent whitish spots aligned on the forewing. The male lacks a costal fold on the forewing. The undersurface of the hindwing has two dark brown bands. The gray palpi easily separate it from the Northern Cloudy Wing (No. 116).

Adults nectar on alfalfa, blueberry, buttonbush, sweet clover, dogbane, common milkweed, black-eyed Susan, thistle and purple vetch.

Early stages and host plants: The caterpillar is reddish brown with paler dorsal and lateral lines and a black head.

Females select a wide variety of legumes on which to lay eggs, including beggar's-ticks, bush clover, goats-rue, milk vetch and wild-bean.

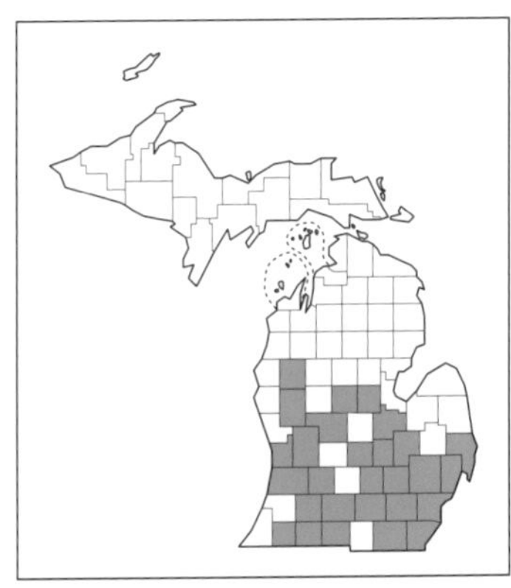

Habitat: Dry open areas, brushy fields, oak barrens, roadsides and rights-of-way.

Distribution: The southern half of the Lower Peninsula.

Flight period: Single brood; May 5 to July 27.

Remarks: Common. It flies with the Northern Cloudy Wing (No. 116) and is easily confused with it.

Male - Upper

Female - Upper

Male - Under

116 Northern Cloudy Wing

Thorybes pylades (Scudder)

Adults and food sources: Upper surfaces are dark brown with small, triangular, semitransparent, unaligned spots. Males have a costal fold. Undersurfaces are darker brown than those of the Southern Cloudy Wing; the hindwing is rounder than the latter's. Palpi are noticeably dark brown.

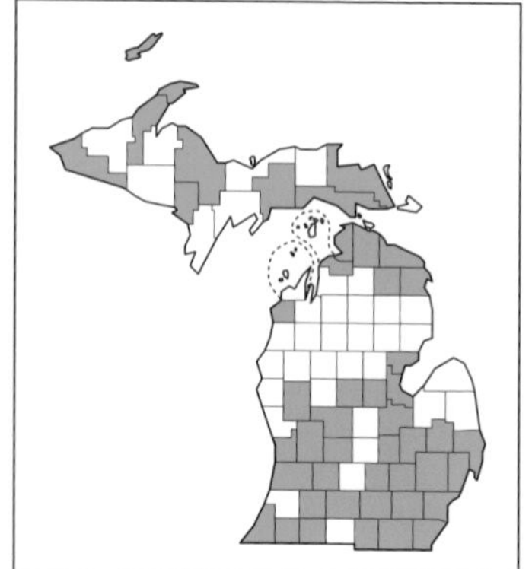

Nectar choices are similar to those of the Southern Cloudy Wing (No. 115); it's also been observed on red clover and downy phlox.

Early stages and host plants: The caterpillar is dark green with brownish dorsal and orange-pink lateral lines.

Females usually lay eggs on beggar's-ticks and bush-clover in Michigan; other legumes such as alfalfa, clover and lead-plant are also used.

Habitat: Open forests and edges, brushy fields, oak-pine barrens and roadsides.

Distribution: Scattered counties throughout the state, including Isle Royale.

Flight period: Single brood; May 7 to August 1.

Remarks: Common. This is the only cloudy wing found in northern counties.

Male - Upper

Female - Upper

Male - Under

117 Dreamy Dusky Wing

Erynnis icelus (Scudder & Burgess)

Adults and food sources: The upper surface of the forewing is blackish brown without prominent white spots near the apex and with a broken chain of dark outlined spots. The upper surface of the hindwing has scattered dull yellowish spots. The undersurface of the hindwing has two rows of dull yellowish spots. Palpi project more than those of the Sleepy Dusky Wing.

Adults nectar on many flowers, including blackberry, blueberry, exotic cherry, alsike clover, daisy, dogbane, bog laurel, lupine, puccoon, wild strawberry and vetch. They also take moisture from damp soils.

Early stages and host plants: The caterpillar is pale green with small, white, scattered, hair-bearing bumps. The black head is angular, with reddish and yellowish spots, and is notched on top.

Eggs are usually laid on aspen and willows in Michigan.

Habitat: Open forest, especially aspen in northern areas, edges, cut-over forest, brushy fields, bogs, disturbed areas and roadsides.

Distribution: Throughout the state, including Isle Royale.

Flight period: Single brood; April 24 to July 12.

Remarks: This is one of our commonest dusky wings.

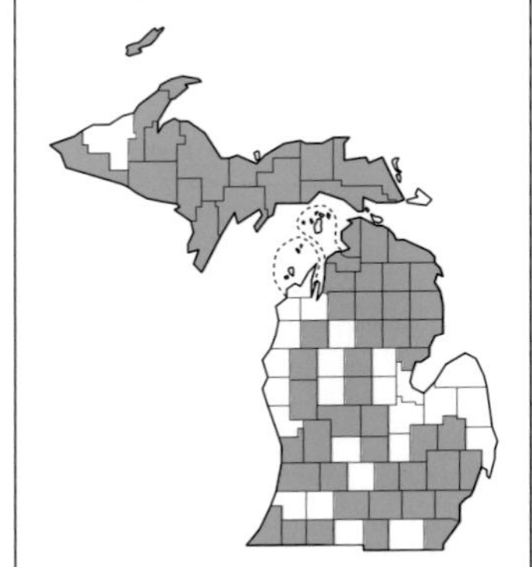

Male - Upper

Female - Upper

Male - Under

118 Sleepy Dusky Wing

Erynnis brizo
(Boisduval & LeConte)

Adults and food sources: The adult is similar to but larger than the Dreamy Dusky Wing (No. 117). The upper surface of the forewing is blackish brown with a distinct, continuous chain of bluish brown spots. The undersurface of the hindwing has more distinct yellowish spots than that of the Dreamy Dusky Wing.

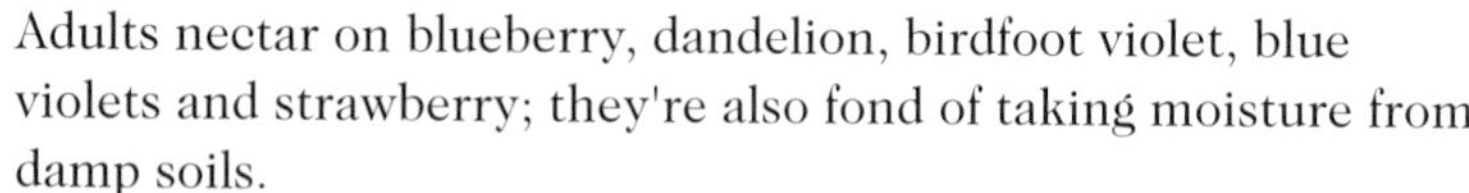

Adults nectar on blueberry, dandelion, birdfoot violet, blue violets and strawberry; they're also fond of taking moisture from damp soils.

Early stages and host plants: The caterpillar is gray-green with purplish ends and a faint lateral white stripe. The head is yellowish to brown with an orange spot.

Eggs are laid on black oak and other oaks.

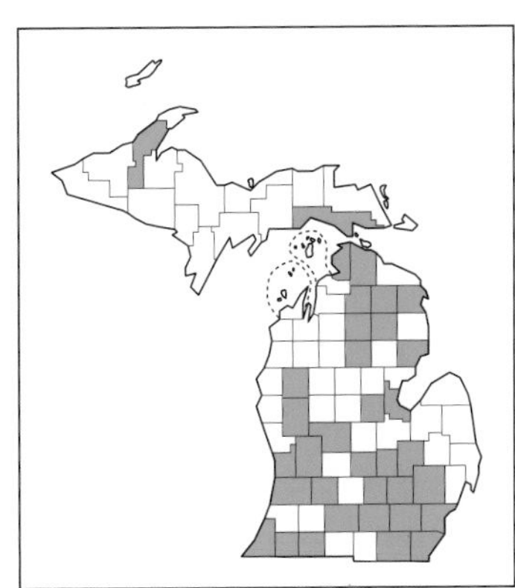

Habitat: Oak-pine barrens and cut-over forests.

Distribution: Scattered counties in the Lower Peninsula and Houghton and Mackinac counties in the Upper Peninsula.

Flight period: Single brood; April 9 to July 7.

Remarks: Common. It is easily confused with the Dreamy Dusky Wing in flight.

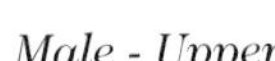

Male - Upper *Female - Upper* *Male - Under*

119 Juvenal's Dusky Wing

Erynnis juvenalis (Fabricius)

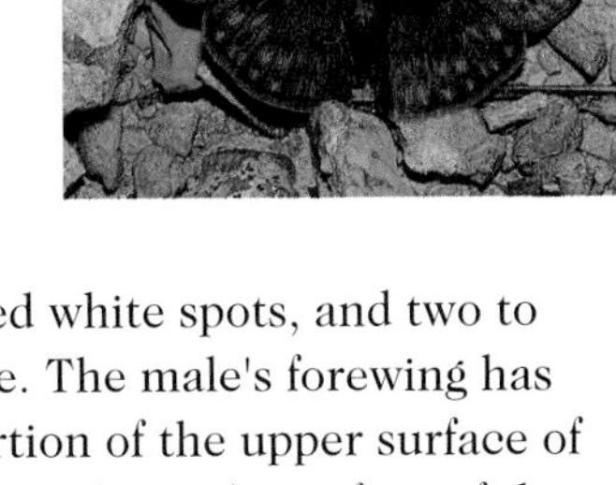

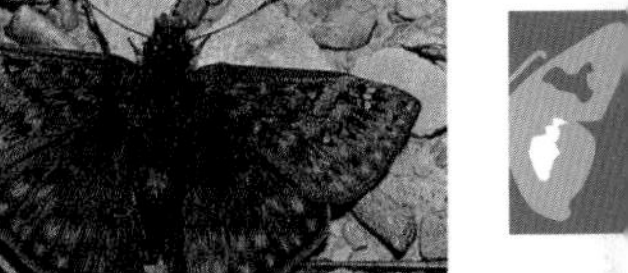

Adults and food sources: The upper surface of the forewing is brown with dark brown mottling; four subapical, semitransparent unaligned white spots, and two to four angular white spots below those. The male's forewing has scattered white hairs. The outer portion of the upper surface of the hindwing has dull yellowish spots. The undersurface of the hindwing has the characteristic two subapical yellowish white spots (these are lacking on Horace's Dusky Wing [No. 120]).

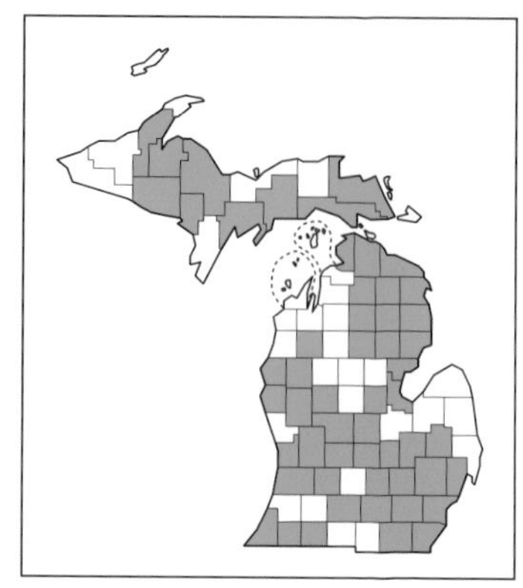

Adults nectar on alfalfa, blackberry, blueberry, chokecherry, honeysuckle, lilac, lupine, wild strawberry and birdfoot violet. They're also fond of taking moisture and minerals from damp soils.

Early stages and host plants: The caterpillar is pale to dark green and covered with tiny, yellowish white dots; the head is brownish with four orange spots.

Eggs are laid on black oak and other oaks.

Habitat: Scrub oak woods, edges, cut-over forests and roadsides.

Distribution: Throughout the Lower Peninsula and scattered counties in the Upper Peninsula.

Flight period: Single brood; April 20 to July 1.

Remarks: Common. It's easily confused with Horace's Dusky Wing in spring. It's frequently seen basking on dead leaves and bare soil.

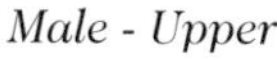

Male - Upper

Female - Upper

Male - Under

(120) Horace's Dusky Wing

Erynnis horatius (Scudder & Burgess)

Adults and food sources: The upper surfaces are very similar to those of Juvenal's Dusky Wing (No. 119); the male's forewing lacks white hairs and is darker. The female's mottling is more contrasting, with larger white spots. The undersurface of the hindwing lacks the two subapical light spots that are present on Juvenal's Dusky Wing.

Nectar sources are blueberry, boneset, buttonbush, sweet clover, dogbane and goldenrod.

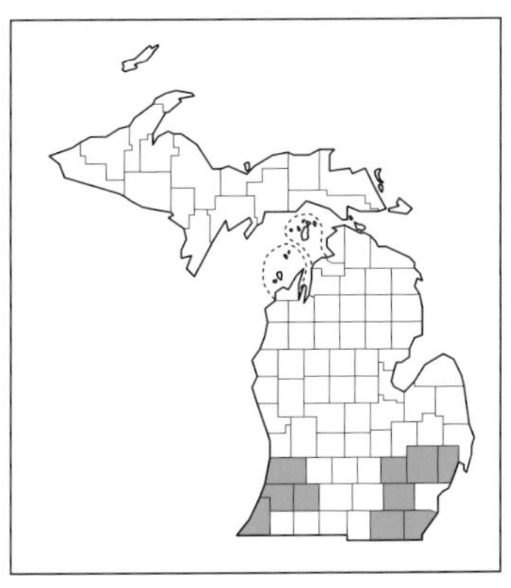

Early stages and host plants: The caterpillar is similar to that of Juvenal's Dusky Wing.

Eggs are laid on black, red and scrub oaks.

Habitat: Open oak forests and edges, brushy fields, swamps and roadsides.

Distribution: Scattered southern counties from Berrien to Macomb.

Flight period: Two broods; April 30 to August 10.

Remarks: Uncommon. Habits are similar to those of Juvenal's Dusky Wing.

Male - Upper

Female - Upper

Male - Under

(121) Mottled Dusky Wing
Erynnis martialis (Scudder)

Adults and food sources: Upper surfaces are strongly mottled with a purplish sheen, especially in fresh specimens; the forewing has small, apical white spots. The undersurface of the hindwing has dull yellowish spots basally highlighted with dark brown scales.

Nectar sources are alfalfa, blackberry, lupine and New Jersey tea in Michigan. Adults also take moisture and minerals from damp soils.

Early stages and host plants: The caterpillar is light green with red marks on a black head.

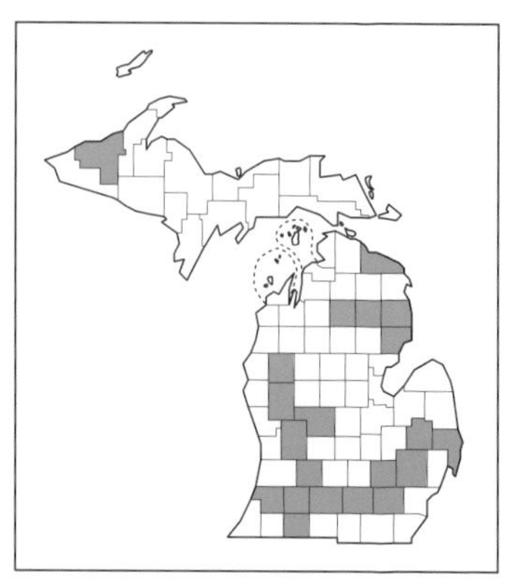

Eggs are laid exclusively on New Jersey tea and wild lilac in Michigan.

Habitat: Oak barrens, brushy fields and prairies.

Distribution: Scattered counties in the Lower Peninsula and the western Upper Peninsula (Ontonagon County, Porcupine Mountains State Park).

Flight period: Two broods; May 13 to August 21.

Remarks: Locally uncommon. This is the most distinctive and easily identified of Michigan's dusky wings.

Male - Upper

Female - Upper

Male - Under

Columbine Dusky Wing

Erynnis lucilius (Scudder & Burgess)

Adults and food sources: Upper surfaces are brown with distinct, subapical, semitransparent white spots irregularly aligned and one to two submarginal white spots. Fresh specimens have a purplish cast. The undersurface of the hindwing has marginal and submarginal rows of pale spots.

No observations of adults nectaring have been made in Michigan; habits are likely similar to those of other dusky wings.

Early stages and host plants: The caterpillar is pale green with a yellowish cast and yellow-green lines and a black head with white or reddish spots. It overwinters in a nest of dried leaves.

Eggs are laid exclusively on wild or garden columbines.

Habitat: Forest openings, edges, limestone outcroppings, trails and roadsides.

Distribution: Scattered counties in the Lower Peninsula and the Upper Peninsula, and Isle Royale.

Flight period: Two broods; May 7 to September 16.

Remarks: It's common in northern Lower Peninsula counties and in the eastern Upper Peninsula, especially on limestone soils.

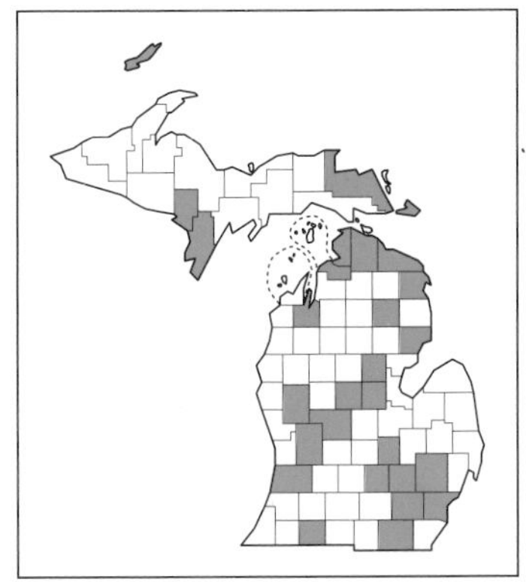

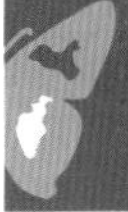

Male - Upper

Female - Upper

Male - Under

123 Wild Indigo Dusky Wing

Erynnis baptisiae (Forbes)

Adults and food sources: The adult is larger than the Columbine Dusky Wing (No. 122). Upper surfaces are chocolate-brown with small, white, subapical, semitransparent spots irregularly aligned; the basal half is darker brown. Fresh specimens have a brassy cast. The undersurface of the hindwing is brown with two irregular rows of dull yellowish spots.

Adults have been observed nectaring on bergamot, blackberry, blueberry, blazing-star, wild strawberry and black-eyed Susan.

Early stages and host plants: The caterpillar is light green with a darker dorsal line and yellowish lateral lines and is sprinkled with raised yellowish dots. The head is blackish brown. It overwinters in a nest of dried leaves.

Eggs are laid on two species of wild indigo in Michigan.

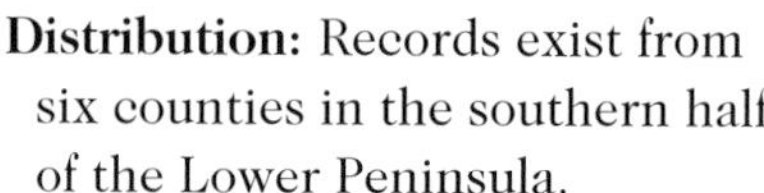

Habitat: Open oak barrens, shrubby fields, prairies and roadsides.

Distribution: Records exist from six counties in the southern half of the Lower Peninsula.

Flight period: Two broods; May 18 to September 25.

Remarks: Locally uncommon. Its range is expanding along highway rights-of-way planted to crown vetch in states south of Michigan.

Male - Upper

Female - Upper

Male - Under

124 Persius Dusky Wing

Erynnis persius (Scudder)

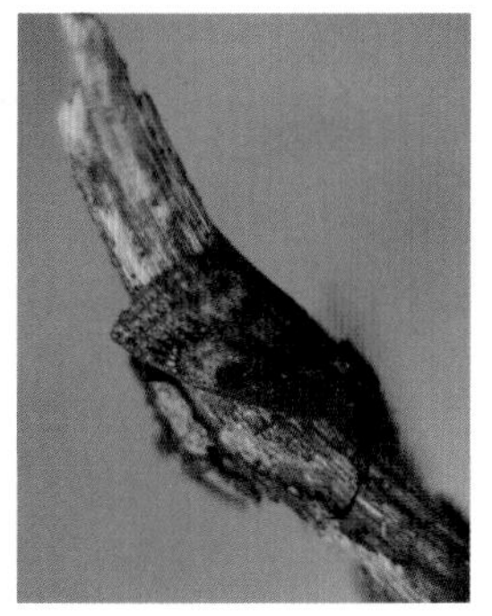

Adults and food sources: Upper surfaces are brown and marked similarly to the previous two dusky wings except that the subapical white spots align basally in a straight line. The male's forewing has abundant white hairs on basal and discal areas. Undersurfaces are similar to those of the previous two dusky wings.

Adults have been observed nectaring on blueberry, wild crab, lupine, downy phlox, wild plum and birdfoot violet.

Early stages and host plants: The caterpillar is pale green sprinkled with white, raised dots with short, white hairs and has yellowish and dark green lateral lines.

The head is reddish brown to yellow-green with vertical lighter streaks. It overwinters as a mature caterpillar.

Eggs are laid on lupine in Michigan.

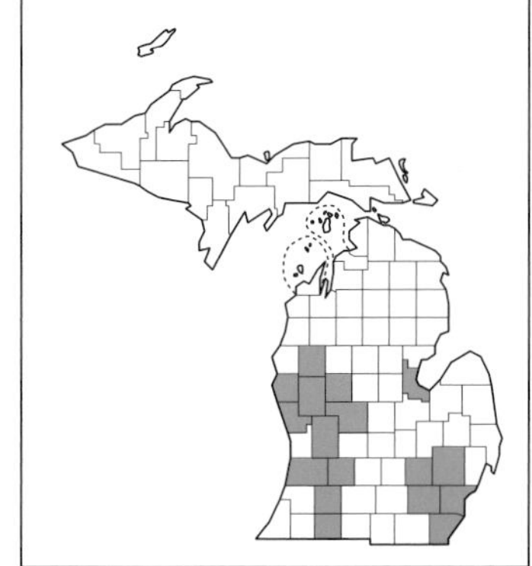

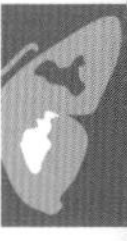

Habitat: Oak-pine barrens and adjacent prairies and brushy fields and along trails and utility rights-of-way through barrens.

Distribution: Essentially the southern half of the Lower Peninsula and northwest to Lake and Manistee counties.

Flight period: Single brood; May 3 to June 10.

Remarks: Locally uncommon. It's currently listed as threatened in the Michigan Natural Features Inventory. It's easily confused with other dusky wings in flight.

Male - Upper

Female - Upper

Female - Under

125 Grizzled Skipper

Pyrgus centaureae wyandot (W.H. Edwards)

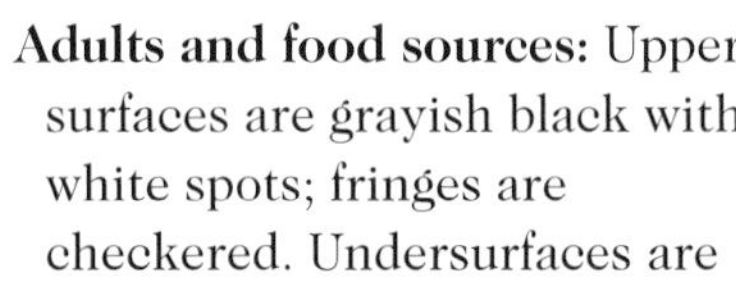

Adults and food sources: Upper surfaces are grayish black with white spots; fringes are checkered. Undersurfaces are similarly marked but with more and larger spots and white lines.

Adults have been observed nectaring on bearberry, blueberry, dandelion, wild strawberry and birdfoot violet.

Early stages and host plants: The caterpillar is light green with a reddish cast and covered with fine, short hairs. The head is blackish brown. The larva overwinters in a nest of dried leaves.

Eggs are laid on wild strawberry in Michigan.

Habitat: Large open areas in oak-pine barrens, disturbed areas and along trails.

Distribution: Scattered counties in the northern half of the Lower Peninsula south to Montcalm County. It ranges throughout the Northern Hemisphere but has not yet been found in the Upper Peninsula.

Flight period: Single brood; May 3 to June 8.

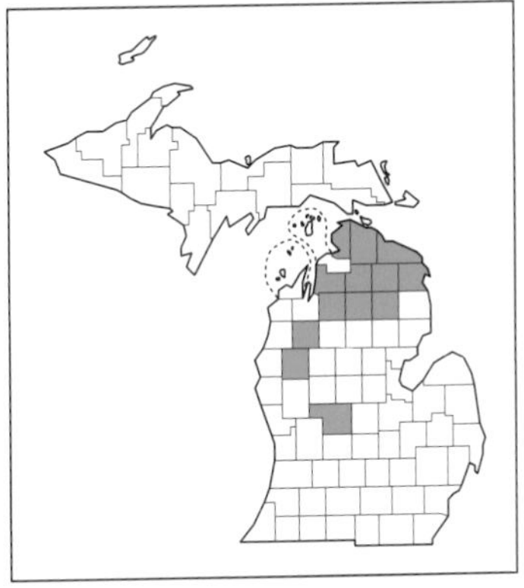

Remarks: Uncommon. This skipper is currently listed as a special concern species by Michigan's Natural Features Inventory. Its flight period is earlier than that of the Checkered Skipper (No. 126). It's usually found in the same habitat as the Chryxus Arctic (No. 108). It flies close to the surface and so is difficult to see.

Male - Upper

Female - Upper

Male - Under

126 Checkered Skipper

Pyrgus communis (Grote)

Adults and food sources: The upper surface of the forewing is grayish black with white spots, usually larger than those on the Grizzled Skipper (No. 125). Some specimens have fewer white spots. Freshly emerged males have a whitish sheen. On the upper surface of the hindwing, the marginal white spots are smaller than the submarginal spots. Females are darker than males.

Adults have been observed nectaring on aster, cheeses, red clover, dandelion, pearly everlasting, garden marigold and thistle.

Early stages and host plants: The caterpillar is yellowish white to brown with brownish and whitish lateral lines and is covered with short, white hairs. The head is black.

Eggs are laid on plants in the mallow family, including hollyhock and common mallow.

Habitat: Open fields, disturbed areas, farmyards, urban gardens and parks.

Distribution: The southern half of the Lower Peninsula and Houghton and Keweenaw counties in the Upper Peninsula.

Flight period: Two broods; June 10 to October 31.

Remarks: This skipper flies close to the surface and is very pugnacious with other butterflies. This southern stray usually occurs in late summer and may breed in Michigan in some years.

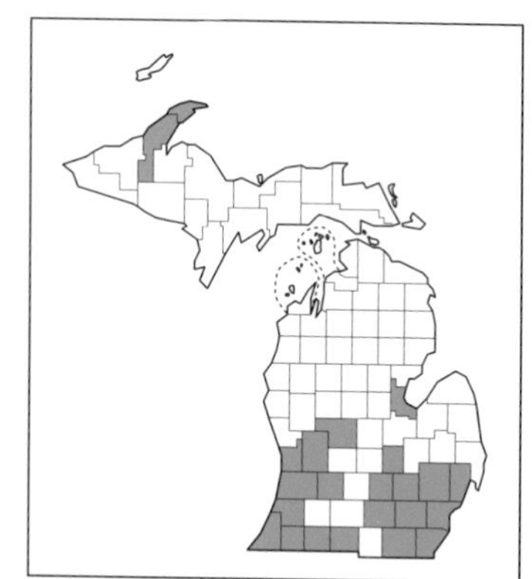

Male - Upper *Female - Upper* *Male - Under*

127 Common Sooty Wing

Pholisora catullus (Fabricius)

Adults and food sources: The upper surface of the forewing is glossy black with scattered, tiny white spots. The upper surface of the hindwing is black without spots. This species cannot be confused with other skippers.

Adults feed on nectar from alfalfa, catnip, white clover, cucumber, dogbane, melon, common milkweed, peppermint and butterfly-weed.

Early stages and host plants: The caterpillar is green and coarsely granulated with pale dots. The head is black.

Lamb's-quarters is the favored host in Michigan; it's also been reported on mint and pigweed.

Habitat: Old fields, disturbed areas, farmyards, vacant city lots, urban gardens, parks, stream banks and roadsides.

Distribution: The southern half of the Lower Peninsula and Alcona and Crawford counties.

Flight period: Two broods; May 2 to October 8.

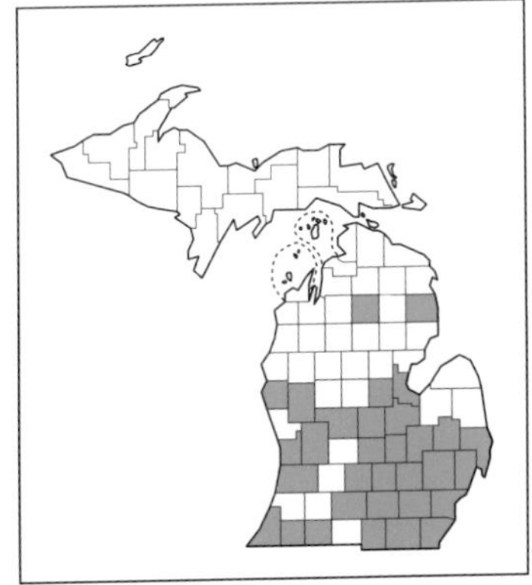

Remarks: It's very common in southern counties; host plants are usually noxious weeds.

Male - Upper

Female - Upper

128 Arctic Skipper

Carterocephalus palaemon mandan (W.H. Edwards)

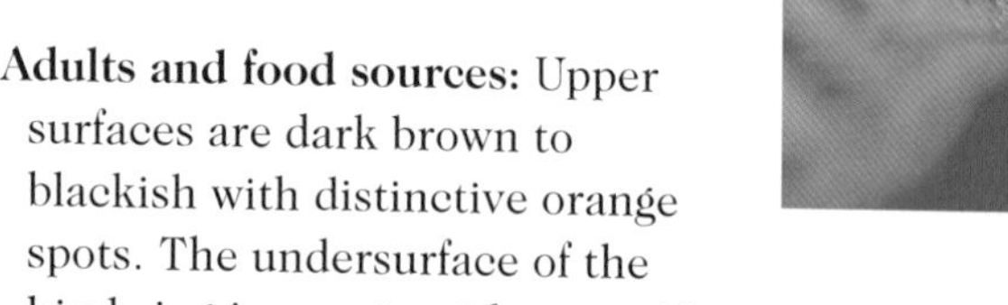

Adults and food sources: Upper surfaces are dark brown to blackish with distinctive orange spots. The undersurface of the hindwing is orange with several large white spots.

Adults have been observed nectaring on wild iris, bog laurel and Labrador tea.

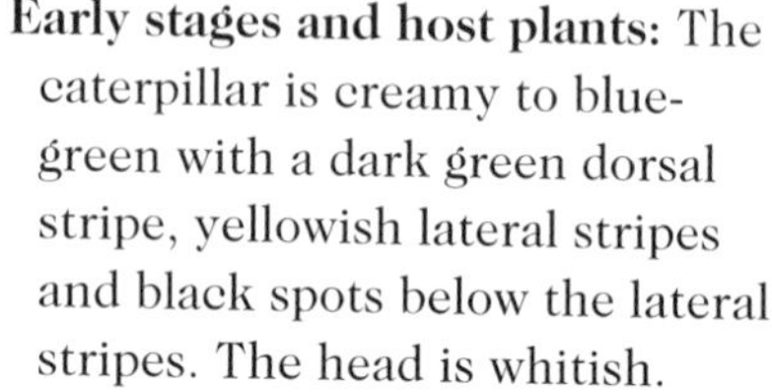

Early stages and host plants: The caterpillar is creamy to blue-green with a dark green dorsal stripe, yellowish lateral stripes and black spots below the lateral stripes. The head is whitish.

The host in Michigan is unknown, though eggs have been reported laid on brome grasses and reed grass.

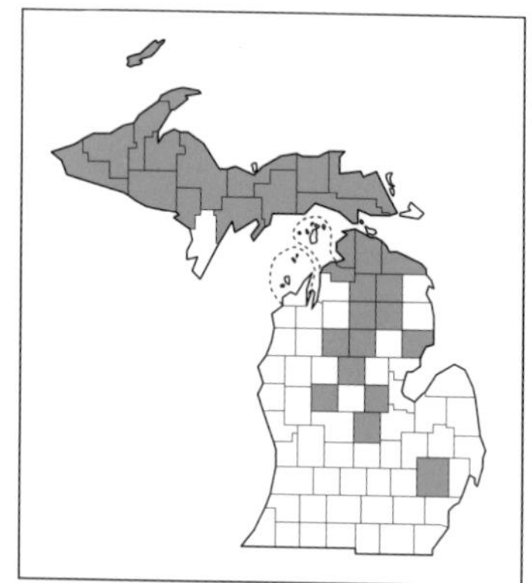

Habitat: Forest openings and edges, stream margins, bogs and swamps.

Distribution: Throughout the Upper Peninsula, including Isle Royale, and several counties of the Lower Peninsula, extending south to Oakland County.

Flight period: Single brood; May 15 to July 1.

Remarks: Locally uncommon. This is a very distinctive skipper. The nominate subspecies, *C. palaemon palaemon* (Pallas), is European; our subspecies occurs throughout the Great Lakes region.

Male - Upper *Male - Under*

129 Swarthy Skipperling

Nastra lherminier (Latreille)

Adults and food sources: This is a small, obscure brown skipper without markings on the upper surfaces. The undersurface of the hindwing is lighter brown with lighter veins.

Adults have been reported to nectar on red clover, peppermint, New Jersey tea, tick-trefoil and purple vetch.

Early stages and host plants: Early stages have not been reported.

Eggs are laid on little bluestem.

Habitat: Dry fields, meadows, disturbed areas and roadsides.

Distribution: One record from Cass County, dated July 17, 1983.

Flight period: Two broods in southern states.

Remarks: Adults fly low to the ground and are easily overlooked and may be confused with other small, dark skippers.

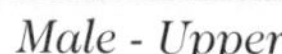

Male - Upper

Male - Under

130 Least Skipper

Ancyloxypha numitor (Fabricius)

Adults and food sources: The upper surface of the forewing is blackish brown to yellowish brown; the hindwing is orange with a black border. The undersurface of the hindwing is essentially orange. Antennae are very short.

Adults nectar on boneset, buttonbush, white clover, water cress, dogbane, goldenrod and common milkweed.

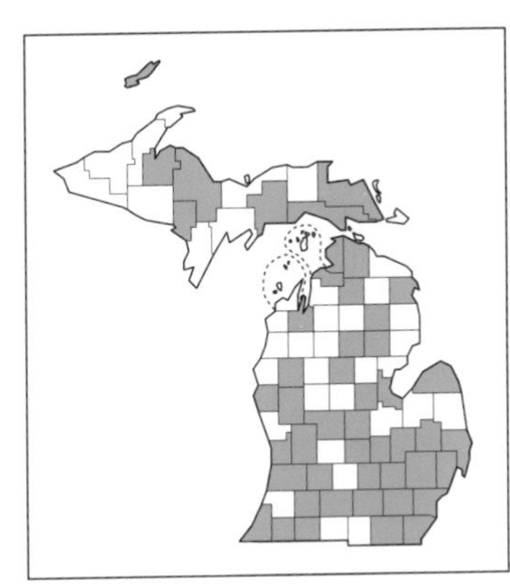

Early stages and host plants: The caterpillar is bright green with a dark brown head rimmed with white on the front.

Eggs are laid on various wetland grasses.

Habitat: Streamsides, marsh borders, brushy swamps, ditches and along drains.

Distribution: Throughout Michigan, including Isle Royale.

Flight period: Two broods; May 16 to September 27.

Remarks: Common. Adults fly weakly and low, usually along streams.

Male - Upper

Female - Upper

Male - Under

131 Powesheik Skipperling

Oarisma poweshiek (Parker)

Adults and food sources: Upper surfaces are dark brown with an orange costal area on the forewing. The undersurface of the hindwing has veins covered with white scales; basal area veins are dark brown without white scales.

Adults nectar on shrubby cinquefoil, white clover, lobelia and black-eyed Susan.

Early stages and host plants: The caterpillar is pale green with a dark green dorsal band outlined by cream lines.

Eggs are laid on spike-rush in Michigan.

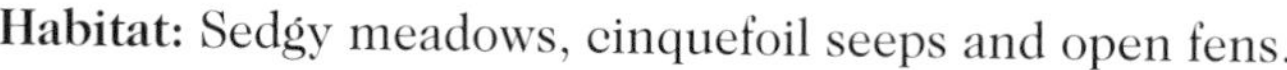

Habitat: Sedgy meadows, cinquefoil seeps and open fens.

Distribution: Six counties in the southern half of the Lower Peninsula.

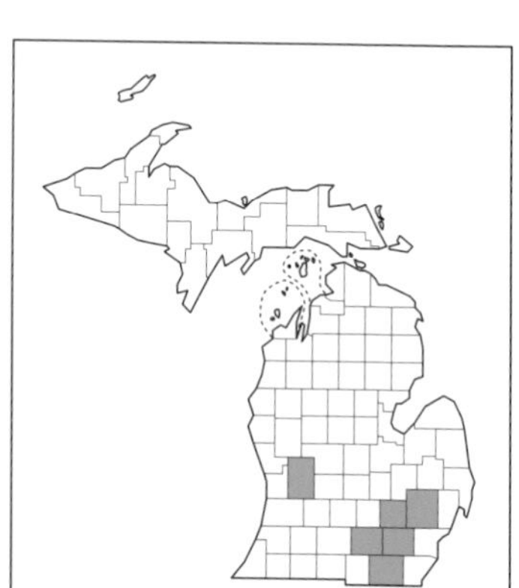

Flight period: Single brood; June 24 to July 19.

Remarks: Locally uncommon. Currently listed as threatened by the Michigan Natural Features Inventory. Adults fly close to the ground and can easily be overlooked.

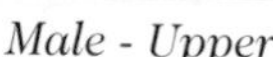

Male - Upper

Male - Under

132 European Skipper

Thymelicus lineola
(Ochsenheimer)

Adults and food sources: Upper surfaces are orange with a narrow black border and veins outlined with black scales; the male has a narrow black stigma on the forewing. Undersurfaces are light orange without distinguishing marks. Pale specimens occur rarely.

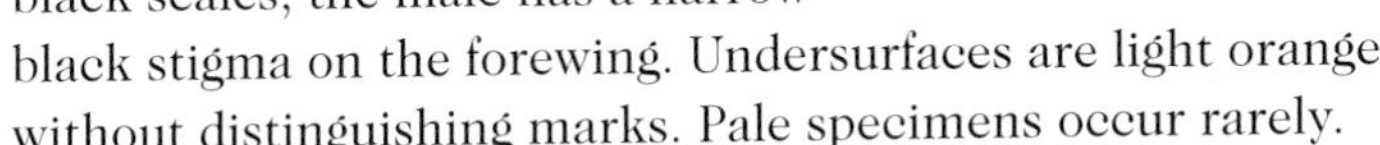

Adults nectar on butterfly bush, alsike and red clover, daisy, pepper-grass, orange and yellow hawkweed, swamp milkweed, mint, black-eyed Susan, New Jersey tea and vetch.

Early stages and host plants: The caterpillar is green with a dark dorsal stripe; the head is light brown with white or yellow stripes.

Eggs are laid on various grasses, especially timothy.

Habitat: Grassy fields, pastures, prairies, urban areas, parks and roadsides.

Distribution: Throughout the state, except Isle Royale.

Flight period: Single brood; May 28 to August 5.

Remarks: Abundant. The European Skipper was discovered in the United States in 1925 in Wayne County, Michigan. A "friendly" skipper, it frequently alights near or on people who are sitting quietly.

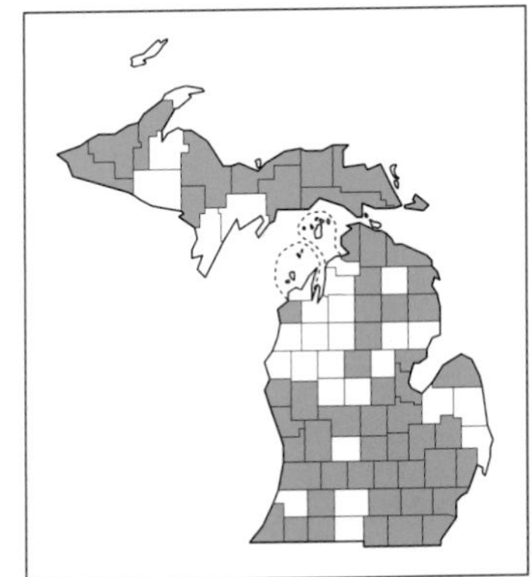

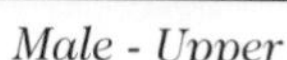

Male - Upper

Female - Upper

Pale male - Upper

Male - Under

133 Fiery Skipper

Hylephila phyleus (Drury)

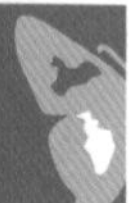

Adults and food sources: Upper surfaces of males are bright yellowish orange with a black, dentate border and a black stigma. Females have a wider black border and an irregular orange band and no stigma. The undersurface of the hindwing is yellowish orange in both sexes with scattered small black spots. Antennae are very short.

Adults nectar on butterfly bush, dandelion and garden marigold in Michigan.

Early stages and host plants: The caterpillar is gray-brown to yellow-brown with three dark stripes; the head is black with reddish brown stripes.

A female has been observed laying eggs on smooth creeping lovegrass; females are reported to lay eggs on bentgrass and crabgrass.

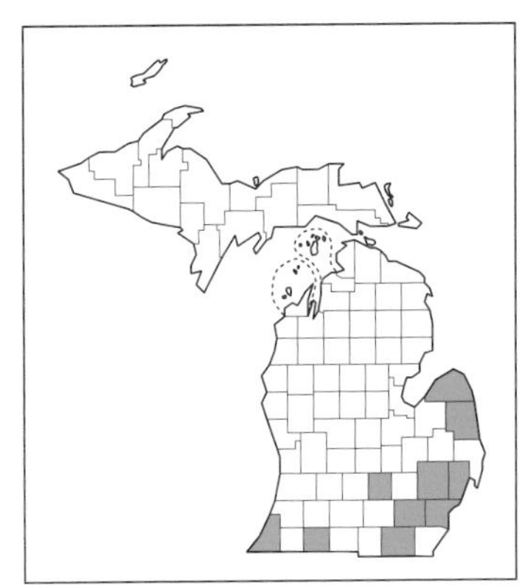

Habitat: Fields, city lawns and gardens, pastures, meadows and stream banks.

Distribution: Scattered counties in the southern half of the Lower Peninsula.

Flight period: At least one brood; July 12 to October 26.

Remarks: Many adults stray into Michigan from southern areas. It's a frequent visitor to flower gardens in late summer and a very fast flyer.

Male - Upper

Female - Upper

Male - Under

134 Laurentian Skipper

Hesperia comma laurentina (Lyman)

Adults and food sources: The upper surface of the male's forewing is dark with an orange basal area, a wide brown border and an elongated black stigma in the central area. The male's hindwing is dark orange above with a lighter band of spots and a brown border. The undersurface of the male's hindwing is golden to golden-green with several white spots. The upper surface of the female's forewing is more brown and has orange spots; the hindwing is brown with an irregular orange band of spots. The hindwing below is dark golden with larger white spots.

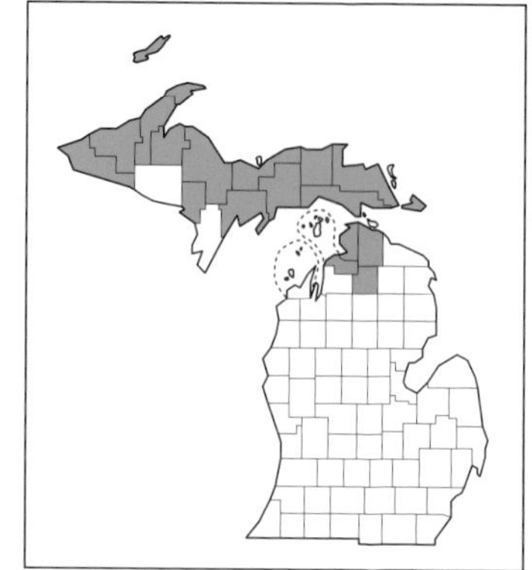

Adults nectar on alfalfa, alsike and red clover, shrubby cinquefoil, dogbane, pearly everlasting, knapweed, common milkweed, black-eyed Susan and pussy-toes. They are fond of taking moisture from damp soils.

Early stages and host plants: The caterpillar is olive-green with a black head.

The specific host plant in Michigan is unknown. Females are reported to lay eggs on various bunchgrasses.

Habitat: Open areas, fields, meadows, roadsides and lakeshores.

Distribution: Throughout the Upper Peninsula, including Isle Royale, and four counties in the northern Lower Peninsula.

Flight period: Single brood; July 6 to September 1.

Remarks: Uncommon. The subspecies *laurentina* is more southern, ranging from Maine to Manitoba; the northern subspecies, *H. comma comma* (Linnaeus), ranges from Labrador to Alaska and occurs in northern Europe.

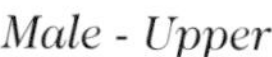

Male - Upper

Female - Upper

Male - Under

135 Ottoe Skipper

Hesperia ottoe W.H. Edwards

Adults and food sources: This is the largest skipper in the genus. The male's upper surfaces are orange with a brown border and black stigma; undersurfaces are orange-yellow without spots. The female's upper forewing is orange-brown with several yellowish white spots; the hindwing is orange-brown with an indistinct band of yellowish spots. The undersurface of the hindwing is ochraceous with ill-defined purplish spots.

Adults nectar on alfalfa, aster, dotted monarda, common milkweed, prickly pear cactus, blazing-star, black-eyed Susan and vetch. Males take moisture from damp soils.

Early stages and host plants: The caterpillar is greenish brown with a dark brown head. It overwinters as a late instar in a grass tubal nest slightly below the soil line.

Eggs are laid on fall witchgrass in Michigan; larvae develop on little bluestem grass in captivity.

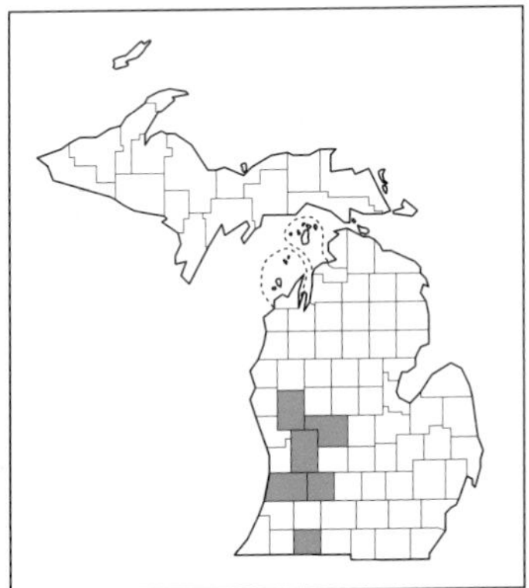

Habitat: Tall-grass prairies and adjacent roadsides.

Distribution: Six counties in the southwestern part of the Lower Peninsula.

Flight period: Single brood; June 18 to August 16.

Remarks: Locally uncommon. It's currently listed as threatened by the Michigan Natural Featues Inventory. It was initially recorded in Michigan as *Hesperia pawnee* Dodge (Nielsen, 1958); this was later corrected to *H. ottoe* (Nielsen, 1960).

Male - Upper

Male - Under

Female - Upper

Female - Under

136 Leonard's Skipper

Hesperia leonardus Harris

Adults and food sources: The upper surface of the male's forewing is dark brown with orange areas and orange scaling bordering a large black stigma in the discal area. The hindwing is dark brown with an orange band. The upper surface of the female's forewing has more brown and yellowish orange spots. The undersurface of the hindwing of both sexes is reddish to yellowish brown with a band of white or yellow spots.

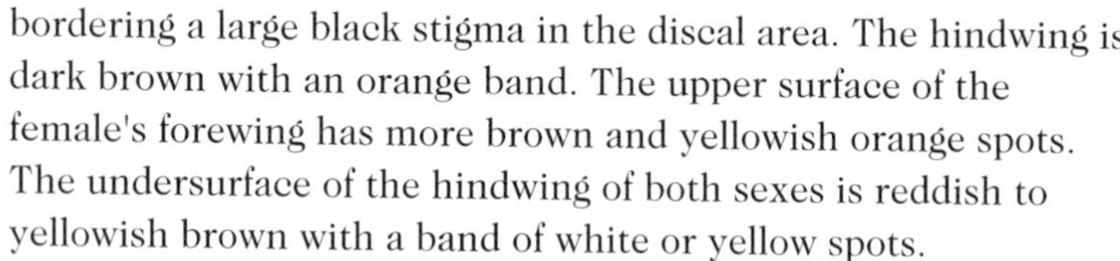

Adults nectar on aster, goldenrod, knapweed, ironweed, blazing-star, bull and swamp thistles, and joe-pye-weed. Males are fond of taking moisture from damp soil.

Early stages and host plants: The caterpillar is olive-green with a blackish head.

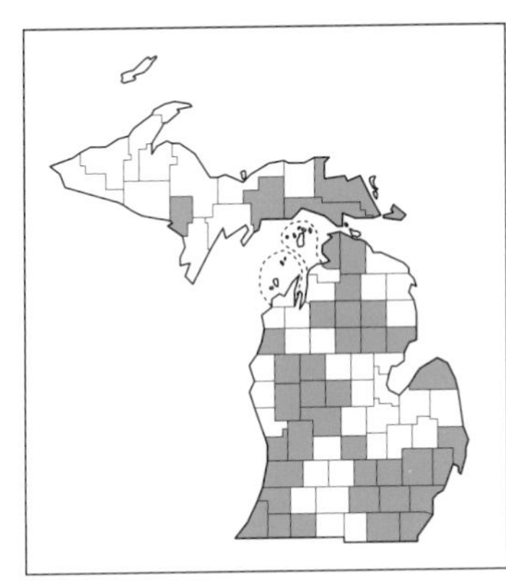

This species overwinters as an early instar caterpillar at the base of the host plant.

Eggs are laid on poverty grass, switch grass and bentgrass.

Habitat: Meadows, tall-grass prairies, oak-pine barrens and roadsides.

Distribution: Four counties in the Upper Peninsula and throughout the Lower Peninsula.

Flight period: Single brood; July 7 to October 14.

Remarks: Common. This skipper is extremely wary and difficult to approach.

Male - Upper *Female - Upper*

Male - Under (White spots) *Male - Under (Yellow spots)*

137 Cobweb Skipper

Hesperia metea Scudder

Adults and food sources: The upper surface of the male's forewing is dark brown with yellowish orange apical spots and orange scaling bordering a black stigma in the discal area. The hindwing is brown with an irregular light yellowish band.

The female's forewing is brown with scattered yellowish spots. The undersurfaces of the hindwings of both sexes are light brown with a V-shaped white band and white scaling on veins.

Adults nectar on blueberry, chokecherry, ornamental cherry, dandelion and wild strawberry.

Early stages and host plants: The caterpillar is olive-green with a blackish head. It overwinters as a late instar at the base of the host plant.

Eggs are laid on beardgrass in Michigan.

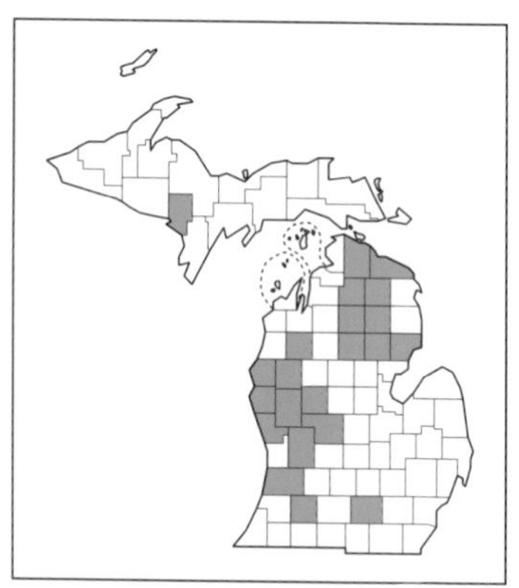

Habitat: Prairies and oak-pine barrens.

Distribution: Dickinson County in the Upper Peninsula and scattered counties in the northern and western Lower Peninsula.

Flight period: Single brood; May 6 to July 1.

Remarks: Locally uncommon. This skipper flies close to the surface and is easily overlooked. It's usually associated with the Dusted Skipper (No. 156).

Male - Upper

Male - Upper

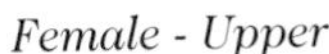

Female - Upper

Male - Under

138 Indian Skipper

Hesperia sassacus Harris

Adults and food sources: The upper surfaces of the male are essentially orange with an irregular black border and a prominent blackish stigma in the discal area.

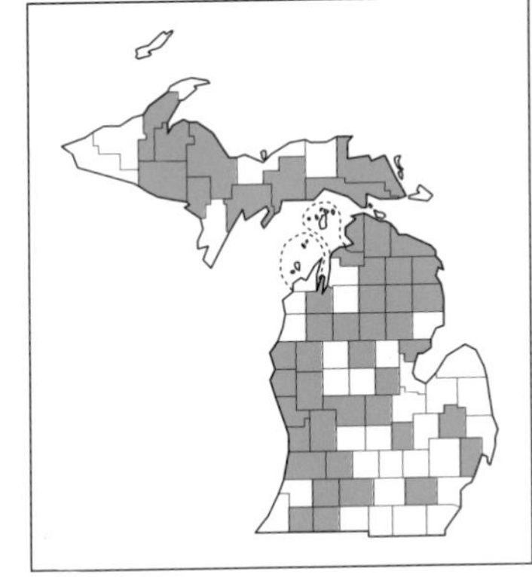

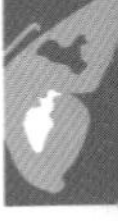

The female is similar, but she lacks the stigma. The undersurfaces of the hindwings of both sexes are light orange with an irregular band of yellowish bars.

Adults nectar on blackberry, briars, prickly pear cactus, red clover, daisy, orange hawkweed, honeysuckle, wild iris, downy phlox, puccoon, Labrador tea and vetch.

Early stages and host plants: The caterpillar is similar to that of the Laurentian Skipper — olive-green with a black head.

Eggs are laid on bunchgrasses.

Habitat: Old fields, prairies, cut-over areas, oak-pine barrens and roadsides.

Distribution: Throughout the state except Isle Royale.

Flight period: Single brood; May 26 to July 20.

Remarks: Common. Females may be confused with orange females of the Hobomok Skipper (No. 148), which has a large yellowish patch.

Male - Upper *Male - Under*

Female - Upper *Female - Under*

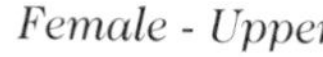

139 Peck's Skipper

Polites peckius (W. Kirby)

Adults and food sources: The upper surface of the male's forewing is dark brown with an orange area along the costal area, three to four subapical rectangular spots, a yellow area on the inner margin and a black stigma. The upper surface of the female is

essentially dark brown with several small elongated spots and no stigma.

The upper surfaces of the hindwings on both sexes are dark brown with irregular orange marks. The undersurface of the hindwing has a distinctive, central yellowish patch.

Adults nectar on red clover, dogbane, wild iris, ironweed, knapweed, common milkweed, downy phlox, blazing-star and bull thistle.

Early stages and host plants: The caterpillar is maroon with light brown mottling; the head is black with white marks.

Eggs are laid on several species of grass, including lawn grasses.

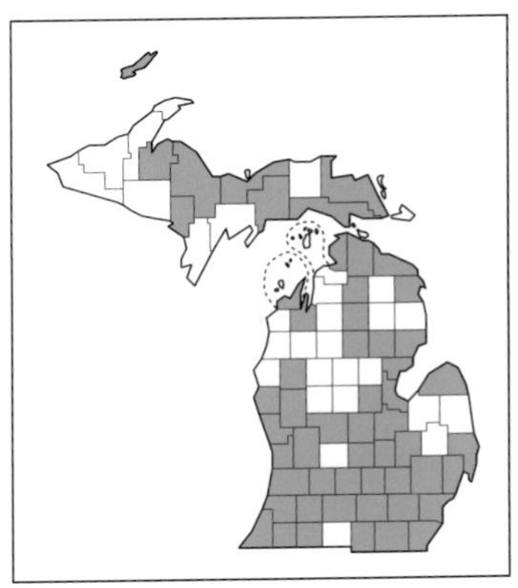

Habitat: Meadows, old fields, urban yards and parks, rights-of-way and roadsides.

Distribution: Throughout the state, including Isle Royale.

Flight period: At least two broods; May 21 to October 8.

Remarks: This is one of Michigan's commonest skippers.

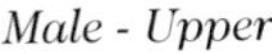

Male - Upper

Female - Upper

Male - Under

140 Tawny-edged Skipper

Polites themistocles (Latreille)

Adults and food sources: The upper surface of the male's forewing is brown with an orange costal area and a black stigma. The upper surface of the female's forewing is similar to the male's except for several small orange spots and no stigma. Upper surfaces of male and female hindwings are brown without spots. Undersurfaces of both sexes are grayish brown with an orange costal area on the forewing.

Adults nectar on alfalfa, prickly pear cactus, red clover, daisy, dogbane, orange hawkweed, knapweed, thistle and vetch.

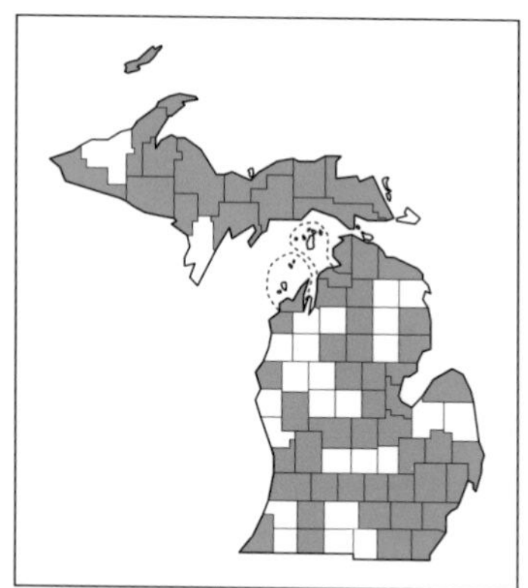

Early stages and host plants: The caterpillar is dark brown with white mottling and a blackish head.

Eggs are laid on panic grasses.

Habitat: Meadows, old fields, pastures, swales, disturbed areas, barrens and roadsides.

Distribution: Throughout Michigan, including Isle Royale.

Flight period: Two broods; May 12 to October 4.

Remarks: Common. Males may be confused with Crossline Skipper (No. 141) males, which are larger and often found in drier localities.

Male - Upper

Female - Upper

Male - Under

141 Crossline Skipper

Polites origenes (Fabricius)

Adults and food sources: The upper surface of the male is similar to that of the Tawny-edged Skipper (No. 140), but the Crossline Skipper is larger and has a few small orange spots on the forewing. The upper surface of the female's forewing is brown with several small yellowish orange spots. The undersurfaces of the hindwings of both sexes have a faint yellowish band of spots (absent in the Tawny-edged Skipper).

Adults nectar on blackberry, prickly pear cactus, knapweed, common milkweed, wild rose, blazing-star, New Jersey tea, thistle, vervain and vetch.

Early stages and host plants: The caterpillar is dark brown with dirty white mottling and a black head.

Eggs are laid on purpletop grass, panic grass and other grasses.

Habitat: Old fields, prairies and oak barrens.

Distribution: Schoolcraft County in the Upper Peninsula and throughout the Lower Peninsula.

Flight period: Single brood; June 3 to August 9.

Remarks: Locally common. It's usually found in drier locations than the Tawny-edged Skipper and easily confused with it where they occur together.

Male - Upper

Female - Upper

Male - Under

142 Long Dash

Polites mystic (W.H. Edwards)

Adults and food sources: The upper surface of the male's forewing is yellowish orange with a brown border and a long, wide blackish stigma; the hindwing has a wide yellowish orange band. The undersurface of the male's hindwing is yellowish brown with a lighter band. The upper surface of the female's forewing is brown with a yellowish orange band and scattered spots; the hindwing has a yellowish orange band. The undersurface of the hindwing is reddish brown with a distinct yellowish band and basal spot.

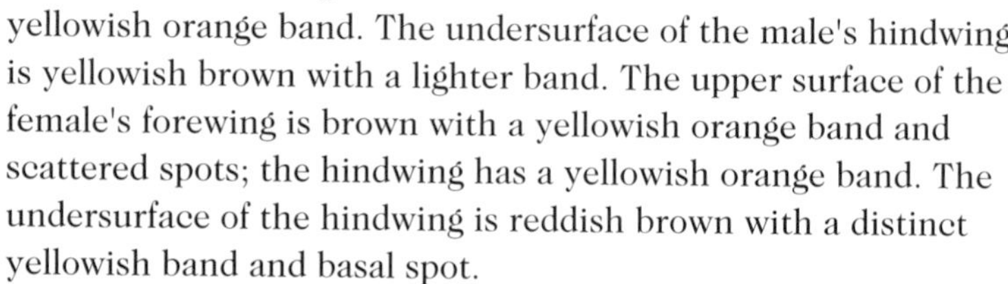

Adults nectar on blackberry, red clover, fleabane, orange hawkweed, wild iris, lupine, downy phlox, thistle and vetch.

Early stages and host plants: The caterpillar is dark brown with white mottling and a black head.

Eggs are laid on bluegrass and other grasses.

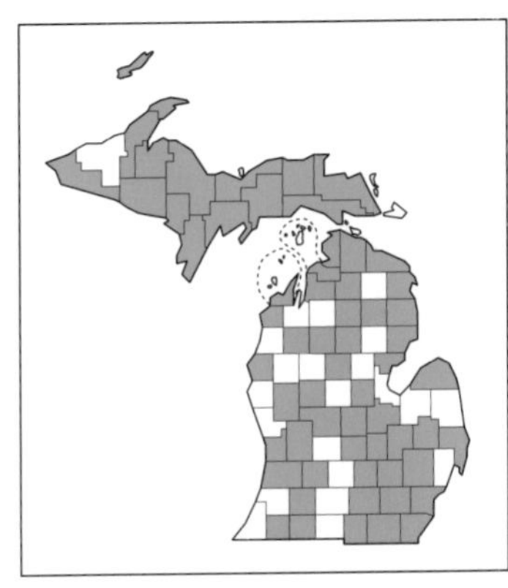

Habitat: Meadows, marsh and forest edges, and wetlands along streams and roads.

Distribution: Throughout Michigan, including Isle Royale.

Flight period: Single brood; May 29 to September 5.

Remarks: This is a very common Michigan skipper.

Male - Upper

Female - Upper

Male - Under

Northern Broken Dash

Wallengrenia egeremet (Scudder)

Adults and food sources: The upper surface of the male's forewing is brown with a distinct broken stigma and yellowish shading along the costal area. The undersurface of the hindwing is lighter purplish brown with a faint band of yellowish spots. The female's upper wing surface is brown with small, rectangular yellow spots; the undersurface of the hindwing is similar to the male's.

Adults nectar on alfalfa, buttonbush, red clover, common milkweed, blazing-star, New Jersey tea and vetch.

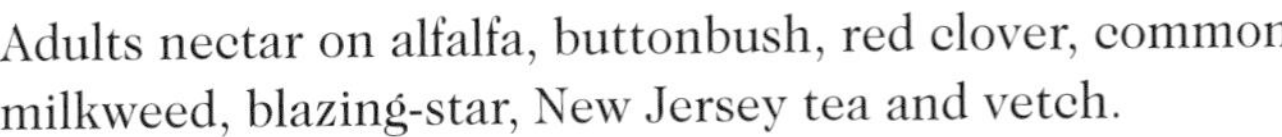

Early stages and host plants: The caterpillar is pale mottled green with indistinct green and yellow lateral stripes and a dark brown head with dark and light stripes.

Eggs are laid on panic grasses.

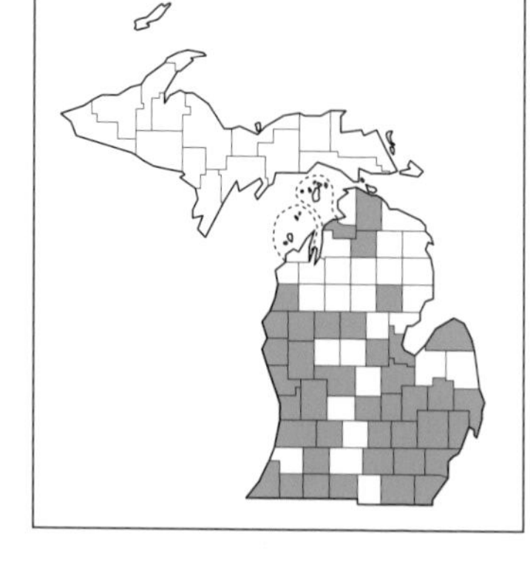

Habitat: Forest edges, brushy fields, meadows, pastures, rural and urban gardens, and roadsides.

Distribution: Throughout the Lower Peninsula; it's not been reported from the Upper Peninsula.

Flight period: Single brood; June 8 to September 26.

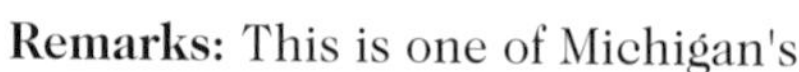

Remarks: This is one of Michigan's commonest skippers. The female may be confused with the Little Glassywing female (No. 144), which has a translucent yellowish spot on the forewing.

Male - Upper *Female - Upper* *Male - Under*

144 Little Glassywing

Pompeius verna (W.H. Edwards)

Adults and food sources: The upper surface of the male's forewing is blackish brown with a black stigma and a large, translucent yellowish spot; the undersurface of the hindwing may have a faint band of yellowish spots. The upper surface of the female's forewing has a large, translucent yellowish spot; the undersurface of the hindwing is purplish brown with a band of small yellowish spots.

Adults nectar on bergamot, red clover, dogbane, common milkweed and thistle.

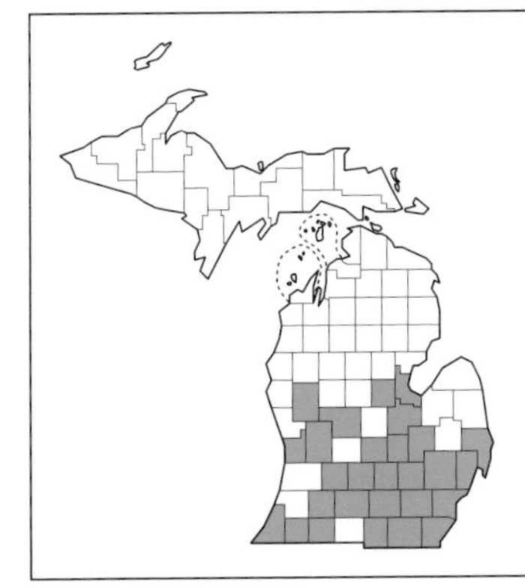

Early stages and host plants: The caterpillar is yellowish green to yellowish brown with brown tubercles and a reddish brown head with a black margin.

Eggs are laid on redtop grass and possibly on other grasses.

Habitat: Forest edges, old fields, meadows, wetlands and roadsides.

Distribution: Throughout the southern half of the Lower Peninsula.

Flight period: Single brood; June 17 to August 19.

Remarks: The Little Glassywing is not as common as the Northern Broken Dash (No. 143).

Male - Upper *Female - Upper*

Male - Under *Male - Under*

145 Sachem Skipper

Atalopedes campestris (Boisduval)

Adults and food sources: The upper surface of the male's forewing is yellowish with an irregular light brown border and a large black stigmal patch; the undersurface of the hindwing is yellowish brown with a large yellow patch. The upper surface of the female's forewing is largely brown with a large, squarish translucent spot; the upper surface of the hindwing is brown with a yellowish band, and the undersurface of the hindwing is yellowish brown with a lighter band.

Adults nectar on asters, red clover, dogbane, ironweed, marigold, common milkweed and thistle.

Early stages and host plants: The caterpillar is dark olive-green with dark tubercles and a black head.

Eggs are laid on Bermuda grass, crabgrass and St. Augustine grass, and possibly other grasses.

Habitat: Old fields, pastures, disturbed areas, rural and urban gardens and lawns, and roadsides.

Distribution: This species is recorded from Houghton County in the Upper Peninsula and Allegan, Ingham and Wayne counties in the southern half of the Lower Peninsula.

Flight period: Probably two broods; July 14 to November 4.

Remarks: This is an occasional southern stray. It is doubtful if the species can overwinter in Michigan. Look for it in formal gardens in late summer.

Male - Upper *Male - Under*

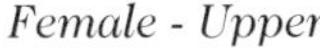

Female - Upper *Female - Under*

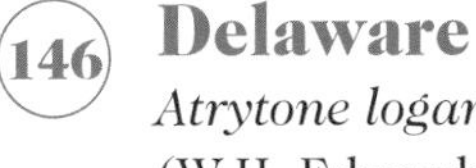

146 Delaware Skipper

Atrytone logan
(W.H. Edwards)

Adults and food sources: The upper surfaces of the male are yellowish orange with a narrow, even black border; the forewing has some black veining and a bar at the end of the discal cell. The female is similar to the male except for heavier black border and markings. The undersurface of the hindwing of both sexes is an immaculate yellowish orange.

Adults nectar on alfalfa, prickly pear cactus, dogbane, fleabane, common milkweed, New Jersey tea, thistle and vetch. Males also take moisture from damp soils.

Early stages and host plants: The caterpillar is bluish white with minute black tubercles and a white head with black stripes.

Eggs are laid on woolly beardgrass, bluestem and panic grasses.

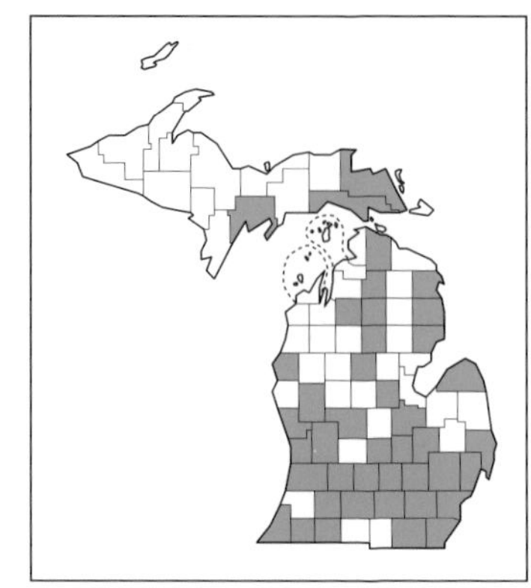

Habitat: Marsh and other wetland edges, meadows, prairies and roadsides.

Distribution: Chippewa, Delta and Mackinac counties in the Upper Peninsula and throughout the Lower Peninsula.

Flight period: Single brood, with partial second brood in some seasons; June 1 to September 18.

Remarks: Locally common. The type locality is Lansing, Michigan. The male may be confused with the Ottoe Skipper male (No. 135) on the undersurface; the latter is slightly larger and a duller yellowish orange.

Male - Upper

Male - Under

Female - Upper

(147) Mulberry Wing

Poanes massasoit (Scudder)

Adults and food sources: Upper surfaces of both sexes are black; some have tiny orange spots on the forewing, and some have larger orange spots on the hindwing. Undersurfaces of the hindwings are black with a large, distinctive yellow patch.

Adults nectar on buttonbush, dogbane, self-heal, common and swamp milkweed, and joe-pye-weed.

Early stages and host plants: Caterpillar stages are unknown.

Eggs are laid on narrow-leaf sedge.

Habitat: Sedge marshes and swamps.

Distribution: Throughout the southern half of the Lower Peninsula, extending north to Clare, Lake and Roscommon counties in the northern half of the Lower Peninsula and Dickinson County in the Upper Peninsula.

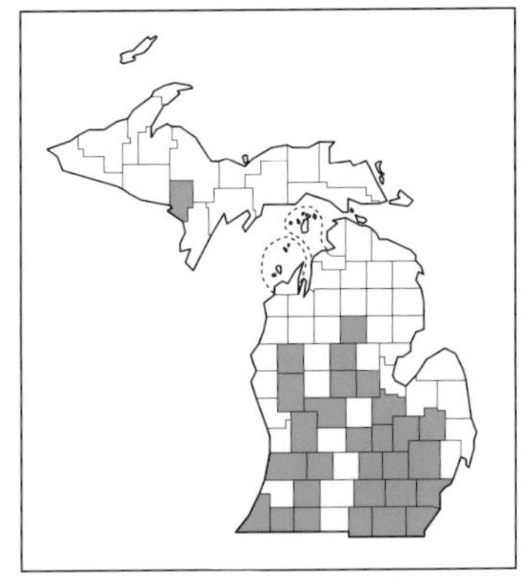

Flight period: Single brood; May 29 to August 22.

Remarks: Locally uncommon. This skipper flies low within sedges. Northern distribution is poorly known in Michigan.

Male - Upper

Male - Under

Female - Upper

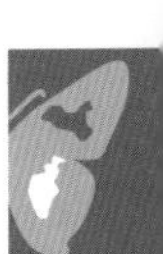

148 Hobomok Skipper

Poanes hobomok (Harris)

Adults and food sources: Upper surfaces of both sexes are yellowish orange with a wide brown border and dark veins; the male lacks a stigma. The undersurface of the hindwing has a large yellowish patch without dots. Some females — form *pocahontas* — are purplish black with a few yellowish white spots on the upper surface of the forewing; the undersurface of the hindwing is purplish black with the faint outline of a lighter patch.

Adults nectar on blackberry, red clover, dandelion, orange hawkweed, honeysuckle, wild iris, lilac, downy phlox, wild strawberry, Labrador tea and vetch.

Early stages and host plants: The caterpillar is unknown.

Eggs are laid on bluegrass and panic grasses.

Habitat: Forest openings and edges, meadows, disturbed areas and roadsides.

Distribution: Throughout Michigan, including Isle Royale.

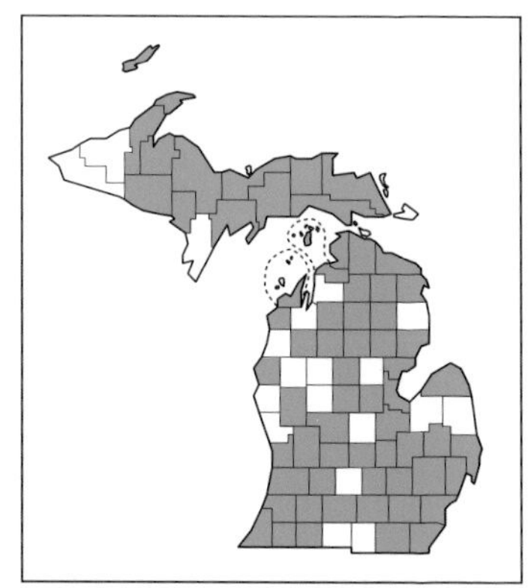

Flight period: Single brood; May 17 to July 26.

Remarks: Common. Northern populations are smaller and darker on the undersurface.

Male - Upper

Female - Upper

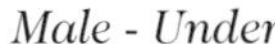

Male - Under

Dark female - Upper

Dark female - Under

149 Zabulon Skipper

Poanes zabulon (Boisduval & LeConte)

Adults and food sources: The upper surfaces of the male are similar to those of the Hobomok Skipper (No. 148); the undersurface of the hindwing has a larger yellow patch than that of the Hobomok Skipper and scattered, small brown spots. The upper surface of the female is blackish brown marked similarly to the Hobomok Skipper, form *pocahontas*. The undersurface of the hindwing is purplish brown with the faint outline of spots and a distinct, white-edged costal margin.

Adults nectar on blackberry, buttonbush, red clover, common milkweed, joe-pye-weed and vetch.

Early stages and host plants: The caterpillar is unknown.

Eggs are laid on purpletop and love grass and probably other grasses.

Habitat: Forest openings, trails and edges, brushy areas and swamp edges.

Distribution: Scattered counties in the southern half of the Lower Peninsula.

Male - Upper

Male - Under

Female - Upper

Female - Under

150 Broad-winged Skipper

Poanes viator (W.H. Edwards)

Adults and food sources: The upper surface of the forewing is dark brown with several angular orange spots; the hindwing is orange with a dark brown border and veins outlined with brown scales. The undersurface of the hindwing is orange-brown with a yellowish streak extending from the base, usually with one small dot above and two below the streak.

Adults nectar on alfalfa, buttonbush, dogbane, common and swamp milkweed, and thistle.

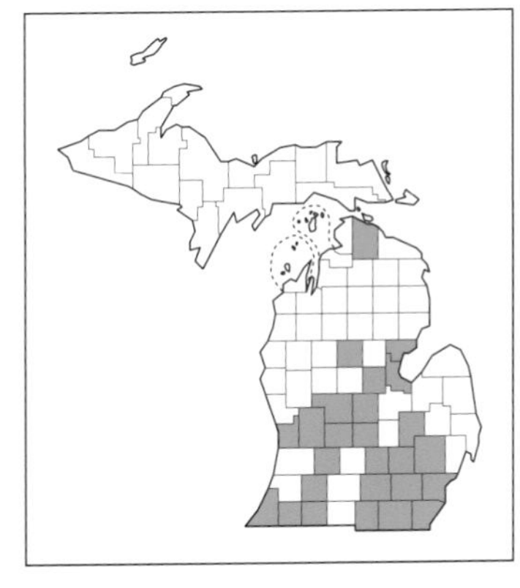

Early stages and host plants: The caterpillar is unknown.

Females may lay eggs on wide-leaf sedge in Michigan.

Habitat: Sedge marshes, brushy swamps and roadsides.

Distribution: Scattered counties in the Lower Peninsula.

Flight period: Single brood; June 30 to August 7.

Remarks: Locally uncommon. It flies within sedges, so it is easily overlooked.

Male - Upper

Female - Upper

Male - Under

151 Dion Skipper

Euphyes dion (W.H. Edwards)

Adults and food sources: The upper surfaces of the male are dark brown with a black stigma surrounded by yellowish orange on the forewing; the hindwing has a yellowish orange streak. The undersurface of the male's hindwing is orange-brown with two yellowish orange streaks. The upper surfaces of the female are dark brown with a band of yellowish spots on the forewing and a yellowish streak on the hindwing; the undersurface of the hindwing is similar to the male's.

Adults nectar on alfalfa, buttonbush, wild iris and common milkweed.

Early stages and host plants: The caterpillar is yellowish green with a black head.

The host is unknown but is probably wide-leaf sedge in Michigan.

Habitat: Sedge marshes, other wetlands with large sedge areas and adjacent roadsides.

Distribution: Scattered counties in the Lower Peninsula.

Flight period: Single brood; June 23 to August 8.

Remarks: Locally uncommon. Males fly above sedges and are very pugnacious with other skippers and flying insects.

Male - Upper

Female - Upper

Male - Under

152 Dukes' Skipper

Euphyes dukesi (Lindsey)

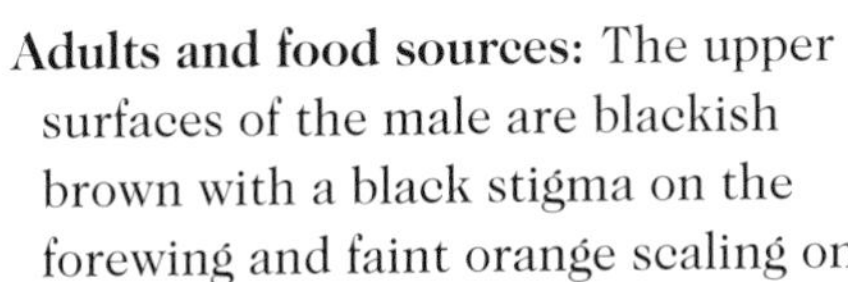

Adults and food sources: The upper surfaces of the male are blackish brown with a black stigma on the forewing and faint orange scaling on the hindwing; the undersurface of the hindwing is yellowish brown with two yellowish streaks. The upper surface of the female is blackish brown with one to three small yellowish spots on the forewing and a faint orange streak on the hindwing; undersurfaces are similar to the male's.

Adults nectar on buttonbush, swamp milkweed and joe-pye-weed.

Early stages and host plants: The caterpillar is light green with a black head. The pupal nest in sedge leaves is bound in the upper portion of the plant with silk.

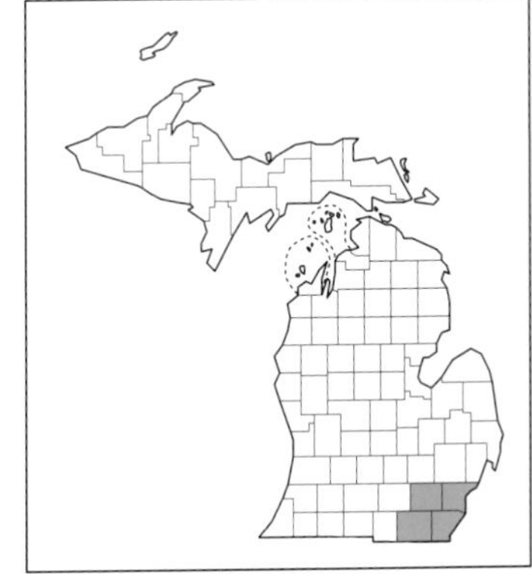

Eggs are laid on wide-leaf sedge.

Habitat: Forested swamps and brushy wetlands with sedges.

Distribution: Four counties in the southeastern Lower Peninsula.

Flight period: Single brood; June 26 to August 10.

Remarks: Locally uncommon. This skipper flies low within sedges and is easily overlooked. It is currently listed as threatened by the Michigan Natural Features Inventory.

Male - Upper

Female - Upper

Male - Under

153 Black Dash

Euphyes conspicuus
(W.H. Edwards)

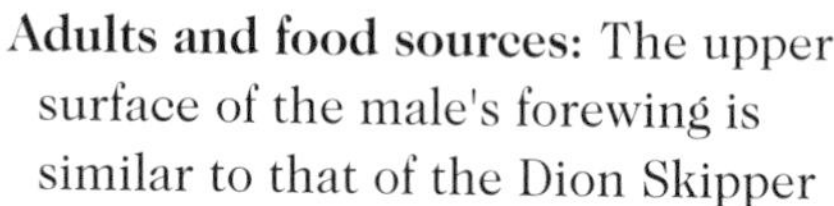

Adults and food sources: The upper surface of the male's forewing is similar to that of the Dion Skipper male (No. 151) — dark brown with a black stigma surrounded by yellowish orange. The hindwing has more orange in the discal area. The upper surface of the female is similar to that of the Dion Skipper — dark brown, though the yellowish spots are smaller. The undersurface of the hindwing in both sexes is orange-brown with a central yellowish orange patch.

Adults nectar on alfalfa, buttonbush, common and swamp milkweed, and swamp thistle.

Early stages and host plants: The caterpillar is unknown.

Eggs are laid on narrow-leaf sedge.

Habitat: Swamps, marshes, fens and other sedgy wetlands.

Distribution: The southern half of the Lower Peninsula north to Clare County.

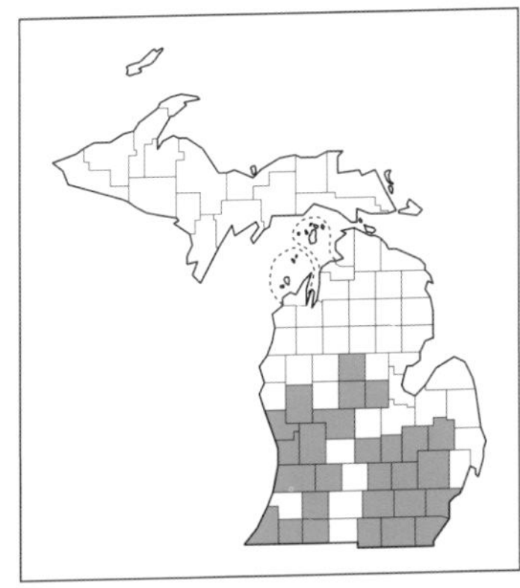

Flight period: Single brood; June 25 to August 10.

Remarks: Locally uncommon. It usually flies with other marsh skippers, such as the Mulberry (No. 147), Broad-winged (No. 150) and Dion (No. 151) skippers. The type locality is Lansing, Michigan.

Male - Upper *Female - Upper* *Male - Under*

154 Two-spotted Skipper

Euphyes bimacula
(Grote & Robinson)

Adults and food sources: The upper surface of the male's forewing is brown with an orange patch centered on a black stigma; the hindwing is brown without markings. The upper surfaces of the female are dark brown with two small spots on the forewing. The undersurfaces of the hindwings of both sexes are orange-brown with a distinctive white fringe along the inner margin. The undersurface of the abdomen is white.

Adults nectar on white campion, red clover, orange hawkweed, wild iris and common milkweed.

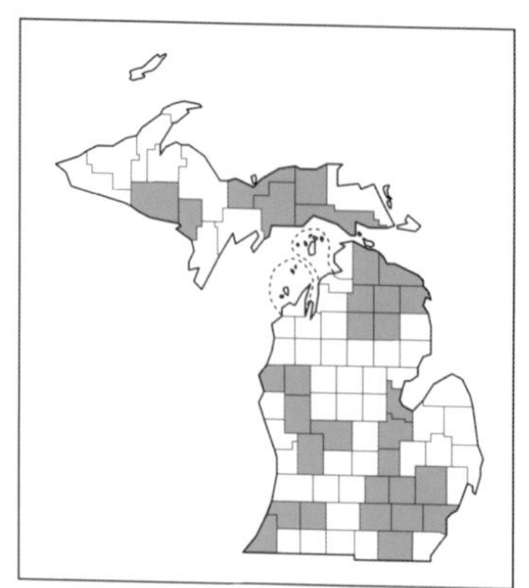

Early stages and host plants: The caterpillar is unknown.

Eggs are laid on wide-leaf sedge.

Habitat: Sedgy marshes, wet meadows and roadsides.

Distribution: Scattered counties throughout the state.

Flight period: Single brood; June 15 to July 26.

Remarks: Locally uncommon. This skipper is more common in northern counties.

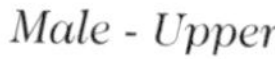

Male - Upper

Female - Upper

Male - Under

155 Dun Skipper

Euphyes vestris metacomet (Harris)

Adults and food sources: The upper surfaces of both sexes are brownish black with a black stigma on the male and two tiny yellowish spots on the female's forewing. The undersurface of the male's hindwing is purplish brown without markings; the female's is purplish brown with a faint yellowish band.

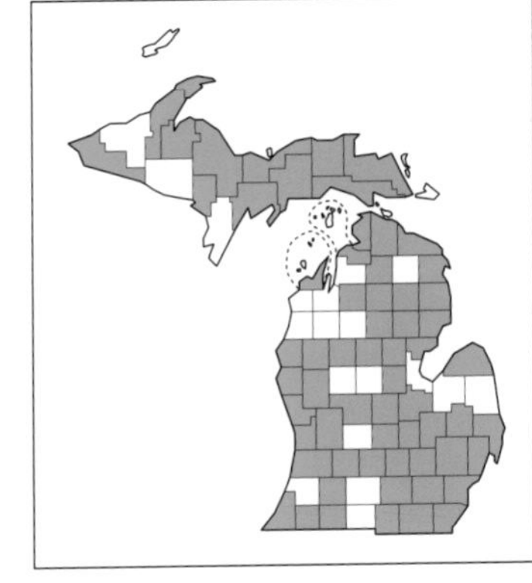

Adults nectar on buttonbush, red clover, fireweed, knapweed, common milkweed, blazing-star, pussy-toes and vetch. Males take nutrients and moisture from carrion and damp soils.

Early stages and host plants: The caterpillar is light green with white dashes; the head is black, brown and cream.

Eggs are laid on nut-grass sedge and probably other sedges in Michigan.

Habitat: Meadows, swamp and marsh edges, disturbed areas and roadsides.

Distribution: Throughout Michigan except Isle Royale.

Flight period: Single brood; June 23 to August 31.

Remarks: This is one of Michigan's commonest skippers. The female may be confused with the female of the Little Glassywing (No. 144), which has a large, transparent white spot on the forewing, and the female of the Northern Broken Dash (No. 143), which has one or two elongated yellowish spots on the forewing.

Male - Upper

Female - Upper

Male - Under

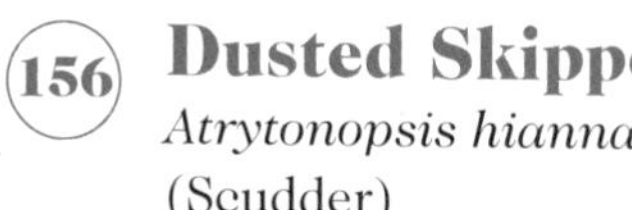

156 Dusted Skipper

Atrytonopsis hianna
(Scudder)

Adults and food sources: The upper surfaces of both are grayish black; the male's forewing lacks a stigma and has one or two small white spots in the median area. The female's forewing has two white spots in the median area. The undersurface of the hindwing is grayish brown with a slight purplish tinge in the outer area, a tiny white spot at the base and a faint darker band in the median.

Adults nectar on blackberry, cinquefoil, lupine, puccoon, vetch and white yarrow.

Early stages and host plants: The caterpillar is pink-lavender dorsally and pale gray on the sides and is covered with long yellow-white hairs. The head is dark reddish purple.

Eggs are laid on little bluestem grass in Michigan.

Habitat: Oak-pine barrens, prairies, rights-of-way in sandy areas and roadsides.

Distribution: Scattered counties in the Lower Peninsula from Cheboygan to Monroe counties.

Flight period: Single brood; May 24 to July 1.

Remarks: Locally uncommon. It's usually found in the same habitat as the Cobweb Skipper (No. 137) but flies several days later. It's currently listed as threatened by the Michigan Natural Features Inventory.

Male - Upper

Female - Upper

Male - Under

157 Pepper and Salt Skipper

Amblyscirtes hegon (Scudder)

Adults and food sources: The upper surfaces of both sexes are grayish brown with a few small, white discal spots on the forewing and have a slight greenish cast to both wings. The undersurface of the hindwings is grayish green with a lighter postmedial band of spots.

Adults nectar on blackberry, blueberry and waterleaf.

Early stages and host plants: The caterpillar is pale greenish white with dark green dorsal and white lateral stripes; the head is dark brown with pale brown bands.

Eggs are laid on Kentucky bluegrass, Indian grass and probably other grasses.

Habitat: Small, sunny forest openings, swamp edges and other partially shaded moist areas.

Distribution: Throughout the Upper Peninsula and scattered counties in the Lower Peninsula.

Flight period: Single brood; May 20 to June 23.

Remarks: Locally uncommon. It usually occurs in the same habitat as the Arctic Skipper (No. 128). It is not as common as the Roadside Skipper (No. 158).

Male - Upper

Female - Upper

Male - Under

158 Roadside Skipper

Amblyscirtes vialis
(W.H. Edwards)

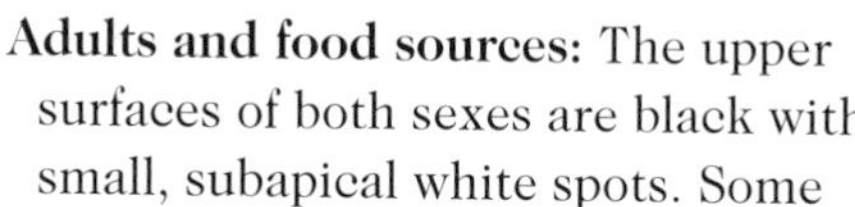

Adults and food sources: The upper surfaces of both sexes are black with small, subapical white spots. Some may have a tiny white spot in the discal area. The undersurface of the hindwing is black with violet-gray scaling on the outer half.

Adults nectar on aster, blueberry, lilac, lupine, wild strawberry and birdfoot violet; they also take moisture from damp soils.

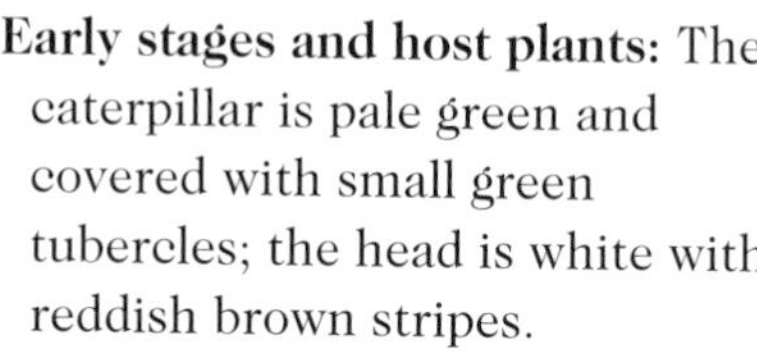

Early stages and host plants: The caterpillar is pale green and covered with small green tubercles; the head is white with reddish brown stripes.

Eggs are laid on beardgrass, bluegrass and several other grasses.

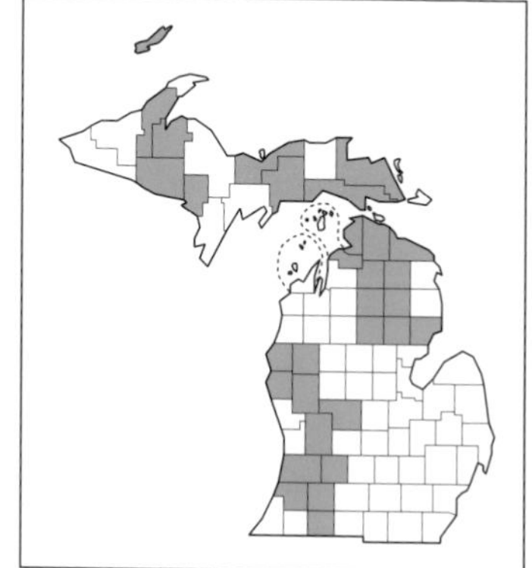

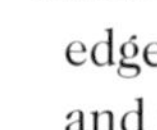

Habitat: Forest openings and edges, oak-pine barrens, prairies and roadsides.

Distribution: Throughout the Upper Peninsula, including Isle Royale, and scattered counties in the Lower Peninsula.

Flight period: Single brood; May 14 to July 27.

Remarks: It is common in dry habitats and flies close to the ground.

Male - Upper

Female - Upper

Male - Under

159 Eufala Skipper

Lerodea eufala (W.H. Edwards)

Adults and food sources: The upper surfaces of both sexes are grayish brown with a few translucent subapical spots and two small spots below these on the forewing; the hindwing is unmarked. The male's forewing has no stigma. The undersurface of the hindwing is gray without markings.

There have been no observations of nectaring in Michigan; they are reported elsewhere on alfalfa and composites.

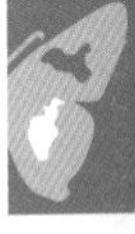

Early stages and host plants: The caterpillar is bright green with a dark dorsal stripe and white lateral lines; the head is white with orange-brown blotches.

The host plant in Michigan is unknown but is probably an upland grass.

Habitat: Upland fields, meadows, prairies and roadsides.

Distribution: Known only from one record from Ontonagon County in the Upper Peninsula.

Flight period: This record is dated August 25, 1959.

Remarks. This is a southern stray that may infrequently occur in late summer in open fields. It is a drab little skipper that can easily be overlooked.

Male - Upper

Female - Upper

Male - Under

Bibliography

Cardé, R.T., A.M. Shapiro and H.K. Clench. 1970. Sibling Species in the *eurydice* group of *Lethe* (Lepidoptera: Satyridae). Psyche, 77 (1): 70-130.

Ebner, J.A. 1970. The Butterflies of Wisconsin. Milwaukee Pub. Mus. Popular Sci. Hdbk. No. 12. Milwaukee, Wis.: Milkwaukee Public Museum.

Fleming, R.C. 1963. An Annotated List of Papilionoidea of Van Buren County, Michigan. Occas. Pap. No. 9. Kalamazoo, Mich.: C.C. Adams Cent. Ecol. Studies, W. Mich. Univ.

Hagen, R.H., R.L. Lederhouse, J.L. Bossart and J.M. Scriber. 1991. *Papilio canadensis* and *P. glaucus* (Papilionidae) are Distinct Species. J. Lepid. Soc., 45(4): 245-258.

Holmes, A.M., Q.F. Hess, R.R. Tasker and A.J. Hanks. 1991. The Ontario Butterfly Atlas. Toronto, Ontario: Toronto Entomol. Assoc.

Howe, W.J. 1975. The Butterflies of North America. Garden City, N.Y.: Doubleday.

Iftner, D.C., J.A. Shuey and J.V. Calhoun. 1992. Butterflies and Skippers of Ohio. Ohio Biol. Surv. Bull. New Series Vol. 9, No.1.

Irwin, R.R. 1970. Notes on *Lethe creola* (Satyridae), with Designation of Lectotype. J. Lepid. Soc., 24 (2): 143-151.

Moore, S. 1960. A Revised Annotated List of the Butterflies of Michigan. Occas. Pap. No. 617. Ann Arbor, Mich.: Mus. Zool., Univ. of Michigan.

Newcomb, W.W. 1910. *Chrysophanus dorcas* Kirby, and Related Species in the Upper Peninsula of Michigan. Canad. Ent., 52: 153-157.

Nielsen, M.C. 1958. Observations on *Hesperia pawnee* in Michigan. Lepid. News, 12:37-40.

Nielsen, M.C. 1960. A Correction on *Hesperia pawnee* in Michigan. J. Lepid. Soc., 14(1): 57. 1970. New Michigan Butterfly Records. J. Lepid. Soc., 24 (1): 42-47.

Opler, P.A., and G.O. Krizek. 1984. Butterflies East of the Great Plains. Baltimore, Md.: Johns Hopkins Univ. Press.

Opler, P.A., and V. Malikul. 1992. A Field Guide to Eastern Butterflies. Boston: Houghton Mifflin Co.

Pyle, R.M. 1981. The Audubon Field Guide to North American Butterflies. New York: Alfred A. Knopf.

Scott, J.A. 1986. The Butterflies of North America, A Natural History and Field Guide. Stanford, Calif.: Stanford Univ. Press.

Shull, E.M. 1977. The Butterflies of Indiana. Bloomington and Indianapolis, Ind.: Indiana Acad. Sci. and Indiana Univ. Press.

U.S. Dept. of Agriculture. 1941. Climate and Man. Yearbook of Agriculture. Washington, D.C.: U.S. Govt. Printing Office.

Voss, E.G. 1972. Michigan Flora. A Guide to the Identification and Occurrence of the Native and Naturalized Seed-plants of the State. Part 1. Gymnosperms and Monocots. Cranbrook Inst. Sci. Bull. 55. Part II. 1985. Dicots (Saururaceae-Cornaceae). Cranbrook Inst. Sci. Bull. No. 59. Part III. 1996. Dicots (Pyrolaceae-Compositae). Cranbrook Inst. Bull. No. 61.

Wolcott, R.H. 1893. The Butterflies of Grand Rapids, Michigan. Canad. Ent., 25: 98-107.

Xerces Society. 1990. Butterfly Gardening — Creating Summer Magic in Your Garden. San Francisco: Sierra Club Books.

Glossary

Androconia – Specialized wing scales of males that produce odors used in courtship.

Apex – The tip of the forewing.

Apical – At the tip or the area near the tip of the forewing.

Artificial bait – A mixture of molasses, fermented fruit, sugar and beer used as an attractant.

Basal – The wing area near the body.

Boreal – Refers to the northern coniferous forest region.

Canadian zone – Part of the state usually covered with conifers and some hardwoods; the average summer high temperatures range from 57 to 65 degrees F (14 to 18 degrees C) and winters may have six months of freezing temperatures.

Chrysalis (chrysalid) – The pupa of a butterfly — the non-feeding stage between the caterpillar and the adult.

Costal fold – A membranous flap along the leading edge of some skipper forewings.

Dentate – A toothed edge.

Discal – The more central area of the wing.

Dorsal – The upper surface of the wing or the upper area of a caterpillar.

Endangered – A species that is in danger of extinction throughout all or a significant portion of its range.

Hibernaculum – A shelter in which the larva spends the winter.

Holarctic – Native to both North America and Eurasia.

Hudsonian zone – A transition zone between the Arctic and Canadian zones, frequently found in Michigan's sphagnum-heath bogs.

Larva (pl.: larvae) – The immature stage between the egg and the pupa (or chrysalis); the caterpillar of a butterfly or moth.

Lateral – Referring to the side.

Marginal – An area at the outer edge of the wing.

Nominate – Refers to the initial species description.

Palpus (pl.: palpi) – The mouthparts, usually extending forward in front of the face.

Postmedial – Part of the wing just beyond the center or median.

Special concern – A species that is likely to become a threatened species within the foreseeable future throughout all or a significant portion of its range.

Stigma – A patch of dark scales on the forewing of many male skippers.

Striated – Marked with parallel fine lines.

Subarctic – Habitats located just below the Arctic Circle.

Submarginal – Near the margin of the wing.

Subspecies – A geographically defined population that differs in some character(s) from other populations of the same species.

Thorax – The portion of the body between the head and the abdomen.

Threatened – A species that appears to have undergone a serious, non-cyclical decline in Michigan, such that it could become endangered in the foreseeable future if the decline continues unchecked.

Type locality – The location from which the species was first collected and described.

Adult Nectar Plants and Larval Host Plants

The names are based on Voss' (1972, 1985, 1996) *Michigan Flora*, except those plants not found in Michigan.

Alder – *Alnus* spp.

Alfalfa – *Medicago sativa* L.

Alpine smartweed – *Polygonum viviparum* L.

Alsike clover – *Trifolium hybridum* L.

Ash – *Fraxinus* spp.

Aster – *Aster* spp.

Baby's breath – *Gypsophila* spp.

Bastard-toadflax – *Comandra umbellata* (L.) Nutt.

Beaked hazelnut – *Corylus cornuta* Marsh.

Bearberry – *Arctostaphylos uva-ursi* (L.)

Beardgrass – *Andropogon* spp.

Beech – *Fagus grandifolia* Ehrh.

Beggar's-ticks – *Bidens* spp.

Bentgrass – *Agrotis* spp.

Bergamot – *Monarda fistulosa* L.

Bermuda grass – *Cynodon dactylon* (L.) Pers.

Birdfoot violet – *Viola pedata* L.

Birch – *Betula* spp.

Black-eyed Susan – *Rudbeckia hirta* L.

Blackberry – *Rubus* spp.

Black cherry – *Prunus serotina* Ehrh.

Black locust – *Robinia pseudoacacia* L.

Black oak – *Quercus velutina* Lam.

Black spruce – *Picea mariana* (Miller) BSP.

Black willow – *Salix nigra* Marsh.

Bladdernut – *Staphylea trifolia* L.

Blazing-star – *Liatris* spp.

Blueberry – *Vaccinium* spp.

Bluegrass – *Poa* spp.

Blue vervain – *Verbena hastata* L.

Bog goldenrod – *Solidago uliginosa* Nutt.

Bog laurel – *Kalmia polifolia* Wangenh.

Bog-rosemary – *Andromeda glaucophylla* Link

Boneset – *Eupatorium perfoliatum* L.

Bottlebrush grass – *Hystrix patula* Moench

Bouncing Bet – *Saponaria officinalis* L.

Broccoli – *Brassica* spp.

Bromegrass – *Bromus* spp.

Brussels sprouts – *Brassica* spp.

Bull thistle – *Cirsim vulgare* (Savi) Tenore

Bunchgrass – *Sporobolus* spp.

Burdock – *Arctium* spp.

Bush-clover – *Lespedeza* spp.

Butterfly-bush – *Buddleia davidii* Franchet

Butterfly-weed – *Asclepias tuberosa* L.

Buttonbush – *Cephalanthus occidentalis* L.

Cabbage – *Brassica* spp.

Cardinal-flower – *Lobelia cardinalis* L.

Catnip – *Nepeta cataria* L.

Cheeses – *Malva neglecta* Wallr.

Chokecherry – *Prunus virginiana* L.

Cockle – *Silene* spp.

Common milkweed – *Asclepias syriaca* L.

Common trillium – *Trillium grandiflorum* (Michaux) Salisa

Cotton-grass – *Eriophorum* spp.

Crabgrass – *Digitaria* spp.

Cranberry – *Vaccinium* spp.

Crown-vetch – *Coronilla varia* L.

Cucumber – *Cucumis sativus* L.

Cudweed – *Gnaphalium* spp.

Currant – *Ribes* spp.

Dandelion – *Taraxacum officinale* Wiggers

Dogbane – *Apocynum* spp.

Dotted monarda – *Monarda punctata* L.

Downy phlox – *Phlox pilosa* L.

Drummond's cress – *Arabis drummondii* A. Gray

Dutchman's pipe – *Aristolochia macrophylla* Lam.

Dwarf bilberry – *Vaccinium cespitosum* Michaux

Dwarf birch – *Betula pumila* L.

Dwarf sumac – *Rhus copallina* L.

Elm – *Ulmus* spp.

Fall witchgrass – *Leptoloma cognatum* (Schultes) Chase

False foxglove – *Aureolaria* spp.

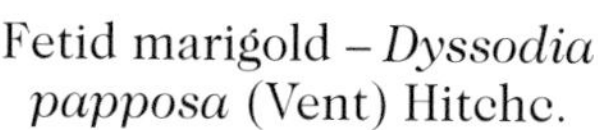

Fetid marigold – *Dyssodia papposa* (Vent) Hitchc.

Fireweed – *Epilobium* spp.

Flat-topped white aster – *Aster umbellatus* Miller

Fleabane – *Erigeron* spp.

Flowering dogwood – *Cornus florida* L.

Garden columbine – *Aquilegia vulgaris* L.

Garden phlox – *Phlox paniculata* L.

Goats-rue – *Tephrosia virginiana* (L.) Pers.

Goatweed – *Croton capitatus* Michx.

Goldenrod – *Solidago* spp.

Gooseberry – *Ribes* spp.

Hackberry – *Celtis occidentalis* L.

Hawthorn – *Crataegus* spp.

Hickory – *Carya* spp.

Highbush blueberry – *Vaccinium corymbosum* L.

Hog peanut – *Amphicarpaea bracteata* (L.) Fern.

Hollyhock – *Alcea rosea* L.

Honey locust – *Gleditisia triacanthos* L.

Honeysuckle – *Lonicera* spp.

Holly – *Ilex* spp.

Hooded ladies' tresses – *Spiranthes romanzoffiana* Cham.

Hops – *Humulus lupulus* L.

Hop-tree – *Ptelea trifoliata* L.

Huckleberry – *Gaylussacia baccata* (Wangenh.) K. Koch

Ironweed – *Vernonia* spp.

Jack pine – *Pinus banksiana* Lamb.

Joe-pye-weed – *Eupatorium maculatum* L.

Juneberry – *Amelanchier* spp.

Kale – *Brassica* spp.

Kentucky bluegrass – *Poa pratensis* L.

Knapweed – *Centaurea* spp.

Knotweed – *Polygonum* spp.

Labrador tea – *Ledum groenlandicum* Oeder

Lamb's-quarters – *Chenopodium album* L.

Lantana – *Lantana* spp.

Lead-plant – *Amorpha canescens* Pursh

Leatherleaf – *Chamaedaphne calyculata* (L.) Moench

Lilac – *Syringa* spp.

Little bluestem – *Andropogon scoparius* Michaux

Lobelia – *Lobelia* spp.

Lovegrass – *Eragrostis* spp.

Lupine – *Lupinus perennis* L.

Mallow – *Malva* spp.

Maple-leaved *viburnum* – *Viburnum acerifolium* L.

Marigold – *Calendula officinalis* L.

May-apple – *Podophyllum peltatum* L.

Melon – *Cucumis melo* L.

Michigan holly – *Ilex verticillata* (L.) A. Gray

Milk-vetch – *Astragalus* spp.

Mint – *Mentha* spp.

Mountain maple – *Acer spicatum* Lam.

Narrow-leaf sedge – *Carex stricta* Lam.

Nut-grass sedge – *Cyperus* spp.

Nettle – *Urtica* spp.

New Jersey tea – *Ceanothus americanus* L.

Orange hawkweed – *Hieracium aurantiacum* L.

Orange milkweed – *Asclepias tuberosa* L.

Ornamental cherry – *Prunus* spp.

Pale vetchling – *Lathyrus ochroleucus* Hooker

Panic grass – *Panicum* spp.

Passion vine – *Passiflora* spp.

Pawpaw – *Asimina triloba* (L.) Dunal

Pearly everlasting – *Anaphalis margaritacea* (L.) Bentham

Pennsylvania sedge – *Carex pennsylvanica* Lam.

Pepper-grass – *Lepidium* spp.

Peppermint – *Mentha xpiperita* L.

Pigweed – *Amaranthus* spp.

Pin cherry – *Prunus pensylvanica* L.

Plains wild indigo – *Baptisia leucophaea* Nutt.

Plantain – *Plantago* spp.

Poison sumac – *Toxicodendron vernix* (L.) Kuntze

Poverty grass – *Danthonia spicata* (L.) R. & S.

Prickly-ash – *Zanthoxylum americanum* Miller

Prickly pear cactus – *Opuntia humifusa* (Raf.) Raf.

Privet – *Ligustrum vulgare* L.

Puccoon – *Lithospermum* spp.

Purple loosestrife – *Lythrum salicaria* L.

Purpletop grass – *Tridens flavus* (L.) Hitchc.

Purple vetch – *Vicia* spp.

Purslane – *Portulaca* spp.

Pussy-toes – *Antennaria* spp.

Quaking aspen – *Populus tremuloides* Michaux

Queen-Anne's-lace – *Daucus carota* L.

Reed grass – *Calamagrotis* spp.

Redbud – *Cercis canadensis* L.

Red clover – *Trifolium pratense* L.

Red oak – *Quercus rubra* L.

Redtop grass – *Agrotis gigantea* Roth

Rock cress – *Arabis lyrata* L.

Rush – *Juncus* spp.

Sandbar willow – *Salix exigua* Nutt.

Sassafras – *Sassafras albidum* (Nutt.) Nees

Scarlet oak – *Quercus coccinea* Muenchh.

Scrub oak – *Quercus* spp.

Senna – *Cassia* spp.

Sheep sorrel – *Rumex acetosella* L.

Shepherd's needle – *Bidens pilosa* L.

Shepherd's-purse – *Capsella bursa-pastoris* (L.) Medicus

Shrubby cinquefoil – *Potentilla fruticosa* L.

Smooth creeping lovegrass – *Eragrotis* spp.

Spicebush – *Lindera benzoin* (L.) Blume

Spike-rush – *Eleocharis* spp.

Spiraea – *Spiraea* spp.

Staghorn sumac – *Rhus typhina* L.

St. Augustine grass – *Stenotaphrum secundatum* (Walt.)

St. John's-wort – *Hypericum* spp.

Swamp milkweed – *Asclepias incarnata* L.

Swamp thistle – *Cirsium muticum* Michaux

Sweet clover – *Melilotus* spp.

Switch cane – *Arundinaria tecta* (Walt.) Muhl.

Switch grass – *Panicum virgatum* L.

Tag alder – *Alnus rugosa* (Duroi) Sprengel

Tall cress – *Arabis drummondii* A. Gray

Tamarack – *Larix laricina* (DuRoi) K. Koch.

Teasel – *Dipsacus* spp.

Thistle – *Cirsium* spp.

Tick-trefoil – *Desmodium* spp.

Timothy – *Phleum pratense* L.

Toadflax – *Comandra* spp.

Toothwort – *Dentaria* spp.

Tulip-tree – *Liriodendron tulipifera* L.

Turtlehead – *Chelone glabra* L.

Vetch – *Vicia* spp.

Vetchling - *Lathyrus* spp.

Violet – *Viola* spp.

Virginia snakeroot – *Aristolochia serpentaria* L.

Walnut – *Juglans nigra* L.

Water cress – *Nasturtium officinale* R. Br.

Water dock – *Rumex verticillatus* L.

Waterleaf – *Hydrophyllum* spp.

Wavy-leafed aster – *Aster undulatus* L.

White campion – *Silene pratenis* (Rafn) Godron & Gren.

White clover – *Trifolium repens* L.

White pine – *Pinus strobus* L.

White sweet-clover – *Melilotus alba* Medicus

White yarrow – *Achillea millefolium* L.

Wide-leaf sedge – *Carex lacustris* Willd.

Wild-bean – *Apios americana* Medicus

Wild bergamot – *Monarda fistulosa* L.

Wild black cherry – *Prunus serotina* Ehrh.

Wild carrot – *Daucus carota* L.

Wild columbine – *Aquilegia canadensis* L.

Wild crab – *Malus coronaria* (L.) Miller

Wild cranberry – *Vaccinium macrocarpon* Aiton & *V. oxycoccos* L.

Wild-ginger – *Asarum canadense* L.

Wild indigo – *Baptisia* spp.

Wild iris – *Iris versicolor* L.

Wild-lilac – *Ceanothus sanguineus* Pursh

Wild lily – *Lilium* spp.

Wild mustard - *Brassica kaber* (DC.) Wheeler

Wild plum – *Prunus americana* Marsh.

Wild-raisin – *Viburnum cassinoides* L.

Wild snapdragon – *Antirrhinum* spp.

Wild strawberry – *Fragaria virginiana* Miller

Willow – *Salix* spp.

Wing-stem – *Verbesina alternifolia* (L.) Kearney

Wisteria – *Wisteria* spp.

Wood lily - *Lilium philadelphicum* L.

Woolly beardgrass – *Erianthus divaricatus* Hitchc.

Yellow hawkweed – *Hieracium piloselloides* Vill.

Zinnia – *Zinnia elegans* Jacq.

"Some finished butterfly,
Some breathing diamond-flake with leaf-gold fans,
That takes the air, no trace of worm it was."

Browning